Marie-Antoinette and Count Axel Fersen

The Untold Love Story

THE AUTHOR

Evelyn Farr is a graduate of University
College London and has published two
other books, *The World of Fanny Burney* and
Before the Deluge, a study of pre-
Revolutionary Parisian society.

EVELYN FARR

Marie-Antoinette and Count Axel Fersen

The Untold Love Story

This edition published in Great Britain in 1997 by
Allison & Busby Ltd
114 New Cavendish Street
London W1M 7FD

First published in Great Britain in 1995 by
Peter Owen Publishers

A catalogue record for this book is available from the
British Library

ISBN 0 74900 370 7

Printed and bound in Great Britain by
Hartnolls Ltd
Bodmin, Cornwall

For
Mollie Gerard Davis

Acknowledgements

I am grateful to Librairie Droz of Geneva for permission to quote and translate from the *Journal (1780–1789)* of the Marquis de Bombelles, edited by J. Grassion and F. Durif (2 vols, 1978–82).

Unless otherwise stated in the notes, all translations of French sources are my own.

E.F.

Contents

Illustrations

between pages 128 and 129

Introduction

For romance, glamour, passion, pain and tragedy, few love-affairs match that between Queen Marie-Antoinette and Count Axel Fersen, yet their love is both little known and misinterpreted. This book peels back layers of myth and misinformation to present a documented history of the all-consuming passion between the ill-fated Queen of France and the handsome Swedish nobleman who tried to save her from a cruel and untimely end.

The lack of an objective appraisal of this eighteenth-century love-affair stems from Marie-Antoinette's status as one of the most controversial figures in French history. Few have been so maligned when alive and so beatified after death. During her lifetime, Marie-Antoinette was 'the Austrian whore', wildly accused of every imaginable sexual and political crime. In the nineteenth century, a guilt-ridden France tried to atone for its wrongs retrospectively by reinventing her as a saint, pure and unsullied. Today attitudes still waver between these two extremes. A careful reading of contemporary sources reveals a more credible and balanced personality. One sees a queen who, from the day she stepped on to French soil in 1770, was the hapless victim of political intrigue, captive to a destiny she rebelled against but never managed to escape. Hated in France from the outset because she was Austrian, neglected and rebuffed by her husband, the young Marie-Antoinette forgot her sorrows by plunging into a hectic social life. She never lived down her image as a reckless and extravagant teenager, although she developed into a woman of immense charm, grace, majesty and intelligence. Above all, she was an exceptionally feminine woman, with deep feelings and an affectionate temperament.

Marie-Antoinette charmed Axel Fersen, and years before revolutionary

9

storm clouds gathered over France she had become the centre of his whole existence. 'No one,' he declared, 'has ever known how to love like her.' For the Queen, Axel was 'the most loved and loving of men', the one man she loved passionately and whole-heartedly until she was snatched from him by the guillotine in 1793. Their doomed love was known to insiders at Court during her lifetime, but was lost in the mass of horrendous libels spread against her by Orléanists and Jacobins during the French Revolution. When the monarchy was restored in 1814, Marie-Antoinette's tarnished reputation was belatedly rehabilitated. Presented as a royal martyr, she ceased to be a human being with human frailties and passions. Memoirs about her (and about the last years of the *ancien régime* generally) were subject to revisionist censorship, and any diverging from the Queen's new image were suppressed. Her loyal *femme de chambre* and confidante, Mme Campan, whose memoirs were published in 1823, maintained a staggering silence about Axel Fersen, even when describing in detail the royal family's flight to Varennes which he masterminded.

Axel Fersen is indeed remarkable by his absence in nineteenth-century biographies of Marie-Antoinette, yet he was the person who probably knew her best, and certainly he appreciated her good qualities and loved her the most. People hoping for scandalous revelations when his diary and letters were finally published in 1877 were sorely disappointed. His great-nephew, who edited them, excised all intimate details about Marie-Antoinette, although he let out interesting snippets by default, because of his ignorance of her life. He presented both the Queen and Axel as models of moral rectitude, reinforcing the Queen's image as a martyr, grateful for the assistance of a devoted, but very respectful Axel Fersen.

Marie-Antoinette's papers were subject to similar restrictions. She burnt many herself during the Revolution, but those surviving in Viennese archives were classified for decades – more to protect the Austrians, who had used her and abandoned her disgracefully, than to shield the Queen herself.

In the twentieth century, as contemporary papers were released for inspection, a more realistic assessment of Marie-Antoinette's character and place in history emerged, but her *grande passion* for Axel Fersen remains in the shadows. It is time to take a fresh look at this fateful love-story, which far from being the chivalrous romance usually portrayed, was a deep, mutual and enduring passion between two truly star-crossed lovers.

A Note on Sources

This book relies solely on contemporary sources to portray the relationship between Marie-Antoinette and Axel Fersen.

According to Mme Campan, the Queen kept all her correspondence, fully intending to write her memoirs after the Revolution. They would have made fascinating reading! Unfortunately many of Marie-Antoinette's letters were destroyed before her death, but those which survive reveal a woman very different from the feather-brained socialite of popular history. Highly significant details about her private life are also to be found in letters the Austrian ambassador in Paris, the Comte de Mercy, wrote to her mother, Empress Maria-Theresa, and brother, Emperor Joseph II – the latter correspondence in particular yields vital clues on the state of Marie-Antoinette's marriage during her liaison with Fersen.

The repeated failure of biographers to connect and compare details of Fersen's life with Marie-Antoinette's has led to ambivalence about the nature of their love – an ambivalence in no small part due to the unprofessional editing of Axel Fersen's papers. According to O.G. Heidenstam, who in 1913 edited letters between Axel, the Queen and French *constitutionnels*, Axel 'loved the Queen without one disloyal or sensual thought that could dim the flame of a love worthy of the troubadours or the knights of the Round Table. The Queen loved him in the same way, without ever forgetting her duty as a wife and her dignity as a Queen'.

Heidenstam's idealism was shared by Baron R.M. Klinckowström, Axel's great-nephew, who produced a much truncated edition of Axel's diary and letters in 1877. Both Heidenstam and Klinckowström were unscrupulous in manipulating the evidence to support their views, and

were clearly governed by a sense of honour which made them determined to protect the Queen's reputation.

Baron Klinckowström published letters between Marie-Antoinette and
Axel Fersen covering only the period June 1791 to June 1792, and even
these suffer from numerous deletions. Klinckowström maintained that
Axel himself erased sensitive financial and political passages before the
letters were forwarded to the King of Sweden. 'Among the papers belonging to Count Fersen,' he averred, 'there is nothing which could
cast a shadow on the Queen's conduct.'

This is untrue. The letters were never sent to the King of Sweden,
and a later Swedish editor discovered that Klinckowström also suppressed
many passages in Axel's diary concerning his love for the Queen. He
even destroyed the 1791–2 correspondence after publication to prevent
his son using chemicals in an attempt to reveal what lay beneath the
black censor's ink. That Axel himself would have erased any word written by Marie-Antoinette is almost inconceivable. He kept every last scrap
of paper from his beloved, and would never have deleted endearments
or expressions of love. Significantly the deletions occur most frequently
at the beginning and end of the letters, exactly where personal matters
would have been recorded, and Marie-Antoinette was not a correspon-
dent who signed off without affectionate words.

Only two fragments of love-letters from Marie-Antoinette to Axel
survive. Klinckowström does not appear to have come across the long
correspondence between Axel and the Queen under her code-name
'Josephine' (see Chapter 6), but his edition of Axel's diary shows he
was unaware of 'Josephine's' true identity. Not content with destroying
Marie-Antoinette's letters and ruthlessly expunging what he considered
compromising material, the baron also suppressed details of Axel's career in France. According to Klinckowström, Axel was in Sweden for
most of the 1780s, when in fact he spent a large part of the decade in
France. Klinckowström was also a snob. He removed Axel's expressions
of distaste for the Swedish establishment, all references to money, and
even 'improved' his great-uncle's not altogether grammatical or elegant
French prose. That he knew of Axel's love-affair with the Queen is
evident from his substitution of 'the Queen' for Axel's *Elle* – *Elle* being
how Axel referred to her when writing on personal rather than political
matters.

Heidenstam imitated Klinckowström's editorial procedures exactly. The most, but by no means totally reliable editor of Axel Fersen's papers was Alma Söderhjelm, who published previously suppressed letters and diary entries in 1930. Axel's diary for the crucial years 1780 to June 1791 was burnt lest it fell into the hands of the Jacobins, but Söderhjelm filled many gaps by publishing letters for this vitally important period from Axel to his sister and confidante Sophie, and to his father. She also traced the elusive 'Josephine' correspondence with Marie-Antoinette through notes in Axel's correspondence book.

Although Söderhjelm undoubtedly cast much fresh light on Axel's life, she produced an incomplete picture of his relationship with Marie-Antoinette. She totally ignored the Queen's side of the affair, overlooking valuable evidence by failing to connect it to crucial dates and events in Marie-Antoinette's life. The most telling phase of the love-affair, and by far the happiest, was during 1783–9, yet Söderhjelm brushed over this period perfunctorily in a few pages. Her forte was Swedish history, not Marie-Antoinette or life at Versailles, and she seemed to share her predecessors' fear of damaging the Queen's reputation.

Perhaps even more details on this long hidden love-affair may one day be revealed. It is, however, possible now to remove the distorted focus of previous biographers by piecing together and analysing all the disparate material they either suppressed or ignored.

PROLOGUE

The Opera Ball

Eighteenth-century Paris was at its liveliest after Christmas, when one of Europe's biggest carnivals began. There were many fairs, street shows and plays, but what most attracted dancing-mad Parisians were the countless balls. The *jeunesse dorée* danced the night away in aristocratic mansions, at Court balls at Versailles, and at the less exclusive and far less sedate masked balls held in the Opera House.

One young man who gavotted and minuetted his way through Parisian high society in the winter of 1773–4 was an eighteen-year-old Swedish nobleman on his first visit to the French capital. Count Axel Fersen, tall, slim and handsome, soon discovered that much more could be enjoyed at an opera ball than mere dancing, as he recorded in his diary.

> *Wednesday 5 January 1774.* At 12 I went to the opera ball with Bolémany [his tutor]. I found a very pretty and amiable mask there, who whispered to me that she was cross I was not her husband, so I could sleep with her. I told her that was no obstacle. I wanted to persuade her of it, but she ran off.[1]

Disappointed, Axel consoled himself by kissing another masked beauty who had been captured by his more fortunate compatriot, Plomenfeldt. They had a long conversation with her, but though they concluded she was 'Mme Bilioni, a singer from the Comédie Italienne who speaks very good Italian and sings prettily', she refused to reveal her identity.[2] Masks gave women a licence to flirt denied them on other occasions, and at opera balls they could approach unknown men without fear of reproach. It was the done thing to be daring, otherwise a mask was valueless.

15

On 30 January 1774, Axel left a supper party hosted by the Comtesse d'Arville to go to an opera ball once again. Little did he foresee the profound consequences of his encounter that night with another teasing mask.

At 1 o'clock I left to go to the opera ball. There was a great crowd of people. Mme la Dauphine, Mgr le Dauphin and the Comte de Provence came, and they were at the ball for half an hour without being recognized. The Dauphine spoke to me for a long time without my knowing her. At last, when she was recognized, everyone pressed around her and she retired to a box. I left the ball at 3 o'clock.[3]

The Dauphine, Marie-Antoinette, wife of the future King Louis XVI, was just two months younger than Axel Fersen and in the full bloom of her giddy youth. Although accompanied by her husband and brother-in-law (which was unusual, as both were poor dancers and disliked balls), she took full advantage of her incognito to speak at length to the handsome Swede. She had probably already cast an appraising eye over him at Versailles, since he had been presented to the royal family and made occasional appearances at Court.

Had any other man than Fersen been involved, this meeting beneath the glittering chandeliers of the Opera House could be dismissed as nothing more than one of the young Marie-Antoinette's flirtatious chats. She invariably tried to speak only to foreigners when she was masked, because Frenchmen penetrated her disguise too quickly. Axel, alas, does not reveal what she spent so much time discussing with him, but judging from a record of another of the Dauphine's conversations with a masked stranger, it may be deduced that 'the talk was light, agreeable, without being indiscreet,' and 'the jokes . . . such as a mask authorizes, especially in France'.[4] In other words, a trifle risqué.

Frivolous their chat may have been, but its repercussions were serious. Marie-Antoinette had fallen in love. She must have been delighted that Axel found the energy to dance for nearly five hours at her ball at Versailles the following day, giving her a chance to renew their acquaintance. Though Axel recorded further conversations, he was maddeningly discreet about her, and his diary gives away nothing. Nevertheless, within the week he had given up dances in Paris altogether. 'I go only to the balls given by Madame la Dauphine,' he wrote.[5] One of eighteenth-century France's deepest, most enduring and tragic love-affairs had been born.

1

A Mésalliance

Chatting to handsome foreigners at opera balls was certainly not the sort of behaviour expected of a future Queen of France. But Marie-Antoinette was not cast in the same mould as the pious Maria Lesczinska, Louis XV's long-suffering wife, or the previous Dauphine, her husband's late mother, who had been a solid and solemn matriarch. Royal marriages were seldom made in heaven, and protracted diplomatic negotiations alone had consigned the vivacious youngest daughter of Empress Maria-Theresa to the arms of one of the most unprepossessing princes in Europe.

Archduchess Marie-Antoinette-Josèphe-Jeanne of Austria was born in Vienna at 7.30 p.m. on 2 November 1755, the penultimate of Maria-Theresa's sixteen children. She enjoyed a happy childhood in the relaxed atmosphere of the Hofburg and the Habsburgs' smaller version of Versailles, Schönbrunn, just outside the Austrian capital. The informality of the Imperial Court was due largely to the influence of Emperor Francis I, Marie-Antoinette's father, whom she adored. He died when she was only nine, and she always remembered how he sent for her at the last minute to kiss her goodbye before setting off on a journey to Innsbruck. Three days later he was dead. His grieving youngest daughter later dated her misfortunes from that moment.

Before his marriage to Empress Maria-Theresa in 1736, Francis I had been Duke of Lorraine. Their union sparked off a bitter war between Austria and the combined forces of France, Prussia and Bavaria. Prussia wrested the valuable province of Silesia from Austria, while France tried to topple Maria-Theresa from her throne and replace her with the Elector of Bavaria. The strategically important

17

duchy of Lorraine was pivotal to French involvement in what was known as the War of the Austrian Succession. Several towns in the duchy had been seized and added to France in the seventeenth century, and although Maria-Theresa eventually retained her right to the Imperial crown, Francis had to cede Lorraine to the King of Poland; it reverted to France on his death in 1766. France would never have tolerated Lorraine passing into Austrian hands, and it was bitter hatred of Austria which lay behind the vicious campaign mounted against Marie-Antoinette from the day she arrived in France – despite the fact that she was a princess of Lorraine as well as an Austrian archduchess.

Marie-Antoinette actually had as much French blood, if not more, than her husband Louis XVI, which makes her nickname *l'Autrichienne* wholly inappropriate. Louis XVI's only French grandparent was Louis XV, and one of his great-grandfathers was a Habsburg: Emperor Joseph I. The House of Lorraine, on the other hand, had frequently intermarried with French nobility and royalty, producing such offshoots as the illustrious Ducs de Guise. Marie-Antoinette was a direct descendant of Louis XIII through her paternal grandmother Princesse Charlotte d'Orléans; combined with her descent from both Anne of Austria (mother of Louis XIV) and Joseph I, this made her Louis XVI's cousin several times over through both the French and Austrian royal families. Her link to the House of Orléans also made her an even closer cousin to 'Philippe Égalité', the Duc d'Orléans, who stirred up French hatred against her as the detested foreigner – 'the Austrian whore'.

The marriage of fourteen-year-old Archduchess Antoinette to the Dauphin of France in 1770 was a triumph of diplomacy over political reality. Chief broker of the marriage, which the Austrians wanted far more than the French, was Louis XV's foreign minister, the Duc de Choiseul. A native of Lorraine and son of one of Francis I's most trusted ambassadors, Choiseul was strongly attached to the interests of both Lorraine and Austria. It would have been enormously beneficial to Marie-Antoinette had he managed to remain in office to assist her through the minefield of French court intrigues and political cabals which greeted her. But barely seven months after her arrival in France he was ousted from power and replaced by a strong anti-Austrian faction at Versailles headed by the Duc d'Aiguillon, who had a most useful ally in Mme du Barry, Louis XV's omnipotent mistress.

France and Austria, traditional enemies, had been uneasy allies since 1756. Marie-Antoinette's marriage to the Dauphin was intended by Choiseul and Maria-Theresa to cement this alliance and deter future French aggression against Austria. The French, however, hankered as always after French hegemony in Europe; an alliance with their most powerful rival was an unwelcome fetter on plans to extend their influence. D'Aiguillon succeeded Choiseul as Foreign Minister in December 1770, precipitating a complete reversal of French policy. Choiseul had been a liberal, a protector of the *philosophes* and the *parlements* (which in a very limited way represented public interests). D'Aiguillon was deeply conservative, pro-Jesuit (Choiseul had banned the order in 1764), and opposed the *parlements*. As a great-nephew of Cardinal Richelieu, he also shared the Cardinal's entrenched anti-Austrian views. Worse still, he had been a close friend of the Dauphin's father. Marie-Antoinette therefore found her young husband guided by her enemies. Apart from d'Aiguillon, both the Dauphin's governor, the Duc de La Vauguyon, and his governess, Mme de Marsan, belonged to the anti-Austrian faction, as did the influential princely Rohan family as a whole. It made for a very difficult marriage indeed. The day Marie-Antoinette stepped on to French soil marked the beginning of her long, unhappy and ultimately disastrous career as a victim of political intrigue.

Archduchess Antoinette (as the Viennese knew her) was ill-prepared for her role as wife to the future King of France. She had received only a superficial education, although Empress Maria-Theresa had ensured her French was perfect by sending for a tutor from Paris, the Abbé de Vermond, who was to prove an admirable Austrian spy when his charge finally settled into her new life at Versailles.

Armed with little more than her charm and good looks, the young Marie-Antoinette left the happy home in Vienna and the mother she was never to see again on 19 April 1770, having already been married by proxy to the Dauphin. The French courtiers who made up her new household, led by the Comtesse de Noailles, met her on the French border near Strasbourg, in a splendid pavilion whose decoration Goethe considered highly unfortunate. 'As I entered,' he recalled, 'my eyes were struck by the subject represented on the tapestry which served as a wall-hanging for the main pavilion. It depicted

Jason, Creon and Medea, that is to say, the image of the most disastrous marriage ever recorded.'[1] It was in this inauspicious setting
that the French subjected their new Dauphine to a humiliating ritual.
With her Viennese retainers, she was ushered into a room while the
French waited outside.

> When Madame la Dauphine had been entirely undressed, so that she
> kept nothing about her belonging to a foreign court, not even her
> shift and stockings ... the doors were opened; the young princess
> advanced, looked for the Comtesse de Noailles, then threw herself
> into her arms, asking her, with tears in her eyes, to direct her, advise
> her, and be her guide and support in everything.[2]

Well might Marie-Antoinette cry for help. She was not even allowed to keep the trousseau she had brought from Vienna, which
became the lawful property of her new French *femmes de chambre*.
Once she was dressed in French clothes, they felt free to admire her,
as Mme Campan records: 'We were seduced by a single smile; and
in this enchanting creature, who shone with all the brilliance of a
French gaiety, a certain majestic serenity, perhaps also the slightly
proud attitude of her head and shoulders, reminded one she was the
daughter of emperors.'[3]

Marie-Antoinette's looks certainly impressed. Louis de Bachaumont,
social columnist of the day, gave 'an exact portrait' of her in his
Mémoires secrets on 27 May 1770.

> This princess is of a height proportionate to her age, slim without
> being gaunt. . . . She is very well made, all her limbs are well propor-
> tioned. Her thick hair is a beautiful blonde; it is supposed it will
> eventually turn light auburn. Her forehead is noble, the shape of her
> face a beautiful oval, but a trifle long. Her eyebrows are as well de-
> fined as a blonde can have them. Her eyes are blue, though far from
> insipid, and gleam with a spirited vivacity. Her nose is aquiline, taper-
> ing towards the end. Her mouth is small; the lips are full, especially
> the lower one, which everyone knows is the Austrian lip. The white-
> ness of her complexion is dazzling, and she has natural colour which
> will spare her the need to use rouge. Her bearing is that of an arch-
> duchess, but her dignity is tempered by gentleness, and when one
> sees this princess, it is difficult not to feel respect mingled with love.

Marie-Antoinette's movements were as light and graceful as her appearance, although the mischievous gleam in her eyes indicated a princess with a rebel streak. 'That child,' remarked Louis XV when she arrived at Versailles, 'is a fresh bouquet of wild flowers.'[4] Mme Campan, then just seventeen, was devoted to the Dauphine from the moment she set eyes on her, and was to serve her as First Woman of the Bedchamber through thick and thin over the following twenty-two years. 'Never,' she wrote, 'in any rank, at any time, have I found a woman with a disposition as captivating as that of Marie-Antoinette. . . . I have never seen another woman as heroic in danger, as eloquent when the occasion required, or as unreservedly gay in prosperity.'[5]

Even the anti-Austrians were forced to admit she was everything a princess should be, but it made them no less anxious to have her sent home. The fifteen-year-old Dauphin, who showed not the slightest interest in matrimony or his bride, seemed likely to aid their schemes. Comte Florimond de Mercy-Argenteau, the Austrian ambassador to France (known simply as the Comte de Mercy), awaited the young couple's first meeting on 14 May 1770 with some trepidation: 'At the first moment, Madame la Dauphine's countenance and speech surpassed my expectations and brought her general applause. All I fear for her is the disgust she may feel for Monsieur le Dauphin's extreme awkwardness, and the traps all the intriguers will set for this young princess.'[6]

This was masterly understatement, typical of Mercy's very diplomatic dispatches. A year earlier, when negotiations for this unholy alliance were conducted, he had written: 'Nature seems to have denied Monsieur le Dauphin everything. This prince . . . displays only limited intelligence, a great deal of awkwardness, and no sensibility.'[7] The French even sent a picture of him following his plough to impress Maria-Theresa. He was hardly the husband of a young girl's dreams, and he went out of his way to make Marie-Antoinette feel unwelcome.

The marriage was nevertheless celebrated with all due pomp at Versailles on 16 May 1770, and was followed by a banquet and fireworks which passed off very well. In Paris, however, disaster struck at a fireworks display held on the Place Louis XV (now Place de la Concorde) on 30 May; 130 people were killed in a stampede as the crowds became uncontrollable. Marie-Antoinette was extremely upset when news of this tragedy reached Versailles. She and the Dauphin immediately sent a month's income to Paris to help the families of the victims.

It was this sensitivity and generosity, coupled with her grace and charm, which made the Dauphine so popular with Parisians during her early years in France. When Marie-Antoinette and her husband finally made their official entry into Paris they were greeted with wild enthusiasm, and had to show themselves several times to well-wishers who flocked into the gardens of the Tuileries to see them appear on a balcony. The Dauphine was overwhelmed. 'When she saw all those heads pressed close together, their eyes raised towards her, she exclaimed, "Great God, what a crowd!" "Madame," replied the old Duc de Brissac, governor of Paris, "without offending Monseigneur le Dauphin, they are all your lovers."'[8]

The Dauphin was far from taking offence. He scarcely ever ad-dressed a word to his wife, and had made no attempt to consummate the marriage. On 26 May 1770, the Comte de Mercy told the Aus-trian Chancellor, Prince Kaunitz, that the Dauphin 'who at the mo-ment of his marriage seemed to be on the point of maturing', had 'now fallen back into the same disagreeable state to which his tem-perament leads him. Since their first meeting, he has not given Madame la Dauphine the slightest sign of liking or interest. Fortunately his rough air of indifference does not overawe the young princess'.[9]

Never was a couple so mismatched. The future Louis XVI, born at Versailles on 23 August 1754, though fifteen months older than Marie-Antoinette, was far les mature. Physically the contrast between them could not have been greater. She was beautiful and graceful, he was unattractive and clumsy. His features were 'noble enough', according to Mme Campan. He had fair hair and lazy blue eyes, which in portraits appear to squint slightly from beneath drooping eyelids, and his nose was prominent and hooked. Louis's mouth was full and sensual, but indicated his love of food more than his interest in the opposite sex. He had a bull-neck and broad shoulders, and carried his not inconsiderable weight very badly indeed; many who met him were appalled by his awkward and undignified gait. They were equally put out by his gruffness, lack of *politesse* and penchant for crude and violent horseplay. He had a sadistic streak which his-torians usually ignore. Gouverneur Morris, when American ambas-sador to France, heard from a boyhood friend of Louis XVI, the

Comte de Montmorin, that he used to enjoy roasting cats alive, and when hunting he was utterly indiscriminate in his kills, shooting young deer and boars, and even dogs.

Louis was always deemed to be a victim of his bad upbringing. He was orphaned at the age of twelve, and his education was entrusted to courtiers whose sole aim was to make themselves indispensable by ensuring he remained dependent on their advice. He was not a clever boy, and in adulthood displayed astonishing ignorance even of his own language; his diary is littered with glaring grammatical faults. Louis's experimental education left him more interested in the blacksmith's art than statecraft, and his manners and appearance were completely neglected. He was dirty, untidy, brutal and shockingly rude, as his young bride soon discovered. The only matters Louis always took seriously were religion and hunting. What he thought about other things is unclear. He was an inarticulate man, very reserved and secretive. Marie-Antoinette found him uncommunicative in the extreme, and would have been amazed at the diverse interests he developed. Revolutionary commissioners who toured his apartments at Versailles in 1792 found not only his blacksmith's forge but stacks of English newspapers and parliamentary debates, numerous maps and globes, a well-stocked library, and, curiously enough, a collection of pornographic literature on Catherine the Great. There was also a belvedere containing a telescope which enabled him to spy on everyone in the environs of his palace – perhaps even on his wife?

At fifteen, however, the Dauphin was totally unsophisticated. His wife loved music and the theatre; he hated them both. When in November 1770 he was presented with a list of plays to be performed for the Court at Fontainebleau, he threw it on the fire without further ado. 'That's what I think of things like that,' he told astonished courtiers. As for dancing, which Marie-Antoinette adored, the Dauphin was too ungainly to partner her, and was unconcerned when she turned to other men. Louis was probably very relieved that she burdened him with her company as little as possible. Marie-Antoinette received more warmth and affection from her pug, which she had sent for from Vienna. The Dauphine's high spirits and humour alone sustained her, and for years she laughed off her unhappiness. To use a Viennese expression, the situation was desperate, but not serious.

Marie-Antoinette had been set an almost impossible task. She was supposed to found a dynasty which would bind France and Austria together with a graceless youth who barely acknowledged her existence. Mme Campan ascribed the Dauphin's behaviour towards his wife to a concerted attempt by anti-Austrians to have the marriage annulled on the grounds of non-consummation.

> A wounding indifference, a coldness which often degenerated into roughness, were the only feelings the young prince showed towards her. So many charms had failed to rouse his senses. Out of duty he used to get into the Dauphine's bed, and often went to sleep without even speaking a word to her. This estrangement, which lasted for a very long time, was, it is said, the work of M. le Duc de La Vauguyon. . . . Will anyone believe that the plans laid against Marie-Antoinette went so far as the possibility of a divorce?[10]

Neither the anti-Austrians nor the Dauphin had reckoned with Marie-Antoinette's character and determination. Within a few weeks she had won the love of her servants. 'She was worshipped by her household,' wrote Alexandre de Tilly, one of her pages.[11] With commendable thoroughness she set about winning the affection of her husband. Her personal feelings could hardly have been involved, but Marie-Antoinette was a dutiful daughter of Austria. The Franco-Austrian alliance would never fail through lack of effort on her part. By dint of ignoring the Dauphin's rudeness and talking to him as though nothing were wrong, Marie-Antoinette penetrated beneath his unattractive exterior. She found a prince who was excessively shy, afraid of his old governor, the Duc de La Vauguyon, and utterly ignorant of even common civility. To everyone's surprise she managed to gain his trust and friendship. By 19 September 1770 Mercy was able to report that the Dauphin was 'gentle, kind and even confiding' towards his wife. Six months later she succeeded in detaching him 'from his former governor, the favourite [Mme du Barry] and all their partisans'.[12]

Viennese charm had for the moment blown the anti-Austrians off course, though it is doubtful the picture was as rosy as Mercy suggests. Although the Dauphine eventually found ways to amuse her boorish husband – Mme Campan stated that Marie-Antoinette first staged private theatricals to draw Louis out of his morosity, with considerable success – she had a greater hurdle to overcome. Her marriage remained unconsummated. The Dauphin was at first unwilling, then unable to make love to his wife. Three years after their wedding an exasperated Louis XV finally ordered the Court physician Lassonne to give them some vital sex education. The Dauphin, Marie-Antoinette informed her mother, 'spoke to him without embarrassment and with a great deal of common sense. Lassonne is quite satisfied and has high hopes'.[13] But four more unfulfilling years passed before those hopes were realized; four years in which Marie-Antoinette earned a reputation as an extravagant socialite as she tried to drown her unhappiness in a constant whirl of amusement.

Not even the smallest detail of Marie-Antoinette's early years at Versailles escaped the eagle eye of the Austrian ambassador, the Comte de Mercy. He was devoted to Empress Maria-Theresa, and played his role of master-spy so perfectly that Marie-Antoinette never suspected him. As he remarked in a letter to Prince Kaunitz, the Dauphine's weekly activities could have been recorded in a mere two pages, but the Empress preferred long reports, which he duly supplied. Maria-Theresa had instructed her daughter to 'follow without hesitation and with confidence everything Mercy tells you or asks of you', and Marie-Antoinette, young, naïve and trusting, obeyed but too well.[14] She became a hapless tool of Austrian foreign policy, convinced by Mercy that she was strengthening the alliance, even though the steps Austria demanded of her frequently undermined her own position as Queen of France.

Mercy, born in 1727 in Liège, in the Austrian Netherlands, was enormously rich and lived in grand style in a private *hôtel* on the Boulevard Richelieu (now Boulevard des Italiens). He was appointed ambassador to France in 1766, and in 1767 was naturalized as a Frenchman to avoid forfeiting the Mercy estates in Lorraine. He rapidly lived up to Parisian expectations by taking a mistress – the soprano Rosalie Levasseur, by whom he had a son.

Mercy's love of theatre and opera was shared by Marie-Antoinette. He must have been a consummate actor himself, for she trusted him implicitly. 'His feelings for me are those of a father for his child,' she told her brother Leopold in 1790.[15] What would she have thought had she known that for twenty years he had been gathering confidential information about her from spies in her household and in those of her friends? His most reliable informant was the Abbé Jacques-Mathieu de Vermond (born 1735), a graduate of the Sorbonne whom Mercy had personally selected as French tutor to the former Archduchess Antoinette. Vermond became her reader when she married, and used his daily audiences with her at Versailles to glean information for Mercy. Though a Frenchman, Vermond too was an ardent champion of Austria. Mme Campan was but one of the many courtiers and servants who detested this 'obscure bourgeois', whom she described as 'vain, garrulous, subtle yet brusque at the same time, very ugly and affecting eccentricity, treating the highest born as his equals and sometimes even as his inferiors'.[16]

Vermond boasted loudly of his influence over Marie-Antoinette, and according to Mme Campan, claimed to revise all the letters she sent to Vienna. This was surely an idle boast. Her clear, concise French never altered, whether Vermond was in attendance or not. It is also unlikely that 'he determined all the actions' of his former pupil.[17] Mercy often complained that the Dauphine failed to heed Vermond's advice, some of which was quite sensible. She unwisely confided far too much in the abbé and Mercy, but certain matters relating to her private life never reached Vienna, either because she concealed them from her two *éminences grises*, or because the latter retained a modicum of decency. Although Mercy painstakingly catalogued all Marie-Antoinette's peccadilloes for the Empress, he toned down and even overlooked some of her more indiscreet and reckless activities. Even so, her mother was not at all amused by the wordy dispatches she received from France.

Life at the French Court was regimented in the extreme. Versailles, built on a magnificent scale by Louis XIV to impress his rebellious nobility, was frighteningly huge and unwelcoming. Besides the royal family and the Court, it housed the entire French government, in all some 12,000 people. To bring order from this chaos, the most minute activities of everyday life were totally regulated. There were rules for everything, from getting out of bed to eating one's meals. Rules which Mme de Noailles, the young Dauphine's lady-in-waiting, enforced so rigorously that she was promptly nicknamed 'Madame Etiquette'. Marie-Antoinette never really adapted to the French royal family's public and formalized life-style. She 'used to relate with delight details of the patriarchal customs of the House of Lorraine', and tried to imitate her beloved father, who had abolished much of the stifling etiquette of the Habsburg Court.[18] In France, however, people took exception to a foreign princess who refused to play by their rules. French royalty lived in public; they dressed, bathed and ate under the gaze of the public. Their apartments were open to all courtiers whose positions gave them a right of entry, at all times. Thus the Dauphine could stand naked and freezing in her room while maids and duchesses sauntered in and out and decided who was meant to hand her her shift. 'It's odious!' she exclaimed. 'What importunity!'[19] As soon as she became Queen, she performed her *toilette* in private. She scandalized old dowagers by walking about the palace accompanied only by a valet and two footmen; a princess was supposed to be followed by a bevy of ladies to safeguard her virtue. And Marie-Antoinette mortally offended many courtiers who found themselves excluded from her inner circle of friends, who received coveted invitations to the Petit Trianon, where she lived 'as a private individual' and the King himself could not enter uninvited.

To do her justice, Marie-Antoinette tried her best to fit into French Court life, and no one ever reproached her for the way she carried out her public duties. 'No woman,' declared the Comte de Tilly, 'knew better than she did how to perform her part of Queen.'[20] She nevertheless fought a constant war against what she saw as unwarrantable intrusions into her privacy, to the despair of both 'Madame Etiquette' and her mother. Court routine was boring beyond belief. A couple of months after her arrival at Versailles, the Dauphine sent her mother details of a typical day. She rose between 9 a.m. and 10 a.m., said her prayers, had breakfast, then paid a visit to her husband's aunts, who had taken her under their wing. Afterwards she had her hair done and dressed in public before going to Mass in the chapel. Dinner followed at 1 p.m. She would then spend an hour and a half either with the Dauphin or alone in her apartments, before amusing herself by playing music, going for a walk or ride, and presenting herself at the public card-table before supper. 'I'm making a waistcoat for the King,' she wrote on 12 July 1770, 'which hardly progresses at all. I hope by the grace of God it will be finished within a few years.'[21]

Such dry humour is typical of Marie-Antoinette. She could not keep to such a tedious regime for very long. Soon Mercy had to report that she was tired of being constantly on public display, disliked having to wear both corsets and heavy Court dress, and had 'developed

an excessive passion for horse-riding'.[22] Worse still, she almost precipitated a diplomatic crisis by refusing to speak to Mme du Barry,
whom she described as 'the silliest and most impertinent creature
imaginable'.[23] It took a great deal of persuasion from Vienna to get
the Dauphine to pacify the favourite by the memorable observation:
'there are a great many people at Versailles today, Madame'.

Marie-Antoinette had perhaps taken her mother's strictures on virtue
a little too much to heart when it came to du Barry, although her
dislike had been fuelled by the Dauphin's aunts, who detested their
father's mistress and doubtless impressed on Marie-Antoinette her
close connections to the anti-Austrian faction. Marie-Antoinette probably had far more dangerous enemies within her own family circle.
She soon saw through the deceit and hypocrisy of her husband's
younger brother, the Comte de Provence ('Monsieur' from 10 May
1774, later Louis XVIII), who bitterly resented the fact that a man
he considered a fool was going to be King, and privately expressed
the strongest opposition to the Franco-Austrian alliance. 'I do not
greatly approve of our alliance with Austria,' he informed Gustav III
of Sweden, 'on the contrary, I think Cardinal Richelieu was very
right to want to destroy this hydra.'[24]

Although the corpulent Comte de Provence did not lack self-esteem,
like the Dauphin he was sexually incompetent (both suffered from
phimosis, an abnormality of the foreskin), and could not provide heirs
to the throne. The Comte d'Artois, however, two years younger than
Marie-Antoinette, was the exact opposite of his older brothers. Slim,
good-looking and decidedly virile, he was the chief purveyor of many
of her amusements, and encouraged her unregal whims; horse-racing,
gambling and dancing all night. It made her mother shudder. This
madness was not without some method. Artois's unloved wife rapidly gave birth to two sons, and while sexual relations between his
oldest brother and Marie-Antoinette remained in limbo he 'had the
imprudence and baseness to say that it would be desirable for his
interests that the Queen had no children, and that if she were widowed, the best thing she could do would be to return to Vienna'.[25]

The elderly Comtesse de La Marck drew a dismal picture of the
French royal household in 1771 in a letter to Gustav III:

> M. le Dauphin displays a few natural virtues, but without intelligence,
> learning or reading (for which he doesn't even have an inclination)

and he is as hard in his principles as he is gross in his actions. M. le Comte de Provence is smooth, clever and polished enough, but he is conceited and . . . I won't say the rest for fear of displeasing Your Majesty. His wife is ugly and ill-tempered, and it is said they do not love each other. M. le Comte d'Artois has wit, the desire to please and to make everyone about him happy . . . he carries all our hopes, for it is quite likely that the Dauphin and the Comte de Provence will not have children. . . . She is pretty, the Dauphine, she has intelligence, and a grace and a charm in her whole person which belong to her alone.[26]

The Dauphin was absolutely no help to Marie-Antoinette in this hostile environment. He was 'too apathetic to be her guide and did not yet love her'. Realizing the great inadequacy of his education he began to try to improve his mind (geography, history and English were his favourite subjects), while 'hunting and mechanical works occupied all his leisure hours'.[27] Hunting was his overriding preoccupation throughout his life. His diary shows that he hunted for 140 to 180 days every year, and the total of his kills between 1774 and 1787 was a breath-taking 190,525 'pieces' – they do not even merit the word animals. This mad pursuit of game left Louis no time for his wife. 'Building and metal work pleased him to such a degree that he admitted a master locksmith into his apartments with whom he used to forge keys and locks, and his hands, blackened by this work, were the subject of complaints and even quite sharp reproaches from Marie-Antoinette.'[28]

She soon found she was wasting her breath. Mercy reported that on one occasion in 1773 when she chided the Dauphin for needlessly exhausting himself and getting dirty, he burst into tears! According to François Gamain, the locksmith who became his close confidant and ultimately betrayed him, Louis XVI employed 'a thousand stratagems' to 'steal away from the Queen and his Court to come and file and forge with me'.[29] He even had a forge built above the library in his private apartments.

Unfortunately for Marie-Antoinette, her own deficient education did not provide her with the mental resources to cope with this impossible marriage. Brought up solely to be a wife and mother, she seemed doomed to fail as both. She spoke fluent French and Italian, very little German, had atrocious handwriting, and excelled at music and dancing. Her youthful reading matter consisted principally of light novels. Yet she was not ignorant. She had a far better grasp of politics than her husband, and expressed her opinions in lucid prose. Had she been allowed to develop her abilities without Austria's malign influence, she might have been as great a queen as her mother; but constant prodding by Mercy and Maria-Theresa merely gave Marie-Antoinette a distaste for politics and all serious subjects. She disliked asking her husband for the political information and favours Austria demanded, and although she could usually be bullied into obeying her mother's wishes, she rebelled by plunging into a frantic social schedule with young people who amused themselves by mocking the fusty old rituals of Versailles.

Marie-Antoinette's flagrant disregard for Court etiquette brought her many enemies among the Court nobility. She enjoyed unprecedented freedom, both as Dauphine and Queen, and used it to dance the nights away in Paris (at private *hôtels* and opera balls), to gamble for high stakes at the Princesse de Guéméné's house, to go to the races at Vincennes, and to advance the unworthy causes of her friends. Closest to Marie-Antoinette were the Princesse de Lamballe, the young widow of a Bourbon prince, and the Comtesse (later Duchesse) de Polignac. Mme de Lamballe proved to be a true friend, unwaveringly loyal, but Mme de Polignac was surrounded by avaricious relatives who used her influence to gain enormous financial favours and prestigious positions at Court.

To the horror of the starchy Court hierarchy, Marie-Antoinette also enjoyed the company of men. Her early amusements nearly always involved her brother-in-law, the Comte d'Artois, and her treacherous cousin, the Duc de Chartres (later Duc d'Orléans). Several other men who tried to start love-affairs with her were backed by Court factions. The Dauphin was widely regarded as weak, ineffectual and strongly influenced by his wife. It therefore seemed logical to conclude that any man who succeeded in winning her affections would wield a powerful influence behind the throne. Marie-Antoinette, however, easily saw through professional seducers like the Duc de Lauzun and the Vicomte de Noailles who paid insincere court to her. She told the Prince de Ligne, a welcome visitor from the Austrian Netherlands, 'a thousand interesting stories concerning her and all the traps which had been laid to give her lovers'.[30] This possibly explains why many of the men admitted to her private circle were

middle aged. Nevertheless, the Duc de Coigny (known to be a perfect gentleman who made a second marriage to Mme de Châlons,
another member of Marie-Antoinette's set), and Comte Valentin
Esterhazy (for whom Marie-Antoinette actually found a wife), were
universally termed her lovers. Among others who enjoyed the same
illusory favour were the British ambassador, the Duke of Dorset, the
Baron de Besenval, the Duc de Guines, and nearly every single man
she spoke to at opera balls.

The tone of Marie-Antoinette's salon did nothing to dispel the
idea that she was utterly wanton and frivolous. 'The latest song, the
bon mot of the day, scandalous little anecdotes, were the sole topics
of conversation', according to Mme Campan.[31] The Dauphine developed many new fashions with her dressmaker, Rose Bertin, and extravagant hair-styles with her hairdresser, Léonard. She also got into
financial straits through the purchase of diamond bracelets and earrings
worth 348,000 *livres* from the Court jewellers Boehmer and Bassenge.
Her husband often came to her rescue by settling her debts, and
paid the 300,000 *livres* she owed on these diamonds in instalments
over six years. Marie-Antoinette's genuine appreciation of music, drama
and the fine arts was matched by her exquisite taste, but her in-
stincts as a connoisseur were not developed fully until she became
Queen.

The young Marie-Antoinette's public image was therefore that of
a wayward social butterfly, who neglected her husband and her royal
role. She confessed to Mercy that she was 'terrified of being bored',
and she fled the stultifying atmosphere of Versailles and the husband who ignored her for the glitter and gaiety of Paris. Even so she
charmed her sternest critics by the goodness of her heart. When the
postilion of her carriage fell and was run over as she returned from
following the hunt in December 1770, the Dauphine staggered all
onlookers by tending to him personally for over an hour, ensuring
he was carried gently back to Versailles, and ordering her own surgeon to treat him. In November 1773 Louis XV's hounds ran a stag
into a garden near Fontainebleau, and the animal severely gored a
gardener. The King uttered only a few words of sympathy and rode
on, but as soon as Marie-Antoinette heard of the accident she made
her coach turn back, did her best to comfort the wounded man's
wife, gave her all the money she had in her purse, and then insisted
she be taken home in the royal carriage, in defiance of all etiquette.

But as Mme Campan testified, 'her heart was always ready to show feelings of compassion'.[32]

Marie-Antoinette's soft heart made her sympathetic towards others, but she seldom demanded sympathy for herself. Although 'deeply hurt' by the Dauphin's behaviour, 'she never permitted herself to utter the slightest complaint . . . a few tears, which dropped involuntarily from her eyes, were the only traces her servants could see of her secret sorrows'.[33] She was a princess, so she grieved in private. Occasionally, however, her guard slipped enough for her misery to become apparent. One of her favourite activities was riding, which greatly worried her mother, particularly as Marie-Antoinette rode astride and at breakneck speed. An old lady attached to her household, fearing it might prejudice her chances of getting pregnant, urged her to give it up. 'In God's name,' snapped the Dauphine, 'leave me in peace, and be assured that I am not compromising any heir.'[34]

For a long time Marie-Antoinette had no hope at all of conceiving children with her husband, but she patiently answered all her mother's queries about her menstrual cycle (which was very irregular), and never betrayed her disappointment. Mercy nevertheless saw her distress when the Comtesse d'Artois became pregnant in 1774, reporting that Marie-Antoinette was 'inwardly affected by it in a very grievous manner'.[35] Her mask of indifference was put to the test when her sister-in-law gave birth to a son, the Duc d'Angoulême, on 6 August 1775. Marie-Antoinette was obliged to witness the birth, and as she returned to her own apartments she was harangued in foul language by Parisian fishwives about her childlessness (her unproductive sexual relations with the King were the subject of many rude songs circulating the capital). Mme Campan takes up the story: 'The Queen arrived at her apartments, very agitated and quickening her steps; she shut herself up alone with me to cry . . . with grief at her position.'[36]

Her unhappiness was not due solely to the political necessity of producing an heir. Marie-Antoinette was genuinely fond of children. She took a keen interest in her nephews and niece, and 'she always had children around her who belonged to members of her household, and lavished tender caresses on them'.[37] She even adopted a five-year-old orphan, Jacques Armand, who narrowly escaped death when he ran out in front of her carriage. 'He was brought to see her every morning at nine o'clock; he breakfasted and dined with her, often even with the King. She enjoyed calling him *my child*.'[38]

None of this had the slightest effect on Louis XVI, who remained as sexually incompetent as he had been on his wedding night. Although he followed the advice of various doctors and tried numerous diets, he seemed to grow only fatter and more lethargic. To compensate for his shortcomings in bed, he indulged all Marie-Antoinette's whims. Indeed, he seemed to encourage her constant pursuit of amusement, probably because it left him free to hunt or work at his forge. It was no help at all that Marie-Antoinette was herself sexually inexperienced and decidedly not in love with a man whose inexpert fumblings succeeded only in driving her out night after night to dance and gamble in Paris. In 1774, shortly after becoming Queen, she confessed to the true state of affairs between herself and 'the poor man' in a light-hearted letter to an Austrian friend, Count von Rosenberg: 'My tastes are not at all the same as the King's; he likes only hunting and mechanical works. You will agree that I would look out of place next to a forge; I could not be Vulcan, and the role of Venus might perhaps displease him more than my interests, of which he does not disapprove.'[39]

Marie-Antoinette also expressed satisfaction at her part in the recent dismissal of the Duc d'Aiguillon and Choiseul's recall from exile (although he never returned to power), and she boasted of her tactics in manipulating her husband – *le pauvre homme* – into granting Choiseul an audience. Horrified, Rosenberg showed the letter to Empress Maria-Theresa. It brought Marie-Antoinette a stinging rebuke from Vienna. 'What a style! What frivolity!' exclaimed her mother. 'Where is the kind, generous heart of the Archduchess Antoinette?'[40] She was displaying far too much independence, and a cynicism which could seriously undermine the Franco-Austrian alliance. Mercy complained that despite being 'gifted with an excellent character, a good deal of intelligence, sagacity, and discernment' Marie-Antoinette still had 'an extreme repugnance for business or serious reflection'.[41] Her flippancy shows what an uphill struggle he had keeping her to the straight and narrow of politics. Austrian demands on her, however, essentially required a successful marriage, and in 1774 it was still unconsummated.

Small wonder that Marie-Antoinette, eighteen, beautiful, isolated from her family and unloved by an unattractive husband, should be susceptible to the charms of a handsome and accomplished young man like Axel Fersen.

2

The Hero of a Novel

When Count Axel Fersen arrived in Paris in December 1773 after his three-and-a-half-year Grand Tour, he had already seen and learnt more than Louis XVI would experience in a lifetime. Tall, dark, very handsome, well educated and well mannered, eighteen-year-old Fersen was ready to embark on his career. As a member of Sweden's most influential noble family, he was expected to have a brilliant future.

On 4 September 1755 Hans Axel Fersen was born in his father's palatial residence on Blaiseholmen, directly across the water from the royal palace in Stockholm. Wealth and power were his birthright. The Fersens had provided Sweden with three marshals and leading senators within a century. Axel's mother, Countess Hedwig De La Gardie, came from an even more illustrious dynasty. Her ancestor General Jacob De La Gardie, who conquered Finland and the Baltic states for Sweden, was rewarded with the title of Count in 1615, and acted as Regent during the minority of Queen Christina. His son Magnus ruled Sweden virtually single-handed from 1660 until his fall from grace under King Karl XI in 1680. As the eldest son of a marriage between two such outstanding families, Axel was heir to castles and estates in both Sweden and Finland, and was strongly encouraged to continue the family tradition of running the country.

The Fersens owed their political influence to the Swedish constitution of 1720, under which power was theoretically shared between the crown, the nobility and the three other estates (merchants, peasants and clergy). In practice, the nobility had total control of the government. The *Riksdag*, or parliament, consisted of four chambers, one for each estate. It met every three years and could be dissolved only by itself. It had almost unlimited power, including the right to raise taxes, to declare war, and to make or break alliances. The *Riksdag* could also choose a new king if the succession were in doubt. Once its sessions ended, its functions were assumed by the Senate. Senators were noblemen, nominated every three years by the *Riksdag*. The King had only two votes in the Senate, and was merely required to sign legislation put in front of him. Although he had a cabinet, his ministers were, of course, drawn from the Senate.

Matters were not so simple as this summary may suggest. The political scene was complicated by the existence of two bitterly opposed parties, who gloried in the names of Hats and Nightcaps. The ruling Hats had been founded by Axel Fersen's grandfather. The De La Gardies were also Hats, and after his marriage to Hedwig De La Gardie in 1752, Marshal Fredrik Axel Fersen, Axel's father, became all-powerful as the leader of this party in the Senate. The Hats pursued liberal policies at home, while their foreign policy was dictated by the need to ward off Russian, Prussian and Danish encroachments on Swedish territory, which then extended well beyond the country's modern borders. To this end they allied themselves with France, while the Nightcaps relied on British, Russian and Danish gold to pursue entirely opposite aims.

So great was the schism in eighteenth-century Swedish politics, the country stood in real danger of being swallowed up by its neighbours. Matters eventually came to a head when in 1771 the twenty-five-year-old King Gustav III came to the throne. Although Gustav was in France when he became King, the Nightcaps claimed he had poisoned his father, and tried to give the crown to his younger brother Karl, Duke of Södermanland. Gustav, however, had not been idle in France. He displeased the fifteen-year-old Marie-Antoinette (perhaps because he paid too much attention to Mme du Barry), but he succeeded in obtaining French financial and political support for an audacious scheme to overturn the Swedish constitution. Gustav sought absolute power to block Russian and Prussian plans to partition his country. Frederick the Great of Prussia was Gustav's uncle, but kinship had not deterred him from signing a secret treaty with Catherine the Great to partition Sweden as they had done Poland.

Gustav III was to be a pivotal figure in the lives of both Axel Fersen and Marie-Antoinette. Historians tend to overlook his statesmanship, concentrating instead on his highly colourful personality.

His education, entirely controlled by the Hats, had been based on a French model, and left him with an enduring love of French literature, art and drama. His father was indolent, his mother an avowed atheist who seemed to despise everyone, particularly her children, while Gustav himself was married to a Danish princess he did not love, chosen for him by the Nightcaps. Many people considered the young Swedish King an effete dandy of ambiguous sexuality who preferred to dress up and act in his private theatre rather than concentrate on affairs of state. Gustav milked this image for all it was worth when he staged his *coup d'état* on 19 August 1772. His plans were exceptionally well laid, and the night before he seized power he was to be found as usual in his finery innocently amusing himself at the theatre and then at a brilliant supper party. Morning saw a very different Gustav in military uniform, haranguing his troops and people in Swedish on the streets of Stockholm, and ordering the arrest of all senators.[1] On 21 August he presented the *Riksdag* with a new constitution, which restored nearly all power to the crown. It was unanimously accepted. Gustav became the undisputed master of Sweden, and not a single drop of blood had been shed.

Gustav did not disappoint those subjects who looked on him as their country's saviour. His French education had brought him into contact with the ideas of the *philosophes* (he corresponded with Voltaire), and he rapidly introduced liberal political reforms. He established freedom of religion, freedom of the press and free trade. He ended legal corruption, abolished torture, and revised the draconian Swedish penal code. He also reduced taxes for large families, encouraged new industries, and brought in progressive agricultural reforms. It made him very popular with the people, but it alienated aristocrats who had wielded power for so long.

Young Axel Fersen was at university in Turin when he heard of the political upheaval in Sweden which deprived his father of power. Fredrik Axel Fersen reacted to what he considered outright despotism by resigning from the King's cabinet. The French ambassador to Sweden, the Comte de Vergennes, wrote an interesting report on 'Marshal Count Fersen, the most illustrious citizen because of the principal role he has played for so long in his country as leader of the Hats' party.' He listed various unsavoury allegations made against Fersen by the Nightcaps, then added: 'I must say that these traits do not agree at all with my own impression of his character. He has sometimes been well able to take advantage of circumstances; he has a great deal of pride, that's true, but I don't believe him to be deficient either in integrity or honesty.'[2]

Gustav could not really afford to lose the services of such a man, particularly as Fersen had strong links with France, which had supplied the money for his *coup* and promised subsidies for several years to come. Fersen was recalled to office, but he remained in the vanguard of attempts to curb the King's authority, and his relationship with Gustav was never easy. The rest of the Fersen family, however, soon accommodated themselves to the new system, enjoying the friendship and protection of the royal family.

Axel's mother, Countess Hedwig Fersen, was chief lady-in-waiting to the Queen Mother, while Axel, his younger brother Fabian, sisters Hedda and Sophie, uncle Count Charles Fersen and two cousins all held posts at Court. Axel was very close to Sophie, two years his junior, and confided in her completely. She had the misfortune to fall in love with Gustav III's younger brother, Prince Fredrik. Fredrik proposed to Sophie twice, but her father rejected him and married her off to Count Adolf Piper, whom she did not love. Axel himself appears to have flirted briefly with the Duchess of Södermanland, Gustav's sister-in-law, but she soon realized his 'friendship . . . was only the work of the moment' and that her love would never be requited.[3] Dallying with royalty seems to have been another family tradition, one which Axel continued; Ebba Brahe, wife of his forebear Jacob De La Gardie, had been mistress to the great Swedish King Gustav Adolf.

Despite the prestige he enjoyed in Sweden, it was almost inevitable that Axel Fersen should be more attracted to life and a career in France. The Franco-Swedish alliance dated back to 1631. The Swedes imported art, fashion, music, philosophy and drama from France, and French was the adopted language of the Swedish Court and nobility. Axel's father had himself been educated in France, and enjoyed a distinguished military career under French colours as proprietary Colonel of the Royal-Suédois regiment. His brother Charles, also a leading politician, developed a lasting interest in French drama, and 'blessed with a handsome face and an imposing figure, had succumbed to this passion so far as to join several provincial French theatre companies under a false name'.[4] Count Charles Fersen went on to play many a role when he returned to Sweden, in Gustav III's private theatre at Drottningholm, which remains the most perfectly preserved Court theatre in Europe. Even Axel's aunt, 'the beautiful Countess Sparre', had spent many years in Paris, where her husband was an attaché at the Swedish Embassy.

Axel was therefore brought up in a French-speaking environment. All his letters to his family are in French, as is his diary. This background, coupled with his father's determination to have him educated on the Continent, meant that ultimately he spent more years abroad than at home, and he never really felt at ease in Sweden. His first taste of foreign travel came on 3 June 1770, when at the age of fourteen he set off on the Grand Tour with his tutor Bolémany. One cannot help noticing the parallel with Marie-Antoinette, also fourteen, who just six weeks earlier had been dispatched to France to be married.

Axel Fersen's tour began with Copenhagen, then Germany, where he started student life at Lüneburg. His education befitted his future roles as courtier, soldier and diplomat. Axel began to keep a diary in which he recorded the regular pattern of his studies. He rose at 6 a.m., and after saying prayers and dressing had lessons in German and history. Between 8 a.m. and 10 a.m. he could be found at the riding school. French, Ancient history and more German lessons followed before dinner at 12.30 p.m. From 2 p.m. to 4 p.m. he received language and piano tuition. Afterwards he was under orders from his fencing-master for an hour or two. Then came a brief period of relaxation and supper before Axel went to bed at 10 p.m. Quite a contrast to the aimless timetable which Marie-Antoinette was following at Versailles!

After some time at Lüneburg, Axel spent several months studying at Strasbourg. He left for Italy in October 1771, passing through Switzerland. While in Geneva he paid a visit to Voltaire at Ferney. The grotesque appearance of the great French satirist and political philosopher seemed to make a much deeper impression on the young Count Fersen than his conversation.

> We talked to him for two hours. He was dressed in a scarlet waistcoat with old embroidered buttons. . . . An old wig (not curled), old-fashioned shoes, woollen stockings pulled up over his breeches, an old dressing-gown – this made up his dress, in admirable harmony with his wrinkled face; but we were struck by the beauty of his eyes and the vivacity of his expression. His whole face had a completely satirical air.[5]

The lack of information on Voltaire's conversation reveals the laconic, intensely practical Axel who seldom recorded others' words unless they were of political or military significance, and also indicates a sixteen-year-old nobleman perhaps a little too concerned with the superficial.

At Turin, where he attended university from November 1771, Axel completed his education and began to make his mark in society. He left the city with regret in April 1773 to see the sights of Italy. He had begun to develop a reputation as a ladies' man in Turin, but was sorely disappointed when he reached Milan. 'The sex at Milan is not at all fair, very ill-dressed, in bad taste, and slovenly, which is common in Italy except in Turin,' he noted.[6] He was certainly a fastidious man where women were concerned, and very few met with his whole-hearted approval.

From Milan, Axel and Bolémany progressed to Rome and Naples, and like all grand tourists they visited Pompeii and Mount Vesuvius. At Naples Axel was befriended by the French ambassador, the Baron de Breteuil, whose previous posts had included Sweden, where he became acquainted with Marshal Fersen. Breteuil later proved a very important connection in France for Axel.

After paying his court in Florence to Marie-Antoinette's brother Leopold, Grand Duke of Tuscany, Axel and his tutor made a brief return visit to Turin before leaving Italy. They reached Paris in December 1773. By now Axel was allowed to spend most of his time displaying his talents in the Parisian *beau monde*. His studies had been nothing if not thorough. In addition to his native Swedish and fluent French he spoke Italian, German and English, and had a good grounding in the required academic disciplines for a man of his rank. His horsemanship and swordsmanship were essential for the military career for which he longed, but he was not deficient in social graces. His early diary indicates a young man who loved to dance and enjoyed the theatre and good music; he always travelled with his own piano. These tastes must have been a potent attraction for the dancing-mad, music- and theatre-loving Marie-Antoinette.

As the son of an influential man, Axel Fersen received a great deal of attention from Parisian hostesses. The Swedish ambassador, Count Creutz, and his First Secretary, Count Ramel, made a point of introducing Axel to all the best families. He also made obligatory appearances at Versailles. On 1 January 1774 he went to Court to watch the investiture of new knights to the Order of the Holy Ghost, and afterwards noted in his diary: 'I went with the Comte de Creutz to pay a visit to Mme du Barry. She spoke to me then for the first time.'[7] It was quite an honour for an eighteen-year-old to be noticed by Louis XV's mistress, though rather galling for her rival, the pretty Dauphine. Marie-Antoinette was not the only member of the royal family to be impressed by Axel. He was regularly invited to balls at the Palais Royal in Paris given by the Duc d'Orléans, but found them somewhat uninspiring. 'As I was leaving,' he wrote after a particularly dull evening there, 'I thought that the French don't know how to enjoy themselves. They have the bad habit of constantly saying "I'm bored", and it poisons all their pleasures.'[8]

Far more enjoyable were the suppers and balls given by the Marquise de Brancas, who treated Axel 'with a great deal of courtesy'. He thought nothing of dancing at her house from 8 p.m. to 6 a.m. with only an hour's rest for supper.[9] But his life was not totally carefree. In mid-February his friend and compatriot Baron Anton de Geer fell ill with gout, and Axel showed the compassionate side of his character by forsaking society to keep him company. 'As I spent all my evenings with him, after the theatre (which I always attended very regularly), the Carnival passed very quietly for me,' he wrote.[10]

In fact, after his long chat with Marie-Antoinette at the opera ball on 30 January, Axel withdrew a little from the Parisian social round to spend more time at Versailles, even though some of the dancers at Court balls failed to meet his exacting standards. On 15 February he went to a ball at the palace attended by Marie-Antoinette, her husband and his brothers. 'They danced different *entrées*,' Axel noted in his diary, 'some very badly, like the Dauphin and M. de Provence, the others quite well.'[11] However he makes no comment on the Dauphine. Did they dance together? It is more than probable. Marie-Antoinette was a very graceful dancer, and had numerous partners at Court balls. She would surely not have overlooked the handsome Swede she had targeted at the opera ball who made such a refreshing change from her clumsy husband.

Axel's highly successful six months in Paris made a lasting impression on his mind. He left for the final leg of his tour, a visit to England, on 12 May 1774 – just two days after Louis XVI ascended the throne and Marie-Antoinette became Queen. The Swedish ambassador, Creutz, was so pleased with his young protégé's behaviour that he made special mention of him in a dispatch to Gustav III on 29 May:

The young Comte de Fersen has just left for London. Of all the Swedes who have been here during my time, it is he who has been most well received in society. He has been extremely well treated by the royal family. It is not possible to have a better or more decent conduct than that which he has maintained. With a most handsome face and intelligence, he could not fail to succeed in society, and he has done so completely. Your Majesty will surely be pleased, but what makes M. de Fersen especially worthy of your kindness, is that he thinks with a singular nobility and loftiness.[12]

High praise indeed for Axel, whose triumph was to have consequences neither he nor Creutz could have foreseen. It is clear that in the royal family it was Marie-Antoinette in particular who treated him 'extremely well', and although he makes few detailed references to her in 1774, Axel's later letters and diary reveal that he was far from insensible to her charms. They were not to meet again for another four years. The young Queen could only try to forget her heartache and distract herself as best she could. And heartache it was. Axel Fersen must have been a revelation to Marie-Antoinette; a handsome young man who asked for no favours and was sociable and yet discreet at the same time. She loved him from the moment they first met.

Marie-Antoinette was certainly not the only woman to love Axel Fersen. He exerted a very powerful attraction over the opposite sex throughout his life, not simply because he was handsome, but because he instinctively gravitated towards women. He enjoyed the company and conversation of women, and many became his friends and advisers. What were the qualities in him which they so admired? The Duc de Lévis, a French courtier, painted a picture of a man in the strong silent mould:

The Comte de Fersen . . . was a great Swedish lord, whose figure was tall and whose face regular without being expressive. His manners were noble and unaffected. His conversation was not very animated, and he showed more judgement than wit. He was circumspect with men and reserved with women, serious without being sad. His face and his manner were perfectly suited to the hero of a novel, though not of a French novel, for he had neither the brilliance nor the frivolity.[13]

Marie-Antoinette's page, Alexandre de Tilly, called Axel 'one of the handsomest men I ever saw, though with an icy countenance,

which women do not dislike if they can hope to give it animation',
while he was generally agreed to possess 'a rare discretion'.[14] According to the Comte de Saint-Priest, a diplomat, Axel's looks were
indeed exceptional: 'He had, in effect, a striking face. Tall, slim,
perfectly well made, with beautiful eyes . . . he was made to create in
the eyes of a woman who sought his [eyes] deeper impressions than
she expected.'[15]

His calm, reserved demeanour and musical and artistic tastes were
all attractive to Marie-Antoinette, although doubtless she fell first
for his 'beautiful eyes' beneath their arched black eyebrows. Temperamentally they were well suited. She was noted for her even temper, and both had a sentimental, romantic view of love. Axel disliked
strident and capricious women; Marie-Antoinette's gentleness, kindness and charm were qualities he praised again and again. He also
greatly admired her figure, the graceful way she walked, her style
and femininity. She should have been flattered, for he was a hard
man to please!

Despite Axel's reserve and even a melancholy streak ('I'm not one
of those men who will find happiness,' he once wrote), he was far
from being an 'icy' character.[16] One woman who loved him and was
rebuffed, the Comtesse de Saint-Priest, vowed that he had 'a burning soul beneath a layer of ice'.[17] She unhappily had to settle for his
'friendship and interest', but to those he loved he was very demonstrative. His expressions of deep feeling are all the more convincing
because of his habitual reticence. Even women he liked were mentioned as merely 'pretty' or 'amiable' in his diary. His outpourings
of love, on the other hand, are worthy of the most ardent romantic
hero. The solemn, soulful expression on Axel Fersen's face was the
outward mask of a passionate man indeed.

Romance, however, was not on Axel's mind during the two months
he spent in London in 1774. He found the freedom Englishwomen
enjoyed and their strict morals remarkable after Paris, and the study
of English proved more productive than exceedingly dull balls at
Almack's Assembly Rooms. He left London in the autumn, and when
he landed at Dunkirk wrote: 'I was very happy to see France again.'[18]
Bypassing Paris, he undertook a circuitous journey back to Sweden
through the Netherlands and Germany, arriving home in December
1774 after an absence of four and a half years.

Axel's father now expected him to prepare for his future role as a key figure in the Swedish establishment. He held a lieutenant's commission in one of the French army's German regiments (the Royal-Bavière), which left the door open to a career in France, while in Sweden he was made a captain in the King's Light Horse, a regiment for scions of the nobility. In military terms this was undemanding, and Axel spent most of his time idly at Court or at home.

Conversations with his beloved sister Sophie relieved the tedium of long evenings in his father's castles, and when she was absent Axel wrote telling her how much he missed her. Their parents spent hours playing piquet after dinner, so Axel often retreated to his room to read, write letters, or play the flute.[19] Court life in Stockholm or at the royal castles of Drottningholm and Gripsholm was a little more lively. There were women to flirt with, balls to attend, and the King's famous theatricals. Gustav III took an instant liking to Axel Fersen, and quickly commandeered him and his family for the numerous productions of French plays which he staged in the Court theatre. On 24 February 1776 during a performance representing the Paris fair of Saint-Germain, Axel 'disguised as an English jockey, made a trained horse perform a hundred tricks. Two months later he appeared with his sister in *La Rosière de Salency*, where both took part in the ballet of shepherds and shepherdesses, while their father, the senator, appeared as "a neighbour" and their Uncle Charles, Chief Huntsman, played the bailiff'.[20]

Axel soon wearied of this unexciting routine. On 24 August 1776 he wrote to Sophie from Ekolsund, where the Court was then in residence: 'I'm exceedingly bored. I would like to be far away from here. All these faces at Court seem so old, they all displease me, but I must nevertheless resolve to see them until November. Patience!'[21]

It was all a far cry from the active and adventurous life he had hoped to have as a soldier. Foreign service seemed most likely to offer Axel the military career he desired, but his father was anxious that he establish himself in Sweden. Senator Fersen unwittingly provided his son with an escape route; he sent him to London to propose marriage to a wealthy young heiress. Neither matrimony nor fortune-hunting were to Axel's taste, but he gladly embarked on the mission to bring his father a rich daughter-in-law. Senator Fersen's dynastic ambitions got the better of his judgement. Little did he know that his son had absolutely no interest in his matchmaking schemes, and would instead find both glory and love in France.

3

From Austria with Love

When Axel Fersen returned to Paris in 1778 he paid court to a Marie-Antoinette considerably changed from the carefree Dauphine he had left four years earlier. She was now a queen. Furthermore, she was pregnant. The whole of France confidently anticipated the birth at last of an heir to the throne. The Comte de Mercy rather optimistically expected a reduction in his roles as super-spy and father-confessor to the Queen as she settled, he hoped, into a more sedate and matronly routine. He should have known her better. Marie-Antoinette was still only twenty-two, wore her majesty lightly, and did not yet appreciate that maternity would curb her exuberant life-style. Mercy could congratulate himself on having restrained her a little, and could take credit for the diplomatic manoeuvres that led to her long-awaited pregnancy. This event, which astonished and delighted France, occurred only after systematic counselling and persuasion by Mercy, Vermond and the Court physician Lassonne, and finally the blunt advice of Marie-Antoinette's brother, Emperor Joseph II. Without Austrian coercion and help, it is unlikely that she and Louis XVI would have conceived a child at all.

The prospect of motherhood was, however, still on the distant horizon when Marie-Antoinette became Queen. Louis XV's sudden death from smallpox on 10 May 1774 thrust a young and politically naïve couple into a position of absolute power. The nineteen-year-old Louis XVI was only just remedying the defects in his education; shy, lacking in confidence and political nous, he did not have the charisma required to enact his enlightened ideas. Deprived of an official political role, Marie-Antoinette used her influence merely to obtain favours or Court positions for her friends. Policy was a matter for the King's ministers.

The French people nevertheless expected much more. Despite his sobriquet, *le bien aimé*, Louis XV had been far from beloved. During his reign the monarchy became isolated from the people, who grew thoroughly disillusioned with the King's debauchery and extravagance. 'The joy displayed by the public on the death of the late King has been carried even to a point of indecency,' Mercy reported on 17 May 1774.[1] Everywhere they went the young Louis XVI and his Queen were greeted with enthusiastic applause from a nation which yearned for radical reform.

Marie-Antoinette told her mother that 'the new King seems to possess the heart of his people. . . . What is certain is that he has an inclination for economy, and the greatest desire to make his subjects happy'. After his coronation at Reims on 20 June 1774, she was concerned about continued high expectations of the new reign: 'It's very true that praise and admiration for the King have resounded everywhere. He certainly merits it for the integrity of his soul and his desire to do good; but I worry about this French enthusiasm for the future.'[2] There were simply too many problems to solve, too many conflicting interests to satisfy.

Marie-Antoinette was now in a position to work harder for the Franco-Austrian alliance, and her mother expected her to exert her influence over Louis XVI to further Austrian foreign policy objectives. Mercy, however, found it extremely difficult to fix the young Queen's attention on such weighty matters, as he informed the Austrian Chancellor Kaunitz: 'The Queen is certainly endowed with the necessary qualities to be able, if she wishes, to reap the benefit of the immense advantages of her position: all depends on the degree of will. In this princess I have to combat a certain levity and too great a readiness to allow herself to be taken by surprise.'[3] Too great a readiness, he might have added, to ignore his unpalatable advice and devote herself solely to pleasure.

Immediately after Louis XV's death the Court left Versailles to prevent other members of the royal family succumbing to smallpox. Louis XVI and his brothers were inoculated against the disease at La Muette in June 1774. When they recovered, the Court moved to the palace of Marly, famous for its magnificent fountains and gardens.

Marie-Antoinette, never very keen on spending her nights in bed, took nocturnal strolls in the grounds with her retinue to refresh herself after the heat of the day. One night she had the romantic notion of going to watch the sun rise, and accordingly set off at 3 a.m. for a distant hill, accompanied by her ladies. A few days later she became a victim for the first time of the sexual slander which ultimately destroyed her reputation, when 'the most wicked libel which ever appeared during the early years of the reign was circulated in Paris' under the innocuous name 'Sunrise'. It is highly significant that 'the Duc d'Orléans, then Duc de Chartres, was one of those who accompanied the young Queen on this nocturnal promenade'.[4] At that time he was seen frequently in her company. As Orléans became Marie-Antoinette's worst enemy, and pornographic libels about her later emanated from pamphlet shops in his Parisian headquarters, the Palais Royal, it is tempting to speculate that he was responsible for giving her amusements at Marly a malicious twist. How did knowledge of this walk reach Paris, if not through one of the participants?

Marie-Antoinette was to find her every move the subject of constant sniping by scurrilous Parisian pamphleteers and song-writers. Even her passion for riding and dancing was criticized by those who considered she was wilfully damaging her chances of conceiving a child. She paid no heed to either criticism or slander; believing she was blameless, she continued to amuse herself openly. A wiser woman would have spoken to no one and remained sequestered in her apartments, for the people with whom Marie-Antoinette chose to share her pleasures were neither loyal nor disinterested.

The young Queen was always sure of her husband's approval, whatever Parisians thought of her activities. Louis XVI's love for his wife manifested itself in indulgence and generosity. Unable to fulfil her emotional or sexual needs, he readily granted all her wishes and pandered to her whims. On becoming King he gave her the Petit Trianon, the villa built by Louis XV near the Grand Trianon, about a mile from Versailles. Designed for Mme de Pompadour, it passed into the ownership of Mme du Barry, who was unceremoniously ejected when Louis XV died.

Marie-Antoinette 'took great delight in her retreat at Trianon'. She made no change to the furniture, 'which had become very shabby', and 'slept there in a very faded bed which had even served for the Comtesse du Barry', but she completely altered the gardens and adjoining land.[5] Over a number of years she laid out an English garden, forsaking the rigid formality and topiary of Versailles for lawns, arbours, a lake, a cascade and a rippling brook. More in hope than expectation she had a Temple of Love built in 1778 amidst this scene of rustic repose – a classical cupola supported by ten columns, it sheltered the copy of a statue of Love by Jacques-Philippe Bouchardon. Perhaps it was no coincidence that Bouchardon was official sculptor to the Swedish Court. Was the Temple of Love possibly dedicated to Axel Fersen? He certainly came to know the Petit Trianon very well. With its own theatre, its mock-Norman farmhouse and dairy, it was a sizeable domain. Above all it was a private domain, which rankled with those courtiers not invited to pass through its fine wrought-iron gates.

Marie-Antoinette was adamant that life at the Petit Trianon should not be subject to the same tyrannical etiquette which so irritated her at Versailles, and she jealously guarded her new-found privacy. She used to drive herself there in a small cabriolet or go on foot, followed by a single footman. Only ladies-in-waiting she had expressly invited joined her. Nevertheless the Duc de Fronsac, First Gentleman of the Bedchamber, repeatedly insisted that it was his right to organize theatricals at the Trianon. 'I have already informed you of my wishes regarding the Trianon,' the Queen told him for the umpteenth time. 'I don't hold court there, I live there as a private individual.'[6] Court officials, so long accustomed to intruding in the royal family's apartments at Versailles as a privilege of office, found themselves excluded from the Queen's private circle. It made her unpopular and created yet another subject for scandalous speculation.

The Petit Trianon's gardens were open to the public with the Queen's permission, and even the house could be viewed freely when she was not in residence. Most courtiers, however, sought a coveted invitation to a Trianon house party. They would have been disappointed by the unpretentious routine, for Marie-Antoinette strove to re-create a relaxed country-house atmosphere.

> The Queen . . . entered her salon, and the ladies neither gave up their embroidery nor stopped playing the piano nor did the gentlemen suspend their billiards or game of *tric-trac*. . . . A white chintz dress, gauze fichu and straw hat formed the attire of the princesses. The pleasure of going over all the buildings of the Hameau, watching the cows being milked, and fishing in the lake, delighted the Queen.[7]

Members of the royal family were always invited to the Queen's parties at the Trianon, particularly her shy and pious young sister-in-law Madame Elisabeth. The King often came from Versailles for dinner or supper, as did most of the guests, for there were few guest rooms. Despite this, critics still found ample scope for censure, and concentrated their firepower on the privileged members of the Queen's 'private society'.

Criticism of Marie-Antoinette's friends was not, it has to be said, entirely unjustified. She formed unwise connections in her youth which later proved extremely difficult to sever. Her first intimate friend, the widowed Princesse de Lamballe, was appointed Superintendent of the Queen's household in 1774 with an enormous salary. Mme de Lamballe was royal, delicate and gentle – qualities which appealed to Marie-Antoinette and met with Louis XVI's approval – but she was also sister-in-law to the Duc d'Orléans. Once established in her position she upset many of the Queen's servants, was negligent in her duties, and pushed by the Orléans family, demanded huge financial favours the Queen refused to grant. She was soon supplanted by an obscure countess whose power over Marie-Antoinette seemed unshakeable, and did incalculable damage to her reputation.

Comtesse Jules de Polignac, as she was known when introduced at Court in 1775, was a pretty, elegant, placid and impecunious brunette who seemed to share Marie-Antoinette's sentimental view of friendship. The Queen took an instant liking to her (Mercy called it an infatuation, having seen through the countess's ingénue disguise from the outset), but was not prepared to commit herself to anything more than esteem until Mme de Polignac wrote a tear-jerking farewell note, saying that lack of money obliged her to leave for the country. The note had been drafted by Mme de Polignac's most ardent supporters – her sister-in-law, Comtesse Diane de Polignac (a lady-in-waiting to Madame Elisabeth), her lover, the Comte de Vaudreuil, and the Baron de Besenval.[8]

Tender-hearted and impressionable, the Queen immediately arranged for her new friend to be given an apartment at Versailles. Mme de Polignac refused a post as lady-in-waiting, but her husband became the Queen's equerry, then a duke, then Director-General of the Post Office, while Vaudreuil (whose arrogance Marie-Antoinette found offensive) received an appointment in the household of his friend, the Comte d'Artois. Mme de Polignac was eventually obliged to work for her favour when she became royal governess in 1782, but not before she and her family had extracted massive financial rewards from the crown, including an 800,000 *livres*' dowry for their daughter in 1780. They had a powerful ally in the government. The Prime Minister, the Comte de Maurepas, eagerly promoted demands made by the Polignacs, who were his relations. The Comte d'Artois was another champion of their cause. The Queen eventually tired of their solicitations, and also disagreed with the Polignac clique politically, but her attachment to Mme de Polignac was too strong to precipitate a complete rupture, which occurred only when her friend left Versailles at the outbreak of the Revolution. How far Mme de Polignac personally was involved in her family's machinations is unclear, but she never refused any of the benefits they obtained on her behalf.

Marie-Antoinette told Mme Campan in the early 1780s of 'the worries which her friends' habits caused her; but that she had to bear pains of which she alone was the author; that fickleness in a friendship such as that which had bound her to the duchess [de Polignac], or a total rupture, carried even more serious drawbacks'.[9] This is a very peculiar statement indeed. Marie-Antoinette grew to dislike nearly all Mme de Polignac's associates, and became much cooler towards her friend after they succeeded in appointing Alexandre de Calonne, whom she neither liked nor trusted, as Finance Minister in 1783. Why, therefore, was she afraid to destroy the Polignacs and their clique? She would have won herself great popularity had she done so, for they were detested by the public. It is most improbable that Marie-Antoinette's friendship with Mme de Polignac was the torrid lesbian affair portrayed in pornographic libels, since both women showed far too much interest in the opposite sex, and the countess's affair with Vaudreuil was no secret. There is nevertheless more than a hint of blackmail about her relationship with the Queen. Mercy was worried that Marie-Antoinette confided in her friend to an alarming degree. Mme de Polignac, he declared in 1777, 'is the depository of all her thoughts, and I very much doubt there are any exceptions to this limitless confidence'.[10]

Mme de Polignac doubtless used these imprudent confidences, which must have concerned the Queen's private life, to strengthen her seemingly impregnable position. Axel Fersen certainly knew her well, and a letter Marie-Antoinette sent her in December 1789 proves that the countess was well informed about her liaison with the Swede.[11] As

Mme de Polignac also possessed Louis XVI's friendship, she was in a powerful position. Marie-Antoinette could not afford to cut her completely for fear of provoking scandalous revelations about her love-life. After the Polignacs' departure from France in 1789, they conspicuously failed to help their Queen, allying themselves instead to the Comte d'Artois.

During the early years of her reign Marie-Antoinette had other friends who were equally dangerous: the Duc de Guines, the fashionable Princesse de Guéméné, and the handsome, suave, seductive Duc de Lauzun. None of them retained her esteem for long. Lauzun was probably the greatest threat. Eight years older than Marie-Antoinette and a protégé of the disgraced Duc de Choiseul, he had soaring political ambitions and a winning way with women. His determined pursuit of the Queen began in 1775, when he met her frequently at Mme de Guéméné's house and at the races. According to Lauzun, during a private audience he even succeeded in embracing Marie-Antoinette; he was quite convinced she had fallen in love with him. Mme Campan recalls this interview differently, vowing that the Queen ordered the amorous duke out of her apartments 'in a loud and angry voice'. Lauzun himself remarked a coolness in Marie-Antoinette's attitude towards him during 1776, but believed she was simply afraid to show her love. A few more months convinced him that his favour had been an illusion. He might have been mortified to learn it was the Comte de Mercy who nipped his promising romance in the bud. Lauzun's political schemes were a threat to Austrian foreign policy, and Mercy advised the Queen not to grant him further audiences. The duke was piqued (few women had the temerity to resist his charms), and later tried to resuscitate his friendship with the Queen – through Axel Fersen.

A rapidly changing circle of acquaintances gave Marie-Antoinette a reputation for fickleness, but she usually had good reasons for dropping people. More durable was her regard for the Duc de Coigny, Louis XVI's equerry. Eighteen years her senior, he was assumed to be her lover despite his known liaison with Mme de Châlons, another member of the Trianon set, whom he eventually married. He was probably more of a surrogate father to the Queen, who had other older male friends such as Comte Valentin Esterhazy and the Prince de Ligne.

Despite the attractions of ladylike farming and simple life at the Trianon, the Queen still often escaped Versailles for reckless nights of gambling and dancing in Paris. Mercy chronicled Marie-Antoinette's frenetic pursuit of pleasure in secret dispatches which greatly worried her mother. The Empress tempered continual remonstrances to her daughter with expressions of love, but neither she, Mercy nor Vermond had any influence on the Queen's behaviour. Her compulsive need for distraction, and in particular her addictive gambling, resulted from an unhappy marriage and poisonous domestic atmosphere.

Louis XVI's character and temperament had considerably improved since his marriage. Marie-Antoinette took the credit for the amelioration of his manners and appearance, but she did not love him even though he had become very affectionate towards her. According to Mme Campan, the marked change in the King's feelings for his wife occurred only in 1776, when 'his long indifference was followed by sentiments of admiration and love: he was a slave to all the Queen's wishes'.[12] There was, however, very little intimacy between them. They met usually for only two or three hours a day. Louis XVI remained dedicated to hunting and his forge when he was not occupied by affairs of state, and the Queen made few efforts to involve him in her amusements or spend more time at home.

One reason for this continued estrangement was the King's sexual deficiency. Although not technically impotent, he was unable to consummate his marriage, and it was no longer because he did not love his wife. The Court physician Lassonne prescribed diets which he hoped would cure Louis XVI's sexual lethargy. Some doctors advised circumcision to correct the abnormality of the foreskin they believed to be the root of the trouble, but in 1776 the eminent surgeon Moreau informed the King that such an operation was unnecessary. It was all a matter of 'temperament' and a sluggish, apathetic constitution. This would seem to indicate a hormonal imbalance. Marie-Antoinette had wearied of the subject long before. In 1775 she simply laughed off songs circulating in Paris about her husband's sexual shortcomings and her own supposed bisexuality. She surely saw the bitter irony of her position; though still a virgin, she was already presumed to have bedded countless lovers of both sexes. She certainly avoided sharing a bed with the King as much as possible, for nights with him were just too humiliating, perhaps even frightening. Gouverneur Morris heard from informed sources at Court that not only were Louis XVI's sexual habits 'unclean', but that on one occasion when young he even beat Marie-Antoinette, being of a 'brutal and nasty' disposition.

The marriage seemed doomed to perpetual sterility, possibly even divorce, until the Austrians decided to take action to check Marie-Antoinette's flamboyance. Her mother accurately foresaw the disaster the Queen's frivolous life-style was likely to bring upon the monarchy, and felt that children would be the most effective method of keeping her under control. Finding out whether she could conceive any was now imperative. Maria-Theresa's eldest son, Emperor Joseph II, who had long been planning to visit his favourite sister in France, finally left Vienna on this delicate mission on 1 April 1777. Though the Empress hoped he would be able to do good, she had doubts about the possibility of success. 'Either my daughter will win over the Emperor through her kindness and charm,' she wrote to Mercy, 'or he will irritate her by trying to preach to her too much. The former seems more probable to me . . . one must not hope that the Emperor's presence will produce a happy crisis.'[13] Prescient mother; she knew her children well, but she greatly underestimated Joseph's powers of magic.

The three months immediately preceding Joseph's visit had produced exceptionally worrying reports from Mercy on the Queen's behaviour. She had debts of almost 500,000 *livres*, chiefly the result of her excessive gambling, and in January and February had grown thin because of her constant activity – riding by day, gambling and dancing by night. The Carnival of 1777 saw her regularly at opera balls in Paris, chatting to 'distinguished foreigners', in particular the Duke of Dorset. Mercy described a typical night for the Queen on 30 January, when she arrived at a ball at the Palais Royal at midnight, left at 4 a.m. for the masked ball in the adjoining Opera House, then returned to dance at the first ball until 6 a.m. She seldom arrived back at Versailles before seven in the morning. When Mercy remonstrated with her, Marie-Antoinette merely declared she had the King's permission to go to Paris as much as she liked. Balls ceased during Lent, so she visited the theatre several times a week, attended the races, and at night played faro for high stakes either at Court or at the Princesse de Guéméné's house in Versailles, where there was 'the double inconvenience of steep play and very mixed company'.[14] The Queen did stop this madcap routine for a few days in March to nurse the King through a short illness, an attention which touched him, but he saw little of her thereafter until her brother's arrival on 19 April 1777.

Joseph II disliked rigid etiquette as much as Marie-Antoinette, and to avoid the restraint imposed by French Court ritual he travelled incognito as Count Falkenstein – Falkenstein being the last remaining fiefdom he held in Lorraine. He even refused an apartment at Versailles, preferring to stay at an hotel. Marie-Antoinette offered him 'a small mezzanine apartment in her *cabinets*', but although Joseph accepted a key, he wanted complete freedom to organize his time as he pleased.[15] The Queen's *cabinets* were small, intimate, exquisitely decorated private rooms overlooking an inner courtyard, and were reached through doors concealed behind tapestries in her public apartments. On the mezzanine floor there was a long private corridor connecting her bedroom to the King's. Joseph made use of a secret entrance to these *cabinets* when he was reunited with his sister, for he did not want their first meeting in seven years to be witnessed by inquisitive courtiers. 'The Abbé de Vermond,' Mercy informed Maria-Theresa, 'met him at the door of his carriage; he conducted the Emperor alone by a secret staircase right to the Queen's *cabinets*, without passing through any of the antechambers, which were full of people.'[16] It was fortunate Joseph took this precaution, for 'the first meeting between him and the Queen was most affecting; they embraced and were silent with emotion for a long time'. Once they regained their composure, they adjoined to an inner room, where 'they remained alone for almost two hours'.

Joseph was overwhelmed by the beautiful stranger he had last seen as a girl, and told her 'that if she were not his sister and he could be united to her, he would not hesitate to remarry to give himself such a charming companion'. He also threw her a lifeline; the promise that if she were to be left a childless widow, she could return home to Vienna. Marie-Antoinette was deeply touched, and fully appreciated the value of this offer. In the long conversation that followed she poured out her heart to Joseph, who was her favourite brother. She told him about her daily routine at Court, her friends, her compulsive gambling, and most importantly, 'talked to him frankly about . . . details relative to her matrimonial intimacy'.[17] This circumlocution is typical of Mercy. As he later informed the Empress, Marie-Antoinette kept nothing back from Joseph, and she probably also encouraged Louis XVI to ask him for sexual advice.

Many more conversations followed during the Emperor's six-week visit, but he first had to be introduced to the French royal family. His comments on Louis XVI's brothers and their wives were acerbic. 'Monsieur,' he told his brother Archduke Leopold, 'is an indefinable being: better than the King: he is mortally cold.' He called Madame 'ugly and gross', whilst 'the Comte d'Artois is a fop in every sense. His wife, who is the only one to produce children, is an absolute idiot.'[18] The King himself provoked a mixed reaction in his brother-in-law, who declared: 'This man is a little weak, but he is no fool; he has ideas, he has judgement, but he is apathetic both in mind and body. He makes rational conversation yet he has no taste for learning nor curiosity; in short, the *fiat lux* has not yet come, his matter is still in suspension.'[19]

The three Bourbon brothers quite amazed Joseph and angered their wives by a display of childish behaviour after supper on 21 April, when they amused themselves by 'running about the room and jumping on the sofas'. Monsieur nevertheless considered himself vastly superior to the Emperor, whom he described as superficial and insincere. Joseph II was unpopular at Court because he ridiculed the arcane etiquette which kept so many courtiers busy doing nothing, at great profit to themselves if not to the Treasury. He was, however, very much liked by the French people, who admired his easy informal manners, and showed their enthusiasm by following him around Paris. When Joseph attended a performance of Gluck's *Iphigénie en Aulide* at the Opera on 25 April, Marie-Antoinette had to pull him to the front of the royal box to acknowledge the audience's spontaneous applause, which lasted several minutes.

Joseph's real business in Paris was not calculated to make him popular with his sister, for between trips to tourist attractions he spent many hours observing her activities. Marie-Antoinette could not flatter herself that she had won his good opinion. He was highly critical of her conduct, and spoke his mind freely. Her very heavy gambling worried him enormously. On 27 April the Princesse de Guéméné had the honour of receiving the Emperor when he accompanied Marie-Antoinette to one of her soirées. He later told Mercy that 'he had been shocked by the low tone of the company, and by the air of licence which reigned at this lady's house', and after watching a game of faro, he 'bluntly told the Queen that the house was an absolute gambling-den'.[20] He suspected systematic cheating, which made the high stakes even more reprehensible.

Joseph also took a dislike to both Mme de Lamballe and Mme de Polignac, and thoroughly disapproved of the Comte d'Artois's over-familiar tone with the Queen. He was nevertheless agreeably sur-prised by Marie-Antoinette's mental abilities, admitting 'that he would never have imagined she possessed so much sagacity and intelligence'.[21] Reports received in Vienna always tended to portray her as a feather-brain, an image her amusements did nothing to dispel. Joseph promptly drew up a reading list for his sister, in the hope she could be per-suaded to spend an hour or two alone each day developing her mind. But Marie-Antoinette detested serious subjects, and was reproved for displaying 'too great a curiosity to know the love-affairs and gossip of the Court'.[22] This was evidently a manifestation of sexual curi-osity resulting from her frustrating experiences with the King, but Joseph had no complaints about her virtue. Her morals, he told their brother Leopold, were very strict – though more by chance than design!

Despite his rank and maturity, Joseph still had to be careful in his dealings with Marie-Antoinette, who told Mercy: 'From my mother I shall take everything respectfully, but as for my brother, I know how to answer him!'[23] She was rather mystified that Joseph seemed so well informed about her life. Mercy's poker-face must have been a sight to behold as he suggested the Emperor merely used his powers of observation more than most men. Joseph had, of course, been reading Mercy's secret dispatches on Marie-Antoinette for over seven years. However, she took all his remonstrances in good part because she loved him, and at her own request he wrote her long instructions for the regulation of her future conduct.

Joseph's main aim was to discover the true state of his sister's marriage; what he learnt was not all comforting to the Empress. Mercy told Joseph that the King 'boasts of the Queen's charms and qualities, that he loves her as much as he is capable of loving, but he fears her at least as much as he loves her. . . . She neglects him too much and often intimidates him'.[24] Hardly a picture of marital bliss. Joseph soon found himself criticizing Marie-Antoinette's 'flippant air towards her husband', her 'disrespectful language' and 'lack of obedience' to him.[25] That she did not love him was all too apparent, and as she later told Mercy, 'the King being so little susceptible to any attentions, she would be troubling herself needlessly to show him any'.[26] In truth, Marie-Antoinette had nothing in common with Louis XVI, and their hope-less sexual relations probably led her to find him physically repellent.

Joseph became the confidant of both his sister and his brother-in-law, and as a sexual athlete himself was utterly appalled by the sorry tale of Louis XVI's seven-year attempt to consummate his marriage. Marie-Antoinette gave Joseph explicit details at their very first meeting, and a fortnight later the King 'of his own accord confessed to His Imperial Majesty his unhappiness at having no children; he entered into the greatest detail on his physical condition, and asked the Emperor for advice'.[27] Joseph listened sympathetically, and two more long private conversations with his brother-in-law followed, as well as a medical briefing by Dr Lassonne. Mercy was denied the intimate details, and Maria-Theresa had to wait until Joseph returned to Vienna for a verbal report, but he had no qualms in expressing his astonishment to his brother Leopold in a revealing letter of 9 June 1777.

> Her [Marie-Antoinette's] situation with the King is very odd; he is only two-thirds of a husband, and although he loves her, he fears her more. . . . Just imagine, in his marital-bed – here is the secret – he has strong, well-conditioned erections; he introduces the member, stays there without moving for perhaps two minutes, withdraws without ejaculating but still erect, and says goodnight; this is incomprehensible because with all that he sometimes has nightly emissions, but once in place and going at it, never, and he is satisfied; he says plainly that he does it all purely from a sense of duty but never for pleasure; oh, if only I could have been there, I would have taken care of him; he should be whipped so that he would ejaculate out of sheer rage like a donkey.[28]

Given Louis XVI's taste for rough horseplay, this might well have been an effective method. The Queen, sexually ignorant and not in love, was in her brother's opinion as much of a 'blunderer' as her husband. What advice he gave them both is unknown, but it would appear he had to give them sex education which would surely have been unnecessary had there been passion on either side. Since Louis did it all purely from a sense of duty' it is possible that as a pious Catholic influenced by the Jesuits in his formative years, he even thought carnal pleasure sinful rather than essential to produce an heir.

When he left Versailles on 30 May 1777, Joseph had won the King's friendship. Marie-Antoinette's grief at parting from her brother was considerable, and she spent the next day in tears at the Petit Trianon.

'My separation from my brother gave me a cruel turn,' she wrote to Maria-Theresa. 'I suffered everything possible, and I can only console myself by thinking he shared my pain.'[29] Joseph was indeed visibly affected at having to leave her, as he told their mother: 'I left Versailles sorrowfully, truly attached to my sister. . . . She is lovable and charming; I spent hours and hours with her without noticing how they had gone. . . . All my strength was needed to force my legs to walk away.'[30]

His feelings for Marie-Antoinette never wavered. She was, Joseph told Mercy four years later, 'the woman I love most in the world . . . my love for her is beyond all expression'.[31] These sentiments were warmly reciprocated, and Marie-Antoinette was to prove a most useful ally to her brother in various foreign policy issues which required French support. 'I shall never be lacking in assiduity or attention in matters which are of personal concern to my dear brother,' she told him in 1784. 'I can never tell you enough times how much I love you with all my soul.'[32]

It is virtually certain that Marie-Antoinette owed the final consummation of her marriage to Joseph's intervention with Louis XVI. He put the entire Paris medical faculty to shame, despite self-proclaimed Gallic superiority in all matters sexual. There is no record that Louis had an operation, yet when the Comtesse d'Artois became pregnant again in June 1777, Marie-Antoinette told her mother that although it was 'a disagreeable perspective' to her, she now had real hope herself of conceiving a child. Finally, at the end of August, came the news Maria-Theresa had waited for so long. 'I'm in the happy state most essential for my whole life,' wrote her daughter from Versailles. 'It is already more than a week since my marriage was perfectly consummated.'[33]

Mercy was obliged to apologize to the Empress for failing to deliver this information first, but his work with the Queen was by no means over. He was supposed to ensure she reformed her life along the lines suggested by Joseph, and for two months she tried hard to live up to her brother's ideals. She drastically reduced her visits to Paris, accompanying the King instead on hunting trips. She was more attentive to older people at Court, started Hume's *History of England*, and stopped spending evenings at the Princesse de Guéméné's house. The Queen, however, remained reluctant to sleep with her husband (in July Mercy, Vermond and Lassonne had to speak to her 'with all the necessary force' to persuade her to share his bed), and her gambling continued unabated.

Marie-Antoinette's youthful fascination with games of chance was truly an addiction. She herself acknowledged to Mercy the dangers gambling held for her, but he did not seem to appreciate the cause of her seemingly unbreakable habit. The Austrian Chancellor Kaunitz assessed her obsession correctly as a substitute for passionate love, while Joseph told Mercy she gambled only to meet people who would amuse her, 'for at heart my sister does not like gaming'.[34] Mercy was convinced Marie-Antoinette was led on by the Comte d'Artois and Duc de Chartres, who continually dared her to play for higher stakes. As she was ordered to give up riding, dancing and long walks in case she prejudiced her chances of getting pregnant, she simply stayed in and lost even more money at the card-table. The Court's annual sojourn at Fontainebleau in the autumn of 1777 saw her relapse completely from the programme Joseph had devised. She no longer even bothered to excuse her conduct to Mercy, telling him that she was simply 'frightened of being bored'. For a while she also stopped answering Joseph's letters. Her visits to Mme de Guéméné resumed, she often stayed out until 2 a.m. and seldom saw the King for more than half an hour before he went out hunting.

Mercy foolishly tried to arouse Marie-Antoinette's interest in her husband by suggesting that now he was sexually active he might be tempted into taking a mistress, but he failed to get the jealous reaction he expected.

> She believes him to be too apathetic and too timid to imagine he could ever indulge in the disorders of gallantry. The Queen is so convinced of this that she has even chanced to say to some of her acquaintances that she would be neither grieved nor angry if the King were to succumb to a passing or momentary fancy, since he might thereby gain more spirit and energy.[35]

Marie-Antoinette made absolutely no attempt to sleep with the King, and from Mercy's dispatch of 19 November 1777 it is obvious that she loathed sexual relations with her husband.

> It is undeniably her fault that the King sleeps in his own bed, and her late nights gambling are the cause. On the 2nd of this month the King began once more to spend his nights with the Queen: on the 3rd this august princess went to gamble at the house of the Princesse

de Lamballe until three in the morning, and on the 4th she went to the masked ball in town and spent part of the night there, which of necessity brought back separate beds.[36]

Despite Mercy's and Vermond's constant lectures, Marie-Antoinette continued to elude her husband's embraces. The 1778 Carnival gave her an ideal opportunity to stay away from Versailles as much as possible, and she was out almost every night in February at opera balls. The only benefit was that her dancing precluded gambling, but Mercy informed the Empress on 20 March 1778: 'The excessive late nights of the Carnival have done the greatest damage to hopes of an imminent pregnancy. I see . . . that the Queen has relapsed into a sort of forgetfulness or indifference on this most important subject.'[37]

The Carnival, however, had to come to an end, and Louis XVI took full advantage of the suspension of balls and other amusements during Lent to keep his wife both at home and in bed. To everyone's surprise, not least the Queen's, he finally succeeded in getting her pregnant. On her doctors' orders Marie-Antoinette immediately adopted a more sedate routine – no dancing, no gambling and few late nights. 'The King,' Mercy reported, 'is utterly enchanted.'[38]

In contrast, Empress Maria-Theresa's reaction was muted. 'I must confess,' she wrote to Mercy on 2 May 1778, 'that I'm almost tempted to doubt it until the moment she has given birth to the child she is supposed to be carrying, so incredulous have I become on this topic.'[39]

4

An Old Acquaintance

The twenty-two-year-old Count Axel Fersen, accompanied by his favourite dog and his valet Joseph, left Sweden on 16 April 1778 for London. The object of this second journey abroad was matrimony. Once settled into lodgings at 7 Suffolk Street, just off Pall Mall, Axel duly hastened to pay his respects to the young lady his father considered would make a perfect daughter-in-law. Miss Catherine Leyell (or Lyall), was, in Senator Fersen's opinion, an heiress worth Axel's attention. Her Swedish father was a naturalized Briton, had made a huge fortune in the East India Company and wanted a title for his daughter.

Axel Fersen possessed both the rank and fortune for this match, but his lukewarm interest in Miss Leyell must have been all too apparent, for she flatly refused him after several weeks of unenthusiastic courtship. He told his sister Sophie of the unproductive outcome of his wooing in a letter dated 30 June 1778, expressing apprehension at his father's reaction:

> It's all over, my dear friend. The girl has assured me she doesn't want to leave her parents, that she won't change her mind, and that she has always begged me to tell my father so. I nevertheless insisted. I said all the most passionate lover could say, but in vain. . . . She informed her father. He spoke to me and told me he was very annoyed about it; and paying me pretty compliments, assured me of his friendship and asked for mine. He expects to write a letter to my father, and I now see myself obliged to send him this news. I'm desperate about it; it will cause him pain, but I've done my utmost. . . .

I could console myself for this loss if I were sure my father were
convinced I had done everything to please him and to obtain Miss
Leyell's consent.[1]

Axel wrote to Senator Fersen the same day, asking to be allowed
to postpone his return to Sweden. His excuse was that time was needed
to efface the memory of his rejection, but wounded pride had little
to do with his motives. He eagerly seized the chance his absence
offered to escape the uncongenial life awaiting him at home. He wanted
to go to war, and Sweden at that time offered few opportunities for
military advancement. To his joy, Axel received his father's permission to travel to Paris, where he hoped to enlist in the French army.

Senator Fersen, displeased with his son's behaviour, nevertheless
demanded an explanation for the Leyell courtship débâcle. On 19
November 1778, safe from further matrimonial schemes, Axel at last
felt free to reveal his true feelings.

You know, my dear father, that I don't love Miss Leyell, but I'm not
so unreasonable not to see that she is a very good match. It's even
the only one which suits me and which I want to make. I've done my
utmost to obtain it, more to please you, my dear father, and through
reason rather than inclination. I wasn't successful, and I confess I
was very happy, once I knew that you consented to let me go to war.[2]

Axel was careful not to let his father think he was closing the door
on this marriage. He even suggested that negotiations could be resumed 'in five or six years' time', should Miss Leyell change her
mind – surely a ludicrous offer, but one that spared him further
unwelcome marital proposals while he concentrated on his military
ambitions. 'I'm young, I still have many things to learn,' he wrote,
'especially in a career where experience is so necessary. I want to be
able to follow in your footsteps, my dear father, and try to make
myself useful to my country.'[3] Senator Fersen had been proprietary
colonel of a regiment in the French army before his successful début
into Swedish public life, and in this instance when Axel said he wanted
to follow his example, he was absolutely sincere.

Owing to French participation in the American War of Independence against Britain, Paris was quieter than usual when Axel arrived there on 22 August 1778. Most army officers were with their

regiments, while their families spent the summer at their country châteaux. Axel immediately renewed his friendship with the Swedish ambassador, Count Creutz, and made new friends who were to play very important roles in his later life – among them the Duchesse de Fitz-James, Marie-Antoinette's lady-in-waiting, and a Mme Stegelmann and her widowed daughter, Mme de Korff, whose house was a meeting-place for Swedes in Paris. Axel liked Mme Stegelmann, but, hypercritical as ever, found forty-year-old Mme de Korff ugly and pretentious. He acknowledged that she was very good-hearted, although he did not appreciate just how good until he asked for her help during the dark days of the Revolution.

During his first week Axel also called on Mme de Boufflers, one of Gustav III's French correspondents. 'She has a daughter-in-law,' he noted in his diary, 'who is as pretty as an angel, but capricious as an angel is not.'[4] He found a woman much more to his taste awaiting him at Versailles, where, as he told his father, he was presented on 25 August: 'It was last Tuesday that I went to Versailles to be presented to the royal family. The Queen, who is charming, said when she saw me: "*Ah, it's an old acquaintance!*" The rest of the family didn't address a word to me.'[5]

This is the first time Axel refers to Marie-Antoinette's charm, and his comment reveals that he had not been immune to it four years earlier. Marie-Antoinette herself could not conceal her joy at seeing him again after such a long absence. It is indeed significant that she remembered him so well. Axel Fersen was not the sort of man she was expected to admire. Quiet, reserved, not known as a brilliant wit or conversationalist, he nevertheless touched her heart as no other man could. The message his 'beautiful eyes' gave her at this unexpected meeting must have been favourable; she made a point of ensuring that he paid frequent visits to Court, as he was pleased to report to his father on 8 September 1778: 'The Queen, who is the most beautiful and amiable princess I know, has had the kindness to ask often about me; she asked Creutz why I was not going to her card-table on Sundays, and having learnt that I went one day when there was no play, she made me a sort of apology. Her pregnancy progresses and is very visible.'[6]

Pregnancy did not diminish Marie-Antoinette's beauty in Axel's eyes, and this praise of her would suggest that he was himself already a little in love: he was usually far less forthcoming to his father.

Axel was also no gambler, but he promptly obeyed the Queen's wishes, becoming a regular at her card-table, where the stakes were high and professional gamblers from Paris held the bank. Marie-Antoinette had, however, finally succeeded in overcoming her ruinous addiction to faro; Mercy informed her mother in April 1778 that 'reform on this point seems to be established in a decided manner'.[7] Her card-table (to which all courtiers were admitted) now served merely as a convenient rendezvous, where she could talk to Axel undisturbed. There is no record that he staked more than a few *louis* at these Sunday gambling sessions, so they must have found much to discuss.

Marie-Antoinette was in fact leading a considerably less hectic life now she was pregnant. She still found it impossible to sleep, and her nocturnal walks along the terrace outside her apartments during the stuffy summer of 1778 gave rise to salacious gossip. But she needed the cool night air. Having given up both riding and trips to Paris, she relied principally on music and conversation to pass long dreary days at Versailles, where her doctors watched anxiously for the slightest warning sign of a miscarriage.

Though flattered by the Queen's attention, Axel had not lost sight of his military ambitions. Determined to see active service with the French army, he left Paris on 10 September to watch manoeuvres in Normandy, accompanied by a fellow-Swede, Count Kurt Stedingk. Nine years older than Axel, Stedingk was already a lieutenant-colonel in the Royal-Suédois regiment and held in high regard at Versailles. Marie-Antoinette later attempted to repay his devotion by arranging two marriages for him, both of which he refused. She certainly never made similar plans for Axel Fersen!

Stedingk and Axel arrived at the French encampment near Bayeux at noon on 12 September 1778. As it was a cold, wet Sunday, no manoeuvres were scheduled, and they spent the afternoon dancing with the wives of French officers. Axel was warmly welcomed, since many of them remembered his father, and he enjoyed his fortnight in Normandy immensely. 'We were overwhelmed with courtesy,' he told his father. 'Everyone treated us with distinction; they looked on us as French, and I would gladly have spent a couple of months in that way.'[8]

Unfortunately, without string-pulling at Court there was little hope of their being allowed to join the French forces in their planned invasion of England, so the two Swedes left for Paris on 25 September.

Romantic curiosity took them on a detour to the monastery of La Trappe near Caen. Founded as a Cistercian house in 1140, it became famous in 1662 when the abbot, Armand de Rancé, heart-broken at the death of his mistress, brought in the austere Trappist regime. Axel Fersen, young, handsome, Protestant, and fond of female company, soon regretted his wish to visit this remote and forbidding monastery. 'I was seized by sadness and a kind of horror as I arrived,' he noted. A tour of the establishment in the company of the only inmate permitted to speak increased his feelings of doom, but he and Stedingk had to spend the night there, the nearest inn being some miles away. 'After supper we were conducted to our room; fortunately we were both in the same one; I was very pleased, because everything inspired me with horror and I wouldn't have wanted to sleep alone.'[9]

They left for Paris early the next morning. Axel's strong emotional reaction against the asceticism of La Trappe shows he was not the cold, impassive character he appeared to French eyes. His urbanity was very deceptive. Marie-Antoinette must have caught more than a glimmer of interest on his inscrutable countenance when he returned to Versailles, for by late autumn their frequent chats had led to greater intimacy than she usually accorded even distinguished courtiers. On 19 November Axel informed his father:

> The Queen still treats me with kindness. I often go to pay my court to her at the card-table, and she always speaks to me. She had heard someone talk of my [Swedish] uniform, and she expressed a great desire to me to see it at her levee. I'm supposed to go there wearing it on Tuesday – not to the levee, but to the Queen's apartments. She is the most amiable princess I know.[10]

He duly wore his uniform to Court, where, according to another Swede, Marie-Antoinette 'examined it very carefully'. One feels sure that despite her enthusiasm for new fashions, she was much more interested in examining Axel than the uniform. Gradually he found himself drawn into the Queen's Trianon set. Stedingk too was invited to her supper parties, but although she was equally gracious to him, he clearly played gooseberry.

French courtiers disliked the Queen's marked preference for these foreigners, but when questioned about it by the Comte de La Marck, she replied: 'At least they don't ask me for anything'. She was tired of constant demands for favours from her so-called friends. Mme de Lamballe had seriously damaged her friendship with Marie-Antoinette, who in September 1778 refused to grant her a lease on lands in Lorraine at half their real value. The princess was encouraged by her brother-in-law the Duc de Chartres, who had earned himself an unenviable reputation as a coward: in command of a naval squadron, he supposedly misread a signal from his admiral and evaded British warships trying to engage the French off Ushant. Despite this he asked the Queen to support his honourable retirement from the navy with the rank of admiral. Although she laughed at news of Chartres's disgrace, she eventually persuaded Louis XVI to grant him the grand title of Colonel-General of Hussars and Light Infantry as recompense for his failure. But Chartres's vanity was not satisfied, and he never forgave Marie-Antoinette for this imaginary insult. No wonder she sought the company of a man like Axel Fersen, who knew how to appreciate both her and his good fortune. 'My stay here becomes more agreeable by the day,' he told his father on 15 December 1778, 'it's a charming place.'[11]

Four days later came an event the whole of France had waited for since 1770: the birth of Louis XVI's and Marie-Antoinette's first child. It was a gruelling ordeal for the Queen. All royal births at that time took place in public (to ensure there was no substitution of the baby), and many loyal subjects exercised their right to cram into the Queen's bedchamber to enjoy her labour pains, as Mme Campan recalled: 'It was no longer possible to move about the room, which was filled by such a motley crowd one could have believed oneself to be in a public square. Two Savoyards climbed up on the furniture to get a better view of the Queen, who was placed facing the chimney on a bed specially prepared for the moment of delivery.'[12]

It was hardly conducive to an easy birth. Marie-Antoinette went into labour at half-past midnight on 19 December 1778, but the waters did not break until 8 a.m. After giving birth to a daughter at 11:30 a.m. she promptly fainted. The King and courtiers were admiring the baby in the next room while doctors bled the unconscious Queen and put her back in her own bed. Mercy did not realize the potential danger until later, as he informed Empress Maria-Theresa. He attributed the fainting fit to 'the movement of too great a number of people present . . . the efforts the Queen made not to complain', and the fact that because the baby did not immediately cry she thought it was stillborn.[13]

The new princess, baptized Marie-Thérèse-Charlotte, was in fact 'big and strong', and a courier from Vienna was permitted to see her before carrying back a description to the grandmother whose name she bore. Mercy too was allowed to monitor the baby's condition every day, since the Empress was very worried she might even be harmed by suspect persons in the royal household. She need not have feared. Anyone who had laid a finger on his child would have had to confront the King. He was so overjoyed he even spoke to the Abbé de Vermond for the first time, and for a week spent every available minute with his wife and baby daughter. 'One cannot imagine anything to outdo the attentions and tenderness he shows the Queen,' wrote Mercy.[14]

Louis XVI adored his daughter. As the royal governess Mme de Tourzel noted, 'the King had a very special fondness for her, and although he was not demonstrative, he never let pass an occasion to show the love he bore her'.[15] Marie-Antoinette, who also loved her daughter dearly, was somewhat alarmed that she had to hand her over to the Princesse de Guémené, who became royal governess as of right. The Queen was even dissuaded from breast-feeding her baby, but interfered as much as she could in her upbringing. Royal children in France belonged more to the state than to their parents, and even after the Queen insisted her daughter's household be reduced to the minimum, eighty people were employed solely in attending to her. Eighty people, needless to say, who were not notably experienced in child care.

The King's brothers reacted well to this birth. Monsieur was openly relieved he had not had to welcome a Dauphin who would have taken his place as heir to the throne, as he told Gustav III of Sweden: 'When my niece came into the world I was very satisfied, I must admit. My sister-in-law has managed things, well this time, but I fear they will not go so well a second time.'[16] He might have been happier had he been privy to her thoughts on both his brother and childbirth. According to Mercy, Marie-Antoinette's feelings for her husband a month after the birth were based solidly on 'esteem and friendship', but although 'she was deeply touched by the tenderness, gentleness and solicitude' he showed her, she still did not love him, and was most reluctant to resume their sexual relations. Mercy was convinced it was simply because she was 'a little disgusted by child-birth' that she 'did not want to get pregnant for several months', but given Marie-Antoinette's character, this seems unlikely.[17] She never shirked physical danger, and fully appreciated the necessity of pro-ducing an heir. It is far more probable that she wanted freedom to enjoy the company of a man she truly loved – Axel Fersen. Sleeping with the King must have been a penance indeed. Eventually, how-ever, she bowed to Austrian bullying and spent some of her nights with Louis XVI, though not always in bed.

Marie-Antoinette instead used the influence conferred by mater-nity to persuade her husband to attend an opera ball during the Carnival in February 1779. 'They remained until six in the morning without being recognized, which seemed to amuse the King greatly.' One ball was enough for him, but he let the Queen go alone to another opera ball on Mardi Gras. She and her lady-in-waiting, the Princesse d'Hénin, changed coaches at the Duc de Coigny's Paris *hôtel*, but their second coach broke down and they were then obliged to hire a fiacre to the Opera House. Marie-Antoinette stayed there all night without being recognized.[18] She may well have spoken to Axel Fersen, for later they met regularly at opera balls, but it was the adventure with the fiacre which caught the Court's imagination. The King thought it was a huge joke, but scandalmongers assumed the Queen had had a passionate rendezvous with the Duc de Coigny, and stolen away in a fiacre to avert suspicion.

The Carnival over, Marie-Antoinette resumed her long daily rides around Versailles and in the Bois de Boulogne, to the consternation of her doctors and the public, who concluded that either she was not sleeping with the King or was recklessly damaging her chances of bearing another child. Axel Fersen probably accompanied the Queen on some of these rides, for her love for him was now becoming ap-parent to her closest friends. Mercy, however, makes no mention of Fersen in any of his dispatches, pointedly referring to other men to whom the Queen deigned to speak. Was he shielding her from the wrath which would surely have erupted in Vienna once her mother knew of this infatuation, or had Marie-Antoinette finally learnt not to confide too much in Mercy? The Abbé de Vermond, upset that she often ignored his advice, now appeared at Versailles only when the Queen summoned him, so Mercy was less well informed of her activities.

Marie-Antoinette's love for Axel was, however, her only crime during the spring of 1779. She spent considerable time every day with the King and her daughter, she seldom visited Paris, her gambling had become 'rarer and more moderate', and she no longer adopted all the unworthy schemes promoted by her friends. Even the Comte d'Artois had been put in his place, although Mme de Polignac, that dangerous confidante, still enjoyed the Queen's friendship. Maria-Theresa nevertheless remained highly dissatisfied with Marie-Antoinette's conduct. She was desperate for the birth of a grandson, and wrote sourly to Mercy on 31 March: 'What my daughter tells me about her conjugal state can hardly satisfy me, and makes me wonder if we must not wait eight more years to see another child born.'[19]

Axel Fersen was exceptionally well received at Court in 1779, and by dint of his connections had been promised the prestigious post of aide-de-camp to the Maréchal de Vaux on a forthcoming French campaign in the American war. He suffered an illness early in the year which left him depressed and looking 'like a ghost' according to the Swedish ambassador Creutz, but he does not appear to have gone to Spa (in Belgium) for a rest-cure as his doctor recommended. Instead Axel spent his time with the woman who could no longer conceal her feelings for him, as Creutz told the King of Sweden.

10 April 1779. I must confide to Your Majesty that young Count Fersen has been so well treated by the Queen that several people have taken umbrage at it. I confess that I cannot help believing she has a strong inclination for him; I've seen too many positive indications to doubt it. Young Count Fersen conducted himself admirably in these circumstances by his modesty and reserve, and above all by the decision he took to go to America. In going away he avoided all the dangers, but it evidently required a strength of will above his age to overcome this seduction. The Queen couldn't take her eyes off him during the final days; when she looked at him they were filled with tears. I beg Your Majesty to keep this secret between yourself and Senator Fersen. When the Count's departure was known all the favourites were delighted. The Duchesse de Fitz-James said to him: 'What, Monsieur, are you thus abandoning your conquest?' 'If I had made one I would not abandon her,' he replied, 'I leave a free man, and unhappily without being regretted.' Your Majesty will acknowledge that this reply showed a wisdom and prudence beyond his years. Besides, the Queen behaves with a great deal more restraint and discretion than formerly.[20]

No wonder the lovesick Marie-Antoinette did not want to sleep with her husband! Her love for her Swedish count was, however, as yet undeclared, and because of her rank he certainly dared not make the first move. His remark to Mme de Fitz-James nevertheless sounds like a heavy hint to Marie-Antoinette that if she loved him or regretted his absence, she would have to make her feelings known unequivocally. That Axel found her interest unwelcome is inconceivable. He could simply have stayed away from Versailles. Instead he seemed unable to stop seeing the Queen; he openly admired her beauty and admitted to being captivated by her charm. She could probably have claimed his love then, but Marie-Antoinette was both timorous and unskilled in affairs of the heart, so doubtless she said goodbye to Axel with a lump in her throat, thinking it might be their last farewell.

In April, soon after Axel joined his regiment, the Queen caught measles and gave Mercy and Vermond a great deal of trouble by her cavalier treatment of the King. Louis XVI had not had measles (a serious illness in the eighteenth century), and the Queen was quarantined first in her apartments, then at the Petit Trianon. Juliet-like she held a conversation with her husband from a balcony overlooking a private courtyard, before setting off for the Trianon accompanied by four men who all had immunity to measles and promised to cheer her up during the three weeks she was confined to bed. Her 'nurses', the Ducs de Guines and Coigny, Comte Valentin Esterhazy and the Baron de Besenval, even proposed remaining in her room all night, more one suspects to shock Mercy (who was duly outraged) than in earnest. Mercy succeeded in turning them out of the Queen's room at 11 p.m., but they came back every morning to bring her breakfast at seven, and kept her amused with gossip and games all day except for the hours they took off for meals.

Scandal naturally ensued. Mercy constantly warned the Queen not to place too much confidence in the Duc de Guines. Fat, florid and over forty, he was a former ambassador to Britain whose political influence the Austrians feared, though gossip-mongers assumed he was the Queen's lover. Vermond persuaded an indifferent Marie-Antoinette to write to the King to counteract rumours circulating at

Versailles. The billet-doux she eventually scrawled produced a loving epistle from Louis XVI and led to a daily correspondence which silenced her critics at Court. Once she was declared out of danger she received senior Court dowagers at the Petit Trianon, finally returning to Versailles for Easter.

According to Mercy, the Queen's reunion with her husband was 'very tender', and bereft of Axel Fersen and other friends who were either in America or involved in what proved to be an abortive attempt to invade England, she made an effort to be a good wife to him during the summer of 1779. This was only after heavy pressure from Mercy, who was convinced that Court cabals had been trying to interest the King in other women while his wife was ill. Louis XVI spoilt this stratagem by confessing to Marie-Antoinette on 4 June that 'he loved her truly with all his heart, and could swear to her that he had never felt either love or desire for any woman, except for her alone'.[21] She was not ungrateful, even though she could not reciprocate. She made few trips to Paris, spent many hours with her baby daughter, held a supper every week at the Petit Trianon for her husband, and even accompanied him on hunting trips which she detested.

This unusual intimacy led to the Queen's second pregnancy, which ended unhappily in July 1779. 'She had spoken of her condition only to the King and her doctor,' recalled Mme Campan, 'when having forcefully raised the window of her coach she felt she had injured herself, and a week later she had a miscarriage.'[22] Louis XVI did his best to comfort her, and was exiled by Marie-Antoinette's doctors to his own bedroom for a month. The Queen spent a very quiet summer at Versailles; even Mme de Polignac left her for several weeks to take the waters.

Axel Fersen, whom Marie-Antoinette undoubtedly missed, was among the crowd of aristocratic officers kicking their heels in Le Havre while the French and Spanish fleets dawdled in the Channel and French troops became disenchanted with the prospect of fighting their way ashore in England. In September Axel wrote a despondent letter to his sister Sophie: 'Many people think we won't go. I don't know what to believe. I fear and I hope. We are now assured that we will embark next month, God willing. If it doesn't happen, I shan't be able to console myself.'[23] Marie-Antoinette, however, was able to console the Swedish aide-de-camp when he returned to Paris after the planned invasion was abandoned early in October 1779. She was also able to support his request for a place in the French force being mustered for an expedition to America itself the following year.

Versailles was more brilliant than usual during the winter of 1779/80. The Queen wanted to attract more people to Court, so she resumed fixed days for receiving visitors, held a ball every Wednesday, reinstated the custom of inviting courtiers to have supper with the royal family in the *cabinets*, and held concerts two or three times weekly in her apartments. She herself used to play the harp and loved singing; as Axel loved music and played both piano and flute, he almost certainly took part in these musical soirées.

The Comte d'Artois and the Duc de Chartres now seldom joined in Marie-Antoinette's amusements, but it is rather suspicious that during December 1779, when the Queen was seeing Axel Fersen frequently (albeit only in public), Mme de Polignac made an outrageous request. Backed by the Comte d'Artois, she demanded no less than the county of Bitche in Lorraine, worth 100,000 *livres* a year, as a gift. The Queen, Mercy reported, was both frightened and shocked, but could not bring herself to refuse her friend outright. Why? The timing suggests that Mme de Polignac, doubtless aware of Marie-Antoinette's passion for Axel, had decided to capitalize on her position of confidence. This blackmail did not succeed as spectacularly as she hoped. Louis XVI agreed to settle her debts and gave a huge dowry to her daughter (the King had to give his consent to all aristocratic marriages, and often provided dowries for impecunious noblewomen), but the Polignacs never received royal lands, either in Lorraine or elsewhere.

Axel Fersen was blissfully ignorant of the intrigues surrounding the Queen's love for him. According to the Comte de Saint-Priest, the Polignacs considered that

An isolated foreigner with an unenterprising character suited them much better than a Frenchman surrounded by relatives who would appropriate to themselves all favours, and who might end as head of a clique which would eclipse them. The Queen was thus encouraged to follow her inclination, and surrendered herself to it without much prudence.[24]

Marie-Antoinette's behaviour soon occasioned many rumours about her interest in Fersen.

There was talk of meetings and prolonged conversations during opera balls, of glances exchanged for lack of conversation during intimate soirées at the Trianon; the Queen had been seen, it was declared,
singing at the piano passionate couplets from the opera *Didon*:

Ah que je fus bien inspirée
Quand je vous reçus dans ma cour
(Ah, how inspired I was
(When I received you at my Court)

meeting Fersen's eyes and ill-concealing her confusion.[25]

The handsome young Swede enjoyed being with Marie-Antoinette,
especially in the informal atmosphere of opera balls, but he kept his
own countenance perfectly, and diligently talked to people who could
further his military career. Early in 1780 Axel came under the powerful
protection of the Baron de Breteuil, former French ambassador to
Sweden, whom he had met in Naples in 1773. Breteuil was taking a
break from his post in Vienna, and as he was well regarded by the
Austrians, Marie-Antoinette treated him very kindly. 'He presents
me everywhere I haven't already been,' Axel told his father in February 1780. 'He always speaks of you, he decides my conduct. I obey
him; I love him like a father, and I flatter myself he has a little friendship for me. The Queen always calls him my Papa. . . .'[26]
Breteuil might have become Axel's father-in-law had his friend
Count Strömfelt had his way. Breteuil's widowed daughter, the wealthy
Comtesse de Matignon, had, Axel reported, 'become very amiable . . .
Strömfelt absolutely insists that I marry her'. Although Axel realized
she was 'a good match' he saw too many difficulties to begin formal
negotiations with Breteuil, and dashed his father's hopes by adding:
'. . . all these obstacles made me abandon the idea'.[27] As with the
Leyell marriage, his motives were purely mercenary. Mme de Matignon
was both a Catholic and in love with someone else, so he probably
mentioned Strömfelt's scheme only to divert his father's attention
from his increasing intimacy with the Queen. He certainly never hinted
at the real reason for Marie-Antoinette's great interest in his welfare, although he was well aware of it, as the following letter shows.

Paris, 23 February 1780. I told you in my last letter, my dear father,
that I had finally been appointed colonel, to the great astonishment

of all the young people. Only older people know the obligations France owes you and find this favour just and merited. The Queen, who was informed by the Baron de Breteuil, said a thousand kind things to me, and added that France had too great an obligation to my father not to do everything which might please him, and that it would always be her pleasure to do so. She then told the Baron de Breteuil that if there were anything I desired in this country I had only to tell her and she would try to obtain it for me. She is a charming princess; she has always treated me kindly, but since the Baron de Breteuil spoke to her, she distinguishes me even more. She almost always walked with me at the opera balls. . . . Her kindness to me and this appointment as colonel have attracted the jealousy of all the young courtiers; they cannot understand or tolerate a foreigner being better treated than they are. I go to Court often, usually two or three times a week.[28]

Two or three times a week for Marie-Antoinette to wear her heart on her sleeve. It was nevertheless invisible to Mercy, who informed Empress Maria Theresa that her daughter spent most nights in February at opera balls, talking to 'distinguished and well-known persons' such as 'the Landgrave of Hesse-Rheinfels and the Princes of Hesse-Darmstadt'.[29] His eyes, or his spies, must have been failing.

Neither Marie-Antoinette nor Breteuil was directly responsible for granting Axel's dearest wish that spring. The French Foreign Minister, Vergennes, a friend of Senator Fersen, finally pulled the right strings to get Axel a place in the expeditionary force to America.

Paris, 2 March 1780. You see me with my wishes fulfilled, my dear father. A big expedition of 12,000 men is being prepared, although it is said it will even be 20,000. I've obtained permission to be part of it as aide-de-camp to the general, M. de Rochambeau, but I've been ordered to keep it secret as many others have been refused. . . . I am in a state of joy which cannot be expressed.[30]

This elation was temporarily dampened by the sudden death of Axel's friend, the twenty-seven-year-old Baron Anton de Geer. Axel had to settle his estate, which included the delicate task of finding and returning unread to King Gustav III letters he had written to 'poor Anton'. Compromising letters, no doubt! Axel then had to make speedy preparations for his departure. His fastidiousness may be gauged by his purchase of no less than thirty-six new shirts for himself, as well as clothes and equipment for his three servants. His valet Joseph was, he wrote, 'too attached to me to leave me, and insists on coming with me', but Axel had to leave his dog behind. Once he had packed he was free to spend his last days in France as he wished. He decided to spend them at Versailles with Marie-Antoinette. 'I've already supped several times in the *cabinets*,' he told his father on 15 March, 'to the great astonishment of the French.'[31]

Jealous French courtiers were surely delighted to see the young Swedish upstart bid the Queen farewell on 23 March 1780. It must have been even more heart-rending for Marie-Antoinette than his departure the previous year, for this time she knew he was definitely going to war, thousands of miles away. On 13 April she wrote with uncharacteristic fervour to her mother: 'The troops . . . are embarked and wait only for a favourable wind to reach port. God grant that they arrive safely!'[32]

5

Worlds Apart

Eager to see military action, Axel Fersen might have thought his ambitions would be thwarted anew when he reached Brest on 25 March 1780, for the French navy's unreadiness meant spending several weeks aboard the 64-gun warship *Jason* merely waiting to sail. On 27 April he wrote to his sister Sophie.

> We are still aboard and we are forbidden to go ashore, except on business. You can imagine that everyone has business or creates some. . . . I like the land and life aboard ship is terrible. I'm nevertheless in good company and with people I know. The captain is a very amiable, lively and agreeable man. He's given me a cabin which I have arranged and where I retire to read, write and work. It's a great comfort to me. I stay here nearly all day and nowhere else do I feel better.[1]

General Rochambeau's army finally sailed from Brest on 4 May 1780, and after a circuitous journey across the Atlantic to avoid British warships, landed at Newport, Rhode Island on 11 July. Twenty British ships promptly blockaded the port, and the much-vaunted French expeditionary force was afraid to venture out to sea again. Rochambeau set up camp at Newport, where his troops spent a whole year 'in perfect idleness'. Early in September Axel accompanied his general on a short tour of New England, where, he declared, 'we saw the most beautiful country in the world, well cultivated, with charming views and comfortable houses'.[2] The rest of his time passed pleasantly enough at Newport, as he told Sophie: 'I'm getting on

75

marvellously here. I have much to do. The women are pretty, amiable and flirtatious.'[3] One amiable flirt he often visited was a Miss Hunter. Axel, the Duc de Lauzun and fellow-officer Dominic Sheldon formed 'a triumvirate', and spent nearly every evening at the Hunter house, talking and making music. Axel practised his English, and gave Miss Hunter French tuition in return. He had not, however, forgotten a certain 'charming countess' he left behind in Sweden in 1778, whose interest in him had cooled. On 18 September 1780 he wrote to Sophie:

> I'm desperate at the decision the charming countess seems to have taken not to write to me any more, and I don't know to what to attribute it. The opening of the letters doesn't seem a valid reason to me. . . . I fear the real reason is indifference caused by my absence. This idea is cruel and torments me – but let's not speak of it again. I would be quite happy to think of her no more.[4]

Here speaks a veritable heart-breaker! Axel appears to have been unconcerned at leaving Marie-Antoinette, although his willingness to consign the 'charming countess' to oblivion indicates that his feelings were engaged. His later actions reveal that he definitely nurtured hopes regarding the Queen, but until his love was requited he remained silent, even to his trusted Sophie. Most young officers, Axel told his father on 8 September, were very miserable in America: 'Far from their mistresses and the pleasures of Paris; no suppers, no plays, no balls. They are desperate; only an order to march on the enemy will console them.' But the order did not come. 'We are vegetating at the enemy's door,' he wrote on 16 October, 'in the most wretched and most dreadful idleness and inactivity.'[5]

Whilst at Newport Axel became very friendly with the Duc de Lauzun, who was convinced Marie-Antoinette loved him even in 1779, when her passion for Axel became known at Court. His motives for befriending his Swedish rival are puzzling. Lauzun commanded his own 1500-strong Legion, and in October 1780 made Axel a generous offer of military advancement. Axel wrote that Lauzun urged him 'to accept the post of colonel-commandant of his Legion, which is vacant, and next year he wants to cede ownership to me because he wants to retire from the army'. Axel had long aspired to own a regiment in the French army. 'The offer is too agreeable and too advantageous for me to be able to refuse it,' he told his father. 'The Duc de Lauzun is writing about it to the Queen, who has a great deal of goodwill for him; she has a little for me, and I'm writing to her about it too.'[6]

The plot is hard to unravel. Lauzun, whom Axel liked, admired and called 'the most noble and upright soul I know', was exceedingly kind and generous to the Swede throughout the American war, but given his serpentine character and reputation for intrigue it is unlikely that his friendship was wholly disinterested. Either Lauzun hoped to frustrate Axel's romantic ambitions by stressing that Marie-Antoinette was really interested only in *him*, or else he foresaw her love-affair with Axel and hoped that by winning his rival's confidence he would open an avenue to the political influence over the Queen he had lost in 1776 as a result of his own rejected advances. A more cynical aim might have been to remove Axel from relative safety as an aide-de-camp to front-line action where he might be wounded or killed. Whatever his motives, Lauzun never regained Marie-Antoinette's trust, and later threw in his lot with her worst enemy, the Duc d'Orléans. Significantly he never once mentioned Axel Fersen in his memoirs.

Marie-Antoinette must have been delighted to receive a letter from Axel, even if only about a military transfer. It showed she was remembered and that he valued her friendship and influence. On the whole, 1780 was an unhappy year for her, and her morale needed a boost. Her first grief was being separated from the man she loved. She tried to distract herself in her usual manner, but in June had to mourn the death of her uncle, Prince Charles of Lorraine, Governor of the Austrian Netherlands. Marie-Antoinette loved him for her father's sake, and abandoned all entertainments for a fortnight.

Versailles was anyway rather forlorn with so many young courtiers absent in America. Marie-Antoinette showed little inclination to fill the void by conceiving another child; Mercy reported on 15 July that 'every day the Queen seems to worry less at not becoming pregnant'.[7] She decided instead to stage theatricals at her new theatre in the grounds of the Petit Trianon. The first performance took place in August, with the Queen, Mme de Polignac, other ladies-in-waiting and Comte Valentin Esterhazy taking leading roles. The royal family alone constituted the audience. Louis XVI hugely enjoyed his wife's acting and singing at the Trianon, clapping loudly and going backstage during the interval to chat to her. Mercy, given special permission by Marie-Antoinette to see performances of the comic operas *Rose et Colas* by Sedaine and Rousseau's *Le Devin du Village*, told the Empress that 'the Queen has a very agreeable and accurate voice; her acting style is noble and full of grace'.[8] He wholly approved of the theatricals, since rehearsals took up hours otherwise spent in harmful gossip with scheming members of the Polignac circle. The King and his brothers had supper with the Queen after performances, and she retired early. To amuse her husband she even played lotto, which she loathed, so Mercy could hardly fault her conduct.

This unwonted peace and harmony soon ended. In September Marie-Antoinette became anxious about her daughter's health, despite assurances from doctors that nothing was wrong. The baby princess was eventually diagnosed as having tertian fever, and for three weeks the Queen spent most of her time nursing her. Louis XVI's sister, Madame Elisabeth, told her friend the Marquise de Bombelles that 'nothing is more touching than the Queen's care for her child'.[9] To most people's surprise she was a very good mother – 'the best possible mother', as Mme de Staël informed the King of Sweden. In an age when high society women farmed out their children to peasant nurses for the first few years of their lives, and royal parents kept their offspring at a suitable distance, Marie-Antoinette was a notable exception. Loving, but not over-indulgent, she played an active role in her children's upbringing. She had the satisfaction of seeing her daughter restored to full health before receiving the shattering news of her mother's death.

Sixty-three-year-old Empress Maria-Theresa, though not in robust health, was as alert and active as usual when she fell ill on 24 November 1780. She died at 8.30 p.m. on 29 November, surrounded by her sons Joseph and Maximilian and three of her daughters, killed by what must have been galloping consumption. Her death was a bolt from the blue for Marie-Antoinette, who penned the following note to Joseph when she heard the fatal news on 10 December:

Stricken by the most dreadful sorrow, I write to you only through my tears. Oh, my brother! Oh, my friend! There is now no one left to me but you in a country which is, and will always be dear to me!

Take care of yourself, preserve yourself; you owe it to everyone. I have only to recommend my sisters to your care. They have lost even more than I have, they will be so wretched! Adieu! I can no longer see what I'm writing. Remember we are your friends, your allies. Love me. I embrace you. [Antoinette][10]

It was typical of Marie-Antoinette to put in a good word for her two older unmarried sisters, Archduchesses Marianne and Elizabeth, both invalids who had been utterly dependent on their mother. Marie-Antoinette had herself lost both a mother she loved and the only person whose advice she respected, who might perhaps have saved her from the disasters waiting to engulf her. Mme Campan recalled that her mistress locked herself in her apartments to give vent to her grief in private for several weeks after the Empress's death. When in late December she caught sight of the Prince de Ligne, one of her mother's Court chamberlains, 'she burst into tears in front of the whole Court who were present at the public Sunday dinner'. Ligne was upset at having caused his adored Queen such public distress, but then as he noted, 'since her marriage to the best, but ugliest and most disgusting of men, I never saw her enjoy a day's perfect happiness'.[11]

Maria-Theresa's death lessened Mercy's work-load considerably. Joseph II was interested principally in his sister's health and well-being, so Mercy no longer had to chronicle the minutiae of her activities. Joseph was, however, keen to see Marie-Antoinette involve herself in politics. Though convinced of the need to strengthen the Franco-Austrian alliance she was very reluctant to exert her supposed influence over Louis XVI, as Mercy informed Joseph on 21 January 1781:

This influence is such that the Queen could effect everything, even in affairs of state, if she so wished; but I cannot conceal from Your Majesty that this august princess has up to now shown such a marked repugnance for all serious business that she only momentarily gives it the necessary attention, and is often distracted by too many other things.[12]

Joseph would have been deeply satisfied had he known that Austrian political machinations were indirectly responsible for Marie-Antoinette's third pregnancy in 1781. More than eighteen months had elapsed since her miscarriage, when in January 1781 Mercy asked her to sound out the King on an Austrian offer to mediate between France and Britain in the American war. On 23 January she informed him that she had tried two or three times to talk to her husband on the subject, but without success. The Queen's bed was evidently the venue for these ineffectual 'pillow talks', for nine months later almost to the day she gave birth to her second child. She most definitely had to lie back and think of Austria as far as sexual relations with Louis XVI were concerned!

The Queen was nevertheless delighted to be pregnant again, informing the Crown Princess of Hesse-Darmstadt that it was 'the most happy and interesting event for me'. In May 1781 she told the Crown Princess: 'My health is perfect, I'm getting very big. Your sorcery is very kind to predict a boy. I have a great deal of faith in it and no doubt about it at all'.[13] Marie-Antoinette was very fond of both the Crown Princess and her sister, Princess Charlotte, who had won her lasting friendship when they visited Paris in 1780. Her German connections were further strengthened when Joseph decided to pay her a short visit in the summer of 1781.

'The Queen,' Mercy told Joseph on 18 July, 'who is waiting for Your Majesty with great impatience, intends to appropriate to herself alone as many moments as she can of such a brief stay.'[14] It was indeed a fleeting opportunity for Marie-Antoinette and Joseph to mourn their mother and talk over family news which no one at Versailles could provide. Travelling once again incognito as Count Falkenstein, Joseph arrived at Versailles on 29 July 1781, and excluding an opera and a supper attended by the French royal family, spent every available moment alone with his sister at the Petit Trianon. When he left her on 5 August, she immediately retreated to her *cabinets* to weep.

Despite the magnificence in which she lived and the hundreds of courtiers who buzzed around her, Marie-Antoinette remained a lonely woman. Mme de Polignac could never take the place of a dearly loved brother, and Louis XVI was even less able to fill the gap. Secretive and shy, in the words of Alexandre de Tilly, though 'he possessed a thousand estimable virtues, he had few of those which compel love, and still less those attractions most compatible with the tastes of the feminine mind'. The Queen, Tilly declared, 'was absolutely devoted to the King', but felt more 'bound to him by duty' than by love.[15]

Louis XVI's love for his wife, however, was never stronger than in 1781, when she gave birth to the boy predicted by the Crown Princess of Hesse-Darmstadt. An interesting account of the Dauphin's birth was sent immediately to Gustav III of Sweden by Axel Fersen's friend, Count Stedingk. Stedingk had distinguished himself in the French capture of Grenada in 1779, and on his return to Versailles took Axel's place in the Queen's circle of friends. On 22 October 1781 he was waiting anxiously in the Polignacs' apartment (Louis XVI had ordered that only princes and ministers had a right to witness the birth) when a maid dashed past at 1.25 p.m. and announced that an heir to the throne had just been born.

> Our joy was too great to be contained. We rushed out of the apartment. . . . The Queen's antechamber was a delight to behold. Joy was overflowing, everybody's head was turned. People were laughing and crying at the same time. . . . No one had dared tell the Queen at first it was a Dauphin, not to cause her too great an excitement. Everyone about her was so well composed that the Queen, seeing nothing but restraint, believed it was a girl. She said, 'You see how rational I am. I'm asking you nothing.' The King . . . said to her, with tears in his eyes: 'M. le Dauphin requests permission to enter.' The child was brought to her, and those who witnessed this scene say they have never seen anything more touching. She told Mme de Guéméné, who took the baby: 'Take him, he belongs to the state; but I will have my daughter back.'[16]

The Dauphin was baptized Louis-Joseph-Xavier-François at 3 p.m. that day. Louis XVI's happiness was overwhelming, as Mme Campan recorded: 'The King's joy was extreme. Tears streamed from his eyes, he offered his hand to everybody, and his happiness made him act entirely out of his usual character. Lively, affable, he constantly sought occasions to say "my son" or "the Dauphin".'[17]

After eleven years waiting, French delight at the Dauphin's birth could scarcely be contained. Even in Sweden, Gustav III expressed enormous satisfaction at the news, and in Vienna Joseph II, who was godfather as well as uncle to the Dauphin, was quite thrilled, telling Mercy on 29 October:

> I did not believe myself any longer capable of feeling a young man's joy, but this event, so desired but which I hardly dared flatter myself

would happen, has really turned my head. . . . To know that this sister, who is the woman I love most in the world, is also the happiest
at this moment, is truly satisfying. Tomorrow I'm holding a grand
gala and I'm opening all the theatres free to the public.[18]

The Dauphin's birth could not have occurred at a better time for
French troops in America either. On 17 October 1781, Generals
Rochambeau and Washington had accepted the surrender of British
forces under Lord Cornwallis at Yorktown. It was a decisive turning-
point in the American war. As Rochambeau's only English-speaking
aide-de-camp, Axel Fersen played a key role in discussions between
the American and French generals. 'This war,' he nevertheless told
his father, 'does honour to the English.' Though cut off from their
supply lines they had fought successfully until Governor Clinton of
New York ordered Cornwallis to hold an untenable position at
Yorktown, where he was surrounded and heavily outnumbered.[19]
Axel was delighted at the prospect of seeing action at last when
Rochambeau's army finally left Newport on 12 June 1781, although
he was tired both of the general and his post as aide-de-camp. He
had hoped to learn military strategy from Rochambeau, but told his
father: 'He is a very limited man; one can see that easily in conversation, and there is no doubt about it when one gets to know the
people around him and those he trusts.' One of Rochambeau's confidants, according to Axel, 'would sell his mother for two *louis*'. The
general's kindness, he declared, meant 'I would do everything for
him, but he bores me like he bores everyone. I don't like the company of fools: one can learn nothing with them.'[20] Axel nevertheless
learnt something about the hardships of war during four months on
the move. After taking part in the siege of Yorktown, he wrote:

> I have no more money, my dear father, and that obliged me to under-
> take the campaign very harshly, with no bed, no tent, and with a
> single portmanteau carried by my horses. I slept on the ground most
> of the time (without straw as there isn't any), and covered only by a
> pitiful soldier's blanket which someone lent me. . . . It's a treat for
> me when I find a barn.[21]

Despite these privations he showed no desire to give up the campaign, unlike many of his colleagues. 'All our young Court colonels

are leaving to spend the winter in Paris,' he wrote on 23 October 1781. 'I'm staying here. My only reason for going to Paris would be for my amusement and pleasure; they must be sacrificed.'[22] This devotion to duty earned him a glowing mention in dispatches by Rochambeau, while his services at Yorktown brought him the Order of Cincinnatus from Washington.

Axel still hoped to accept a colonel's commission in Lauzun's regiment, but having heard nothing from Paris, left with Rochambeau for Williamsburg ('a wretched hole'), where he remained 'bored to death' for some months. The only excitement was a mission in April 1782 to collect dispatches from Philadelphia – inadvertently left behind by a courier who brought only private letters to the camp! Axel won further praise by accomplishing this 700-mile journey in seven days. A month later he received news to gladden his heart: he had been awarded a salary of 6,000 *livres* a year for the duration of the war, and Marie-Antoinette had obtained his military promotion, though not, significantly, as commanding officer of Lauzun's regiment.

Williamsburg, 22 May 1782. . . . I confess, my dear father, that the hope of commanding a corps in battle under the orders of my friend gave me inexpressible joy . . . I must now give up this agreeable idea. Lauzun and Staël write to tell me it cannot be arranged at the moment, for reasons which Lauzun will tell me when he arrives, but that the Queen, who has always been very kind and still takes an interest in me, has done something else for me. Lauzun tells me she is arranging with M. de Castries for me to be a colonel attached to his legion with a salary of 6,000 *livres*, and Staël tells me she has asked for the post of second colonel in the Royal-Deux-Ponts regiment, and that I'm going to get it. Their letters bear the same date, and I don't know which to believe.[23]

The Baron de Staël proved to be better informed. On 30 October 1782 Axel told his father: 'I'm in full possession of my post as second colonel in the Royal-Deux-Ponts regiment, and I'm delighted to be an aide-de-camp no longer. The regiment is a fine one, well disciplined and well trained.' He had, however, a fresh worry. The King of Sweden was threatening to recall him to become Captain of his Bodyguard. Axel begged his father to 'obtain the King's permission for me to finish the American War. My reputation in France depends on it'.[24] Why was he so concerned about his reputation in France? Was his desire to remain in the French army motivated solely by his avowed wish to learn more about the practical aspects of warfare, or did he really want to impress the woman who had gone to so much trouble over his promotion? The Swedish post was far more prestigious than any he could hope to obtain in France, so Axel was surely thinking of something other than his career when he insisted on remaining under French colours.

Marie-Antoinette was doubtless well informed of Axel's activities by friends of his who had returned to Paris. During 1781 and 1782 her friendship for the widowed Comtesse de Lameth (who was pious and middle aged, unlike most of her circle) may well have been fuelled by a desire to hear news of Axel, for Mme de Lameth's son Alexandre was also on Rochambeau's staff. The Queen's love for the Swedish colonel had not diminished during his absence, but she had many months to wait before she could discover if it was requited. Meanwhile the inexorable Court routine continued, though Marie-Antoinette's activities were now far less newsworthy. She suffered a nasty attack of erysipelas in May 1782, received a visit from Grand Duke Paul of Russia and his wife during June, and finally learnt to keep the Polignacs in the dark about political affairs. Mercy informed Joseph II that 'on several recent occasions I have seen the Queen rather weary of their avidity', but although she kept Mme de Polignac's hangers-on at arm's length, her close friendship with the duchess herself was unbroken.

As Louis XVI still spent his free time hunting, and her children were cosseted by an army of nurses, the Queen took lessons to improve her handwriting, and even spent several weeks learning German, which Mercy claimed 'she has not forgotten although she has lost the usage'.[25] He was over-confident. Although her handwriting showed definite improvement, Marie-Antoinette gave up German in despair. She soon found a more useful way to pass the time, for in October 1782 the Prince de Guéméné's bankruptcy precipitated major changes in the royal household.

Guéméné was rumoured to be 'a fraudulent bankrupt', so he and his wife resigned their Court posts. This left the royal children without a governess. Marie-Antoinette immediately decided that Mme de Polignac would be the ideal replacement for Mme de Guéméné, but only the personal persuasion of Louis XVI forced the duchess to accept this unwelcome responsibility. A bevy of assistants saw to the day-to-day running of the royal nursery, and she actually spent little time with her charges, but she objected to having to keep an open salon for the Queen's visitors every day.

This change in governesses led Marie-Antoinette to implement the bold decision to take charge of her daughter. It created a considerable stir at Court, and greatly annoyed Mercy, who wrote to Prince Kaunitz in December 1782: 'Since she [the Queen] has taken charge of her august daughter's education and has her continually in her *cabinets*, it is hardly possible to discuss any important or serious subject without being constantly interrupted by the little incidents of the royal child's games.'[26]

Unfortunately Marie-Antoinette's great affection for her daughter was not reciprocated. Madame, as she was called, preferred her father, and let her feelings be known in a way which cut her mother to the quick. On 12 April 1783, the Queen told the Abbé de Vermond she had nearly broken her head in a fall from her horse the previous day. Hoping to elicit a sympathetic response from four-year-old Madame, he asked her if she were worried that her mother could have died. Madame reacted with stunning indifference, as the Marquis de Bombelles reported:

> 'But Madame surely doesn't know what death is?'
> 'Yes, Monsieur l'abbé, I know. You don't see people who are dead. I would no longer have to see the Queen and I would be quite happy, because then I could do what I like.'
> ... The Queen felt ill, and, listening only to her first impulse, ordered her daughter to be taken away and punished. Then she went to Mme de Polignac's apartment and burst into tears.[27]

Investigations revealed that Madame's governess, Mme d'Aumale, constantly threatened her charge with the Queen's wrath if she were naughty, and Marie-Antoinette attributed the child's behaviour to these fabricated menaces. Mme d'Aumale was sacked, as were seven of Madame's maids, but the little girl was unrepentant; she vowed she did not love her mother, and even made fun of the nurse who put her to bed early as a punishment. According to Bombelles, whose mother-in-law the Baronne de Mackau took over as Madame's governess, the young princess was very wayward. When she was six, he wrote: 'Her faults become worse and more difficult to correct by the day. My mother-in-law was forced to speak about them very seriously and frankly to the Queen, who loves her daughter too much; full of spirit, the child knows how great an influence over her mother this love gives her, and she makes a singular misuse of it.'[28] It was perhaps no surprise that Marie-Antoinette was adored by her sons, while Madame became '*la pauvre petite*', the darling child of Louis XVI – '*le pauvre homme*'.

Nevertheless 1783 brought the Queen compensation for all her domestic woes and her long years of unhappy marriage. The American War of Independence ended under the Treaty of Versailles on 20 January 1783, and French forces were ordered to return home. After Yorktown, the campaign on the American mainland virtually ceased. The French switched their attention to more profitable colony-snatching in the West Indies, but were heavily defeated at the naval Battle of the Saintes in September 1782, whilst in Europe their combined assault on Gibraltar with the Spanish was equally disastrous. Hence their relief when the British decided to grant American independence and opened peace negotiations. As soon as the treaty was signed, British tourists flocked to Paris, and Marie-Antoinette showed what she really thought of the dangerous republicanism unleashed by the war by being particularly gracious to all British visitors to Versailles. They were suitably impressed by the twenty-seven-year-old Queen, who was even in the anti-Austrian Marquis de Bombelles's opinion 'a charming woman'.

> The Queen, perfectly brought up, bestowed on France the freshness of Hebe, her graces, and every power of pleasing. . . . People have tried to say she has abused her freedom. Perhaps they have attempted to trouble the King's peace of mind by making insinuations about the Queen, but this prince has not allowed himself to entertain unjust suspicions.[29]

Suspicions which would soon be unjust no longer. Axel Fersen was on his way back to Versailles, and this time Marie-Antoinette had every intention of deploying the full battery of her charms against him.

Axel was overjoyed when he learnt that the war was finally over. After dawdling in Williamsburg, his regiment went to Porto Cabello in Venezuela to rendezvous with Spanish forces and prepare to invade British Caribbean islands. News of the peace had not yet reached Axel when he wrote to his father on 10 March 1783, telling him that 'Porto Cabello is a wretched place, with no resources of any kind.'[30] The French were very demoralized, having lost 700 men in a war-ship sunk by the British navy on the voyage from America. Axel, suffering from the tropical climate (which left him with recurrent fevers), unburdened himself further in a letter to Sophie.

> *Porto Cabello.* I want your news. It's the only consolation we have in this vile country. We're dying of boredom here; we're becoming thin and drying up, growing old and yellow with heat and boredom. There is nothing to do in this wretched country; one cannot satisfy any of the five senses. Everything is black – not a white feature anywhere. Man is not made to live here, but rather tigers, bears and caymans. We are told that Caracas, which is 36 leagues away, is a fine town, that there is society there and pretty women who have nothing black about them except their eyes. I expect to go and find out in a few days.[31]

Axel instead received orders to return to France, and arrived with his regiment at Le Cap, the capital of Saint-Domingue (now Haiti), on 13 April 1783. He informed King Gustav III that the French campaign in the West Indies 'was simply tiring and boring, and we all received news of the peace with great pleasure'.[32] At Le Cap Axel had received a letter from Gustav with a colonel's commission in the Swedish Light Horse and the promise of a company of the King's Bodyguard, but he had no intention of returning to Sweden. On 26 April he wrote to his father, asking to postpone his homecoming until the following spring: 'I have been through three campaigns with the French army. I would be very annoyed not to reap the reward, and I need the winter to obtain what I seek. . . . I'm almost certain I can have my own regiment; this position does not require my presence, it's simply honorary and lucrative.'[33]

Axel was juggling with the truth. He had already told Sophie his plans and sworn her to secrecy, so he must have known his father's reaction would be unfavourable. Ownership of a regiment in the French army certainly required both expenditure and his presence in France from time to time, and although he vowed he did not want to become an expatriate, Axel showed no desire to return to Sweden. He felt happy and at home in France, and after three years in the wilderness,

Paris and Versailles must have seemed far more attractive than a gloomy Swedish castle. To please his father, he therefore suggested that he might at last settle down. 'I'm at an age when marriage, despite the little inclination I have for this sacrament, becomes a necessary thing.'[34] Axel said he had written to Miss Leyell to ask if she had changed her mind; were she still unwilling, he thought wealthy young Germaine Necker, daughter of the French Finance Minister, might be a suitable match, and told his father: 'This project depends entirely on your wishes; I have no other interest in it but yours. . . . I've only seen her once in passing, and I don't remember her face; I only recall that there is nothing disagreeable about her and she isn't deformed.'[35]

However, the Baron de Staël had already unsuccessfully proposed to Mlle Necker, and Axel declared that 'if he still has any hope, I shall abandon the idea altogether'. Soon he was to abandon every thought of marriage, for his life was to revolve around another woman entirely. A woman who wrote to Gustav III on 11 May 1783 to express her regret at news of the Swedish ambassador Creutz's recall from Paris, then added: 'Your Majesty cannot fail to know that in the war now happily terminated, Swedish officers particularly distinguished themselves. I applauded with all my heart the King's public praise of their conduct, and I seized the occasion to show my sincere attachment to you. [Marie-Antoinette].'[36]

Axel Fersen was still very much on the Queen's mind, three years after she had last seen him. What were his feelings for her? Would he come to Versailles only to leave her heart-broken yet again?

6

'Josephine'

Shortly after his return to Paris, Axel wrote to his sister Sophie.

Paris, 27 June 1783. I arrived at Brest on the 17th and here on the 23rd. I've been received marvellously. The Comte de Creutz will tell you what is being arranged for me, my dear friend. If it happens, I'll be the happiest of men, if not it will make me utterly wretched. My dear friend, persuade my father to consent; he will make me happy for life. I've written to him about it, but press him strongly. It's a question of money – speak to him for me. Adieu, my dear, tender, true, my only friend. Love your brother as much as he loves you.[1]

Something in France clearly exerted a very powerful attraction for Axel, and it could hardly have been the prospect of owning a regiment, since he could have obtained one far more easily in Sweden.

Despite Sophie's best efforts to persuade their father to agree to Axel's demands for a French regiment, negotiations proceeded neither quickly nor smoothly. Senator Fersen was strongly opposed to his son's wishes, and in France Axel encountered numerous obstacles. The free offer of Lauzun's legion seems to have been withdrawn; instead he was given the opportunity to buy the Royal-Suédois regiment for the not inconsiderable sum of 100,000 *livres*. His friendship with the Duc de Lauzun must have ended very abruptly; Marie-Antoinette, who deeply mistrusted the duke, was probably instrumental in detaching Axel from Lauzun and finding an alternative regiment. She may also have suggested he ask Gustav III of Sweden to intercede with Louis XVI to bypass interminable bureaucratic deliberations. Axel sent a letter to Gustav on 27 June 1783, begging him 'to consent to an arrangement on which depends my existence, my future and the happiness of my life'. Why such emotive language for a regiment? 'There is now a chance for me to have the Royal-Suédois,' he added, 'and if Your Majesty would ask for it for me I'm sure I would get it.' Axel later told Gustav the Royal-Suédois had been chosen 'because it was thought here it would be the one which would most please Your Majesty'.[2] One need not go far to *chercher la reine*.

Gustav III, always susceptible to flattery from his valued allies, the French, promptly took up Axel's cause with both Senator Fersen and Louis XVI. On 31 July Countess Hedda Fersen (later Klinck-kowström) told her father: ' . . . the King [Gustav] spoke to me of my brother Axel's business, and seems to think it an advantage for Swedes in general . . . doubtless he has given you his views'. After further discussions, Gustav wrote directly to Louis XVI in early September: 'The Comte de Fersen having served with general approval in Your Majesty's armies in America, thereby having proved himself worthy of your benevolence, I do not believe I am committing an indiscretion in asking for a proprietary regiment for him.'[3]

Louis XVI replied diplomatically on 19 September 1783 that he hoped soon 'to find a way to place him as he merits', but Marie-Antoinette was far more forthcoming in a letter she wrote the same day, taken personally by Axel to the Swedish King.

> I am taking advantage of the Comte de Fersen's departure to renew the sentiments which attach me to Your Majesty. Your recommendation to the King was received as it ought to be, coming from you and in favour of such a worthy subject. His father is not forgotten here; his services to France and his good reputation have been renewed by his son, who greatly distinguished himself in the American War, and who, because of his character and good qualities, has earned the esteem and affection of all those who have had occasion to meet him. I hope it will not be long before he is provided with a regiment. I will neglect nothing which may further Your Majesty's views. . . .[4]

Certainly not. Marie-Antoinette was desperate for Axel to get his regiment. Her suspense was speedily ended. On 20 September 1783 Axel told Sophie: 'My business is decided, my dear friend. I'm proprietary colonel of the Royal-Suédois, but I haven't yet received my commission. Don't say anything to my father if he doesn't mention it to you – there's still the matter of the 100,000 [*livres*] to be arranged with him.'[5]

Senator Fersen found himself outmanoeuvred by his son. Although he had given his consent he had not yet promised the 100,000 *livres*, but Axel had agreed to buy the regiment, convinced he could borrow the money against his inheritance and pay the interest from his annual salary of 12,000 *livres*. He hoped to win his father round when their long-delayed reunion took place in October 1783.

The Marquis de Bombelles, diplomat, courtier and close friend of Axel's protector, the Baron de Breteuil (now a government minister), followed negotiations for this regiment with interest. The twenty-seven-year-old Swede often dined at Breteuil's house during the summer of 1783, and in July spent three days with the baron at his daughter's country estate, Dangu. Bombelles, aware that Axel was expected to become an important figure in Sweden, studied him very carefully during this brief visit.

In the short time he was here, he displayed his good nature, good conversation, and signs of enthusiasm directed by noble opinions. He did not seem to us particularly gifted with wit; the vivacity of youth is often mistaken for it. . . . I believe he will always fall short of what was expected of him when he came into the world. His father is going to recall him to Sweden in a couple of months' time. . . . He will find a polished young man who has not done a single foolish thing on his travels or whilst serving for three years in the French army in America.[6]

Bombelles credited Breteuil with bringing discussions over Axel's regiment to a successful conclusion – apparently the War Minister, the Maréchal de Ségur, had created all the difficulties. On 24 September 1783 Bombelles alluded directly to Marie-Antoinette's interest in '*le jeune Comte de Fersen*':

Calumny is pleased to report that the Queen is in love with this young man, and wanted above all to place him more solidly in the King's service. I have been in a position to see that her interest in him is as straightforward as it is honourable. The Comte de Fersen went to Versailles only when the Baron de Breteuil forced him to show himself there. If the Queen had really had a passion for him, nothing

would have been easier than to make him spend the winter here, instead of which he left for Stockholm eight or ten days ago. This, it is
said, is the master-stroke of Her Majesty's dissimulation, as is the
noticeably nonchalant way she treated M. de Fersen in public. It seems
to me that a Queen whose standing and authority are so well known
has no need of such tricks.[7]

Marie-Antoinette's acting skills must have been exceptional if they
fooled the usually shrewd Bombelles, who also appears to have been
taken in by Axel Fersen's demure air. It was Marie-Antoinette herself who urged Breteuil to pull strings to get Axel the Royal-Suédois,
and she was also the cause of his great reluctance to leave France –
for in the summer of 1783 she and Axel became lovers. Her acting at
the Petit Trianon and his performances on Gustav III's stage at
Drottningholm proved invaluable training for the double lives they
immediately commenced.

As Axel's diary from 1779 to June 1791 was destroyed during the
French Revolution, it is impossible to state when he first went to
Court after arriving in Paris on 23 June 1783. Probably on the 25th
or 26th, since he needed to speak urgently to people at Versailles
who could help him obtain a regiment. The Queen, who had already
eagerly assisted him during the American war, would have been the
first person on his list. Not purely for business reasons, however.
Events in July 1783 prove that Axel's feelings for Marie-Antoinette
had been much more than friendly for a very long time. His return
to Versailles coincided with disagreement between Marie-Antoinette
and Louis XVI over her brother Joseph's alliance with Russia against
the Ottoman Empire. This even led to a rift between the Queen and
Mme de Polignac, who supported the King.

Axel could not have timed his return better. Marie-Antoinette felt
lonely and isolated, she still loved him deeply, and the birth of a
Dauphin meant she could now indulge in an affair without compromising the succession. She was free at last to declare her love, but
had no intention this time of allowing her feelings to be read by
courtiers who could sabotage her happiness. Some, more perspicacious
than Bombelles, nevertheless noticed her changed behaviour towards
Axel and correctly concluded it was a smokescreen. Axel's very correct, formal manner towards the Queen was also what most caused
the Comte de Tilly 'to suspect the high degree of his favour'.[8]

Publicly Marie-Antoinette could congratulate the handsome Swedish colonel on his successful campaign, and she was well within her rights to offer him a private audience to discuss his demands for a regiment. It was a rendezvous he never forgot. On 15 July 1783, Bombelles recorded that Axel left Mme de Matignon's house party at Dangu 'to go hunting at Versailles with the King'. This was undoubtedly an excuse. On 15 July 1798, Axel noted in his diary: 'I remember this day, when I . . . stayed at Madame de Matignon's house, and I went to *Her* privately for the first time.'[9] Fifteen years had passed, fifteen years in which he had experienced supreme happiness and utter despair, yet he still vividly recalled the very day he first went '*chez Elle*'. *Elle* was Marie-Antoinette's code-name in Axel's diary. He surely always remembered 15 July because it was the day they first made love.

Where did this long-awaited consummation take place? '*Chez Elle*' indicates Marie-Antoinette's private *cabinets*, possibly the *méridienne*, an intimate octagonal room built in 1782 which contained a large ottoman set in a curtained alcove. Or possibly the small mezzanine apartment Marie-Antoinette had offered her brother on his 1777 visit might have been the setting. In either case, Axel Fersen would have climbed the same secret staircase Joseph had used to reach Marie-Antoinette's *cabinets* unobserved. The reason Axel appeared at Court that summer only when Breteuil forced him was because he had many other secret rendezvous with the woman he loved. Versailles was deserted in the summer, according to Bombelles, and the Queen had more hours to spend undisturbed in her *cabinets* during the long hot afternoons.

After so many years nurturing what she probably feared was a hopeless love, Marie-Antoinette must have been overwhelmed by the ardour of Axel's response when she finally dared tell him her feelings. There was absolutely no hesitation on his part, and his excessive joy indicates that he too must have loved in silent hope of a return for a very long time. His letter to Sophie of 31 July 1783 says it all:

I received a letter 3 days ago from my friend Creutz which has given me the greatest of all pleasures. How happy I am now, my dear Sophie; he tells me the King and my father have agreed to everything. Imagine my happiness! I'm writing to my father today to thank him and to express all my joy. I can hardly believe I'm so happy – I've more than one reason for that, which I'll tell you when we meet.

I shall leave here around 13 September, and I'll be in Sweden on 15 October.... Despite all the pleasure I shall feel in seeing you I cannot leave Paris without sorrow. You will find it very natural when you know why; I'll tell you because I don't want to keep anything hidden from you.

I'm very pleased Miss Leyell is married. They won't speak of her to me any more, and I hope they don't find anyone else. I've made up my mind; I never want to tie the conjugal knot, it's against nature. When I have the misfortune to lose my father and mother, you will take their place, my dear friend, even that of a wife. You will be the mistress of my house; it will be yours, and we can stay together. If this arrangement suits you it would make me happy for life. I cannot belong to the only person I want to belong to, the only one who truly loves me, and so I don't want to belong to anyone.[10]

After losing Miss Leyell to the Earl of Delawarr, and Germaine Necker to the Baron de Staël, Axel turned his back on matrimony. If only he could have married Marie-Antoinette, the one woman he wanted, if only she had not been born a princess . . . they could have been the happiest couple in the world. That would have been too perfect, of course, and both Axel and Marie-Antoinette were realists. They accepted the hand fate had dealt them, and seized what happiness they could.

Despite the innocent gloss prudish nineteenth-century historians put on the relationship between Axel Fersen and Queen Marie-Antoinette, presenting their love as a charming example of romantic idealism unsullied by a single erotic thought, there is no doubt it was a sexual affair. Axel's diary shows that in later life he judged women with whom he had physical affairs against Marie-Antoinette – usually unfavourably. Had his relationship with her been merely platonic, the comparison would have been irrelevant. Napoleon would not accept him as Swedish negotiator at the Congress of Rastatt in 1796 because, Axel noted in his diary, 'he said he refused to deal with a man who had slept with the Queen of France'. By that time there was no danger in writing about the nature of their liaison. How could Marie-Antoinette have maintained such a powerful hold on Axel's affection, had they not been linked physically as well as emotionally? And had they been simply friends, however close, there would have been no need for elaborate subterfuge to conceal their affair; no letters in invisible ink or secret meetings in Marie-Antoinette's private apartments.

How passionate Axel's love-making was cannot be known, but with his 'burning soul', he was surely far more virile, tender and sensual than Louis XVI. Marie-Antoinette probably inherited a strong sex drive from both her parents. Just because her husband failed to arouse her, there is no reason to assume she could not respond to a man she loved and desired; but though tactile, she could hardly have been the rabid sexual acrobat of popular myth. Axel might have been surprised by her inexperience. Nevertheless for him she was, and always remained, the perfection of womanhood. He never found her grace, charm, tenderness and warmth elsewhere. 'How perfect *She* was in everything,' he wrote in 1794. 'Never have there been nor will there be other women like *Her*.'[11] Axel's love for Marie-Antoinette was all-embracing; she was in every sense the wife he never had. Lover, friend, confidante, she became the centre of his whole existence.

Loving Axel Fersen must have been a sweet pastime for Marie-Antoinette in the summer of 1783, and she was soon sweetly recompensed. She became pregnant. That this pregnancy resulted from a renewed burst of energy from Louis XVI, who had grown very fat and even more unattractive, is doubtful. It had taken him eighteen months to achieve the conception of the Dauphin, whose birth was followed by a further eighteen months of occasional and unproductive intercourse with the Queen. Yet from July 1783 when her affair with Axel began, she became pregnant no less than three times, in 1783, 1784 and 1785.

Despite Marie-Antoinette's love of children, she seemed decidedly unhappy when her pregnancy was confirmed. On 25 August 1783, the Marquis de Bombelles wrote: 'The news of the day is the Queen's pregnancy. Not having taken enough care of herself she has had, in the words of M. de Vermond, her male midwife, a "shaking of the embryo", and will spend the next nine days in bed or on a *chaise-longue*.'[12] Four days later the situation was even worse.

29 August 1783. There is a worrying silence about the Queen's condition. Many people think she had a miscarriage last Sunday, and conclude this from the fact that at 11 a.m. that same day Her Majesty sent urgently for Mme la Duchesse de Polignac, who seemed sad and very worried when she returned to the Dauphin's apartment. What served to confirm this suspicion even more was that the Queen told Mme la Princesse de Chimay she would not see her, nor the other ladies in waiting. Mme de Chimay, as a *dame d'honneur*, has the right to enter the Queen's apartment whenever she wishes. . . . All in all there is noticeable and considerable ill-humour in the domestic life of the palace.[13]

Was it possible that Marie-Antoinette, frightened of giving birth to an illegitimate child, had tried to contrive a miscarriage? Her behaviour during this pregnancy was wholly uncharacteristic. It is more than probable that she confided in Mme de Polignac. The Princesse de Lamballe also regained Marie-Antoinette's confidence during this period, although she may have served to ward off intruders. Axel wrote letters home from Versailles during August, so his meetings with Marie-Antoinette must have been frequent. On the evening of 10 September 1783, the Queen again refused to receive visitors – 'She was closeted with Mme la Princesse de Lamballe,' noted Bombelles, 'with whom she had already spent a part of the morning and dined.'[14] She might well have spent the afternoon instead saying goodbye to Axel, who was about to leave for Stockholm. They had to arrange a means of correspondence and discuss their reunion. Axel counted on returning to France in the spring of 1784, and spending a whole year with the Queen. He originally intended to leave Paris on 12 September, but final negotiations for his regiment delayed his departure by a week; a welcome delay for the lovers.

On 20 September Axel set off for a long-overdue meeting with his father in Stockholm, stopping off at Strasbourg for a few days to see his younger brother Fabian, who was on the Grand Tour. On arriving at Wismar, Axel received an order from the Swedish ambassador at Hamburg to await a letter from Gustav III, who had just embarked on a journey through Europe. It came on 8 October and threw all his plans into confusion. 'The King's order is clear and precise,' he told his father on 9 October. 'I must join him at Rostock, and if he has already left there follow his route, which is via Brunswick, Augsburg, Innsbruck, Brixen and Verona. I must accompany him as Captain of the Bodyguard, and he expects to see me very soon.'[15]

This news, as Axel well knew, would be very badly received by Senator Fersen, who had evidently written expressing disapproval of his son's conduct. It also denied Axel the opportunity to settle his affairs in Sweden and return to France the following spring as he had planned.

> This order, however flattering it may be, makes me desperate. It deprives me of the great satisfaction of seeing a father I love and whom I cherish for so many reasons. It prevents me from talking to you. . . . It prevents me from destroying in part the bad opinion you have of me and of 'my extreme penchant for pleasure, which is my only guide and sole master'. Time will prove, my dear father, the injustice of this opinion. If I followed only my pleasure, I would not carry out the King's orders at this moment.
>
> Be my judge, my dear father, and be just. It would be dreadful to bear a grudge against me because I am carrying out my duty at the expense of my pleasure; seeing you would have given me great joy . . . but duty prevents it, and I must obey. As long as I serve I shall know no other law. I must sacrifice everything to it, even my life; I have already often sacrificed my pleasures.[16]

True, Axel had forgone pleasures for three years during the American war, but he had no intention of giving up Marie-Antoinette now she had surrendered herself to him body and soul. King Gustav's command, coming at this moment, could not have been more inopportune for Axel's love-life or his strained relations with his father. Nevertheless he joined the Swedish royal party at Erlanger as Captain of the Bodyguard.

Although Gustav III travelled incognito as the 'Comte de Haga', he was accompanied by a large retinue, including his court chamberlains Barons Sparre, Armfelt and Taube, not to mention various artists and sculptors. His Italian journey was primarily a cultural pilgrimage, but he wasted no opportunities to forge useful diplomatic and political connections.

The Swedish party visited Marie-Antoinette's brother Leopold, Grand Duke of Tuscany, but found Court life in Florence exceedingly dull. They were instead royally entertained by two English expatriates, Sir Horace Mann and Lord Cowper. Axel Fersen became friendly with Cowper's sister, Emily, and a marriage may even have been mooted between them. In his correspondence book Axel records a letter to Emily on 30 April 1784 telling her 'that it can never happen and to think about it no more', and another letter to her brother the same day, asking Cowper 'to console her'. The key to this mystery was probably revealed to Lady Elizabeth Foster, another English visitor to Florence. The long-standing mistress of the Duke of Devonshire, by whom she had three children, she was travelling to escape scandal at home, and found a sympathetic listener in Axel, who noted she was 'very unhappy'. He corresponded with Lady Elizabeth regularly right up to 1795. She appears to have known about his liaison with Marie-Antoinette, for the Queen was frequently mentioned in their letters. On 7 December 1784 Axel sent her a letter in which he 'declared everything' – possibly that he could not marry Emily Cowper because his feelings were engaged elsewhere.

Axel also had to contend with his father's anger over his purchase of the Royal-Suédois and the whole Italian trip. He received a letter from Senator Fersen on 3 April 1784 which, he wrote, 'made me desperate'.[17] But duty called. Axel accompanied Gustav to all the main cities and sights of Italy, even to an audience with the Pope at the Vatican on 26 December 1783. On their travels, the Swedish party frequently encountered Emperor Joseph II, also touring the country. Gustav irritated Joseph intensely, probably because of his bisexuality. Joseph told his sister Marie-Christine: 'The King of Sweden is a type who isn't at all homogeneous to me; false, small, miserable, a dandy in front of his mirror. He's going to pass through France, and if you see him, I recommend him to you in advance.'[18] Some recommendation!

Axel admired Joseph's simplicity and good manners, ruefully contrasting his own gaudy Swedish uniform with the Emperor's plain dress. This tedious and unwelcome journey in Gustav's company doubtless made Axel glad he had found a way to spend more time in France, for the King constantly demanded his presence. Gustav liked to impress, and Axel's height compensated for his own insignificant stature. The King was nevertheless well received by Marie-Antoinette's sister, the Queen of Naples. 'She is amiable and attentive,' wrote Axel, 'like the whole House of Austria, and like them she likes to govern and she rules.'[19]

Though he displeased Joseph and Leopold, Gustav was assured of a warm welcome in France from their sister Marie-Antoinette. On 15 October 1783 she wrote and told him that 'if, as I hope, Your Majesty's travels bring you to Versailles, you cannot doubt the welcome due to an old and good ally of France'.[20] She later renewed her invitation, approved by the French Foreign Minister, Vergennes, who was worried Gustav might form an alliance with Russia. Gustav could not possibly refuse, though Marie-Antoinette was surely motivated more by her great desire to be reunited with Axel than a wish to renew her acquaintance with his foppish King.

The Queen's chief concern in the autumn of 1783 was her pregnancy. Marie-Antoinette informed Joseph of it in September 1783, and told him of her 'little accident'. Heeding his plea to take care of herself, she travelled by boat to Fontainebleau when the Court moved there on 9 October. Bombelles, whose mother-in-law looked after young Madame, saw the Queen on her arrival. 'She was wearing a loose white dress which is called a *pierrot*, and she looked as though she were six months pregnant. It did not detract from her freshness or the charm of her face.'[21] She was so large, he thought she might even have twins.

Fontainebleau was very crowded that year. Louis XVI went hunting nearly every day while Marie-Antoinette stayed with her daughter and sister-in-law, Elisabeth. Deprived of Mme de Polignac's company, she discussed instead the merits of various runners in local races with the Comte d'Artois. On Saturday 1 November 1783 she held an open salon and dined with the King in public, but during the night she fell ill, and on the 2nd was bled twice by her doctors. Her pains however continued, and on 3 November at 3 a.m. she had a miscarriage. According to Bombelles, 'it was very fortunate, because H.M. had been pregnant with a deformed foetus'.[22] Mercy sent the same news to Vienna, adding that the Queen's health had not suffered. She spent a week in bed and reappeared in public on 11 November, looking 'very well recovered' in Bombelles's opinion.

Doubts about the pregnancy are raised by Marie-Antoinette's evident relief at this miscarriage. When she miscarried in 1779, she was extremely upset. This time she resumed her public life with barely a sigh, writing very uncharacteristically to Joseph on 20 December 1783: 'My health continues to be very good, my dear brother. But although I have a great desire to have another son, I believe a few months' rest will put me in a better position to carry it through.'[23]

Was this the Marie-Antoinette who loved her daughter too much, always played with children at Versailles, who ought to have been eager to ensure the succession by producing a second son? It is interesting that at Fontainebleau in 1784 news broke of the Comtesse d'Artois's pregnancy. Everyone knew she had not slept with her husband for a long time, and Marie-Antoinette entered into negotiations on the frantic countess's behalf with the Comte d'Artois. The Queen's sister-in-law gave birth on 4 April 1785 to a child fathered by one of her bodyguards. The infant was immediately sent away, and its mother is rumoured to have defended herself afterwards by saying her conduct was still better than the Queen's.[24] Did she therefore know the truth about Marie-Antoinette's 1783 pregnancy?

Axel Fersen must have quickly received news of the miscarriage, since he wrote many letters to the Queen during his Italian journey. His reaction is unknown, but King Gustav wrote to the Baron de Staël on 7 November from Pisa: 'I felt the accident which happened to the Queen of France much more keenly than her relatives here; I really am desperate about it.'[25] He was deeply sympathetic, having only recently lost his second son (Marie-Antoinette's godson). It was the start of a warm, active friendship for her which proved very valuable in the dark years to come.

The first six months of 1784 were equally stressful for Marie-Antoinette. The winter was exceedingly cold, and she set an example to courtiers in February by giving 1,000 *louis* to help the poor. She then had to nurse her daughter through a minor illness, before discovering her son was seriously ill. The two-and-a-half-year-old Dauphin displayed symptoms which alarmed his mother, but doctors assured her in April that all was well. Mercy was sceptical. The young prince, he declared, had a 'scorbutic humour'. He had stopped growing, and was languorous and feverish. Mercy was particularly concerned because there seemed little likelihood the Dauphin would have a brother. 'His existence is all the more precious because the regime and habits of the King do not give any hope at all that he will have a numerous posterity.'[26]

By mid-May the Dauphin was suffering from convulsions, and the King and Queen spent hours each day together at his bedside. Doctors hoped the child's fever would cure his condition, about which none of them agreed. On 30 May 1784, Bombelles reported that his whole body was swollen, he was shaking, could neither sleep nor pass water but was deemed at last to be improving. 'The King, who came to see his son, after looking at him tenderly for a long time, could not hold back several big tears which he tried to hide but which were noticed by all those around him, as well by M. le Dauphin.'[27]

The crisis passed and with further tender nursing, the Dauphin steadily recovered; but this was unhappily the first sign of the recurrent tuberculosis which eventually killed him.

Marie-Antoinette must have been more anxious than ever to see Axel, who always took a keen interest in her children's welfare and education. She wrote to him often during his eight months in Italy, but had to go to elaborate lengths to receive his replies. The French police had a department devoted solely to intercepting and opening private mail, including diplomatic dispatches and royal letters. Hence the need for couriers. Axel kept a correspondence book for many years, in which he noted the dates and destinations of all letters he sent, often jotting down a précis of their contents. When he left Paris on 20 September 1783 he commenced a long correspondence with 'Josephine'. By 18 May 1783 he had written her no less than twenty-seven letters. 'Josephine' designated his private letters to Marie-Antoinette. She was only 'the Queen' when he wrote to her officially – two or three times in the 1780s about his regiment, and often during 1791–2 when he represented the Swedish government and their correspondence was political.

Not one of the innumerable letters Axel received from 'Josephine' has yet been found. Probably they were destroyed by his prudish great-nephew, Baron Klinckowström. Marie-Antoinette certainly never dared keep Axel's letters after 1789, and disposed of batches of her personal papers three or four times during the Revolution. There is no doubt at all, however, that she was 'Josephine'. Axel numbered all the letters he sent to her, so she could be sure none went astray. He numbered only important letters; to Marie-Antoinette, General Bouillé and occasionally to Eleonore Sullivan (the last two series dealing with the flight to Varennes). Each series of letters to 'Josephine' began when he left Paris and ceased when he returned to the capital, so 'Josephine' was unquestionably based in or near Paris for the duration of their correspondence. The letters were often written in invisible ink, which surely indicates a great need for secrecy and they were frequently sent through intermediaries.

Proof that 'Josephine' was Marie-Antoinette occurs in an entry in Axel's correspondence book for 1788: '*Josephine 23 August* Letter by Est[erhazy] which I begin with "My dear Comte, it's for *Her*."'[28] '*C'est pour Elle.' Elle* was how Axel mentioned the Queen to his sister and a few close friends. Esterhazy, Marie-Antoinette's old and

trusted friend, would have been a reliable courier. Many other intermediaries are mentioned, and letters were even sometimes sent through
the post. Axel only occasionally noted the contents of his letters to
'Josephine', so many must have been simply love-letters. In a few he
refers to political or military topics, her children, music, mutual friends
and arrangements for secret visits to her at Versailles.

Incontrovertible proof of 'Josephine's' identity occurs in Axel's diary
entry for 7 November 1792, when he was preparing to leave Brussels
in the face of advancing French troops.

> I went to see Mercy to ask if he had taken care of Josephine's dia-
> monds. He had the effrontery to tell me he didn't know he had them;
> that he had certainly received a box, but that he had given the key to
> the Archduchess [Marie-Christine] when she arrived. Yet it was I
> who wrote him a letter about it at the time and sent him the box.[29]

This is a very clear reference to Marie-Antoinette's diamonds, sent
to Mercy for safe-keeping through Axel in 1791.

Little did 'Josephine' know that a dastardly plot involving a magnificent diamond necklace was being hatched in the spring of 1784, a
plot which would do her irreversible harm. One wonders if Axel called
her 'Josephine' or Antoinette in private; she probably chose the code-
name for the letters, since her third name was Josèphe, and of course
Joseph was her favourite brother. She would have been extremely
interested to hear what Axel had to say about him when he eventually reached Paris in June 1784, but arranging a rendezvous was not
easy. Axel had written on 21 May to tell her 'that I cannot come
before the King'.[30] He was under Gustav's orders, and Gustav intended to steal as much limelight as possible.

The King of Sweden lived up to his theatrical reputation when he
arrived unannounced at Versailles on 7 June 1784. Louis XVI had
been on his way to Rambouillet for a hunting trip, but was urgently
recalled by Marie-Antoinette when she heard of Gustav's impending
arrival. Louis dressed in such haste to meet him that he put on different
coloured stockings and had a buckle missing from one shoe. Axel
Fersen and Baron Stettin were the only members of the Swedish
party to accompany their King, who had a brief audience with Louis
XVI before the monarchs went to the Queen's apartments for supper.

Marie-Antoinette may just have been able to slip Axel a note before he was dismissed by Gustav, who, according to Bombelles, 'sent word to the Comte de Fersen (with whom I was waiting in the Queen's antechamber) that he was free to sup and go to bed. I went with him as far as the Hôtel des Ambassadeurs, which adjoins my house'.[31]

During the next six weeks Gustav frequently dropped in for supper at Versailles, although he refused the magnificent apartment specially prepared for him, preferring to keep his transparent incognito as the Comte de Haga by staying in the same hotel Joseph used on his visits to France. He developed a particular fondness for Marie-Antoinette and her children, and the evening after his arrival she showed him round the gardens of the Petit Trianon. Bombelles saw her as she left Versailles.

The Queen went to the Petit Trianon without being accompanied by her retinue. I saw her going there in a cabriolet with a single horse, which she drove, her coachman seated behind and two outriders in front of this light equipage. I was walking by the Dragon fountain with my eldest son. . . . The Queen had the kindness to wish him good evening as she passed, calling him Bombon [his nickname].[32]

Marie-Antoinette may possibly have managed to see Axel privately later that evening at the Petit Trianon, since according to Louis XVI's diary, Gustav had supper at Versailles with him and his sister-in-law, Madame.[33] Meetings between the lovers must nevertheless have been difficult to arrange, for Gustav was an energetic tourist, went frequently to operas and plays, and Axel was a favourite companion. On 20 June 1784 Axel told his father: 'I was obliged to feign an illness which confined me to my room, in order to be free to write to you and attend to my affairs. I'm going out only this evening, to sup at Versailles.'[34] He was probably going to console Marie-Antoinette, who was annoyed with the Baron de Breteuil for not inviting her to a fête he had held for the Swedes the previous evening, doubtless because she had missed a chance to see Axel.

A highlight of Gustav's visit was the Queen's own fête in his honour held at the Petit Trianon on the evening of 21 June, when the gardens were illuminated. The whole royal family attended, and Marie-Antoinette captivated the Swedish King. He was delighted that 'she spoke to all the Swedes, and took care of them with extreme solicitude and attention'.[35] Despite all the entertainments he was offered,

Gustav did not neglect politics during his French visit. He obtained
the French Caribbean island of Saint-Barthélemy in exchange for
granting France trading concessions in Sweden, and also negotiated
a renewal of the Franco-Swedish alliance, which provided an annual
French subsidy to Sweden of 1,200,000 *livres* for a further six years.

Axel also benefited from Gustav's negotiating skills. Evidently he
had some difficulty in financing the purchase of the Royal-Suédois,
probably because of continued paternal opposition, and the King
managed to obtain an increase in Axel's colonel's salary to 20,000
livres a year – enough to grant him a measure of independence from
his father, whom he had yet to meet in Sweden.

The last few weeks of the Swedish visit, when Gustav's curiosity
waned a little, gave Marie-Antoinette many more opportunities for
romantic encounters with Axel. Their farewell must have been tender indeed, for after leaving Paris with Gustav on 20 July, he wrote
her six letters in nine days – from Chantilly, Sedan, Düsseldorf,
Lüneburg and Warnemünde. Axel arrived home in Stockholm, after
an absence of six and a half years, on 2 August 1784, fully determined to return to the woman he loved as soon as possible.

7

'Le Chou d'Amour'

Axel Fersen's first task on arriving home was to reconcile his father to his purchase of a regiment in the French army. They met at the family castle at Ljung, where Axel remained for six weeks. Only his sister Sophie knew the true reason for his burning desire to return to Paris, though it is doubtful she knew at this stage the full extent of his liaison with Marie-Antoinette. She was certainly sympathetic; in later correspondence with her brother Sophie displayed a touching warmth for the Queen of France, who reciprocated by sending her friendly messages through Axel.

The autumn of 1784 saw Axel playing his part at Gustav's court at Gripsholm, and buying a Swedish dog for Marie-Antoinette. He had written to 'Josephine' about it twice in July – 'asked what name to give the dog, and if I should make a secret of it'. There is no indication of the animal's breed, which was probably the same as Axel's own dog. He nevertheless had some difficulty in obtaining this present for his loved one. On 22 October 1784 he noted in his correspondence book: 'To Mr de Boye. That the dog has not arrived; what must I do to get it'; and on 9 November: 'to Mr de Boye. Asked him to send me a dog which was not small, of the same size as those which Monsieur Pollett had, said that *it was for the Queen of France*'.[1] The magic words 'Queen of France' seem to have had the desired effect, for we hear no more of Axel's problems in securing a dog for Marie-Antoinette.

Axel's departure from Versailles must have left the Queen feeling bereft, but at least she had the satisfaction of knowing he missed her; they corresponded often during his stay in Sweden. Marie-Antoinette

was now completely reassured about the Dauphin's health. Her son
had been sent to fresher air at the Château de la Muette near Paris
during King Gustav's visit, and on 21 July, the Marquis de Bombelles
reported that he was in fine form: 'The prince now walks wonderfully
well; I found him digging in his garden and showing by the activity
of his movements and his gaiety that his health is completely restored.'[2]

There was now a possibility the Dauphin might yet have a younger
brother to ensure the succession, for early in August 1784 Marie-
Antoinette discovered she was pregnant again. 'My health is still very
good,' she told her brother Joseph on 17 August, 'despite the beginning of my pregnancy.'[3] She did not seem displeased and immediately adopted a quieter routine, spending most of her time in calm
seclusion at the Petit Trianon. This peace and tranquillity was unfortunately of short duration, and the Queen's beloved brother himself shattered it.

Joseph II's foreign policy was often a source of embarassment to
Marie-Antoinette, who, indoctrinated to regard the Franco-Austrian
alliance as sacrosanct, usually failed to distinguish between French
and Austrian interests. In her opinion, allies could have no policy
differences, otherwise what price an alliance? In the summer of 1784
Joseph called on France to support his demand that the Dutch open
the Scheldt to shipping from the Austrian Netherlands. After promising to back the Emperor, the French Foreign Minister Vergennes
then changed his mind. Joseph was furious, and told his sister on 1
September that 'the conduct of M. de Vergennes is hardly made to
strengthen, but rather even to break the ties of alliance and policy
which unite us'.[4] He strongly suspected French fickleness and Prussian intrigue and even accused Marie-Antoinette of being duped by
Vergennes. She had, of course, been bullied by Mercy to intervene
on her brother's behalf. It was a role she hated, and on 22 September she wrote Joseph a letter which illustrates her extremely awkward political position, and is also very revealing about her relations
with Louis XVI and his difficult character.

> I won't contradict you, my dear brother, on our government's lack of
> direction . . . I have spoken of it more than once to the King; but you
> would need to know him well to judge the few resources and means
> available to me, given his character and prejudices. He is of a taciturn
> disposition, and often he doesn't tell me about important matters,

even if he has no desire to conceal them from me. He answers when I speak to him, but he hardly ever informs me first; and when I know a quarter of the business I need some skill to get his ministers to tell me the rest, by letting them think the King has told me everything. . . . I confess that political affairs are those over which I have the least command. The King's natural mistrust was first strengthened by his governor. Even before my marriage M. de La Vauguyon had frightened him about the control his wife would want to exert over him, and his black soul took pleasure in terrifying his pupil with all the phantoms invented about the House of Austria. . . . M. de Vergennes follows the same plan, and possibly uses Foreign Ministry correspondence to spread lies and falsehoods. I've spoken about it openly to the King, and more than once. He has on occasion answered me with ill-humour, and, as he is incapable of discussing anything, I haven't been able to persuade him that either his minister was deceived or was deceiving him. I don't blind myself as to my influence; I know that in politics above all else I do not have much influence over the King's mind. Would it be prudent for me to have scenes with his minister about issues when it is almost certain the King would not support me?

Without ostentation or falsehood I let the public think I have more influence than I really have, because if I were believed to have none I should have even less.[5]

This letter was tantamount to a plea by Marie-Antoinette to be spared further unwelcome political missions, and shows a woeful lack of understanding and communication with her husband. Joseph responded on 9 October by promising he would not make her life difficult. The Queen was, however, indispensable to Austria in the resolution of what developed into a full-blown crisis. Not only did Vergennes refuse to back Austrian demands over the Scheldt, he even deployed French troops to support the Dutch. Marie-Antoinette was truly alarmed: 'What will my position be if we cannot stifle this deadly seed of division!'[6]

Louis XVI was governed entirely by Vergennes, and even though he professed himself in favour of the Franco-Austrian alliance, allowed matters to go to the brink of war. Perhaps by way of compensation he bought the Château de Saint-Cloud from the Duc d'Orléans for 6 million *livres* in November 1784 as a present for Marie-Antoinette. She was very pleased, because she could bequeath it to any of her children (one feels sure she intended it as an inheritance for her daughter), but it was not a popular gesture with the public. A Queen of France was supposed to be wholly dependent on her husband, and Marie-Antoinette's ownership of a château was considered outrageous. It was a large gift, but not by comparison with the many millions Louis XVI spent on hunting parks for himself, and the huge sums he gave his brothers.

Mercy had no doubt that French ministers hoped the Queen would be too busy refurbishing Saint-Cloud to pay much attention to their attempts to wreck the Austrian alliance. If so, they badly miscalculated. After unsuccessful skirmishes with the Dutch, Joseph complicated matters by offering to withdraw his demand for access to the Scheldt if France helped him negotiate an exchange of the Austrian Netherlands for Bavaria. The Dutch then asked to buy back the strategic border town of Maastricht from Austria, and discussions and sabrerattling alternated for almost a year before a treaty was eventually signed. French involvement was crucial, and Marie-Antoinette, coached by Mercy, was active in bringing matters to a successful conclusion. According to Mercy, by May 1785 she had made real progress in her handling of political affairs: 'She often brings to them an astonishing wisdom, which more than once has greatly embarrassed the Comte de Vergennes.'[7]

Despite political vexations and her pregnancy, Marie-Antoinette by no means forgot Sweden during the winter of 1784/5. At Gustav III's request she had a portrait of herself and her children walking in the gardens of the Petit Trianon painted by Werthemuller. Mme Campan considered this one of only two good likenesses of the Queen, but Gustav was not very impressed. When the portrait eventually reached Stockholm in 1786, he wrote to the Baron de Staël: 'It is well painted, but it doesn't do her justice; it is indeed difficult to catch the graces and charm of her face. Little Madame is charming; my son calls her his little wife . . . the Dauphin is very tall and resembles his father the King.'[8]

The year 1785 was a happy one for Marie-Antoinette personally, although it marked the beginning of successive attempts to undermine her public image which eventually proved catastrophic. Her first happiness was the birth of her second son. The Marquis de Bombelles was among the crowd which flocked to Versailles to hear the good news on 27 March 1785.

I learnt that the Queen had suffered a little this morning, that when she returned from Mass and saw lots of people already in her ante-chamber it annoyed her, and she said she felt so well she would go and sup with Mme la princesse de Lamballe; afterwards she informed Mme de Polignac of her real condition and ordered her to keep it secret, which was done in such a manner that many people, begin-ning with some of the Princes of the Blood, did not arrive on time. At four in the evening her pains began to be serious, and labour then following, Her Majesty was delivered before seven o'clock. . . . The little prince was baptized an hour after his birth.

He was called Louis-Charles, Duc de Normandie. Bombelles was allowed to see him the following day. 'M. le Duc de Normandie is a superb infant, very strong, well made, and who shows signs of being easy to rear. . . . The Queen is wonderfully well, and the palace as well as the courtyards offer the agreeable sight of a crowd of people anxious to know the details of this happy event.'[9]

'I was very sure, my dear brother,' Marie-Antoinette wrote to Joseph on 18 April, 'that you would share my joy. There has been a great deal here for the birth of my son, who is very well and has all the signs of a good constitution.'[10] The Dauphin and Madame were de-lighted with their baby brother, but few people realized just how dear he would become to Marie-Antoinette. The Duc de Normandie was unquestionably her favourite child; she adored him, and he re-sponded with a warmth and gaiety that made him even more precious. There was none of the emotional coldness she had experienced with her daughter, and even at times with the Dauphin, both of whom had inherited facets of Louis XVI's temperament which greatly hurt their mother.

When writing about Normandie to Mme de Polignac, Marie-Antoinette employed a private nickname – 'le Chou d'Amour' (liter-ally: 'the darling of love'), a sure indication of her fondness for him. This rather odd expression seems to imply that Normandie was a fruit of love, not duty, in which case Louis XVI's paternity seems doubtful. It was often alleged during the Revolution that the King's second son was illegitimate, and although Louis never openly questioned his paternity, he displayed little affection for his wife's handsome, lively *Chou d'Amour*. His diary entry for Normandie's birth possibly confirms suspicions about the child's conception, which coincided with Axel Fersen's 1784 visit to Versailles with Gustav III. When his daughter was born, Louis XVI affixed an extra page to his diary with full details; for the Dauphin, he added two pages. Yet Normandie's entry into the world was recorded very concisely in the following ambiguous passage.

> *27 March 1785.* The Queen was delivered of the Duc de Normandie at half-past seven; everything happened just as to my son [the Dauphin]; the baptism was at eight o'clock and the Te Deum; the only prince present was the Duc de Chartres; there were neither congratulations nor compliments. Monsieur and the Queen of Naples godparents.[11]

This does not sound like the proud and happy father of a healthy prince; Louis XVI was himself responsible for the lack of celebrations, for he had to pay for illuminations and parties to celebrate the birth. Evidently he did not think that Normandie warranted such expense. One is tempted to ask why, when the Dauphin's poor health made the birth of another son essential to ensure the succession.

Axel certainly took a fatherly interest in Marie-Antoinette's children, particularly in her younger son. He was soon able to share her delight at Normandie's birth, for the possibility of a Franco-Austrian war over the Scheldt affair required him to take command of his regiment in France. His father was not at all pleased, for he was breaking a promise to spend at least two years in Sweden. 'Your brother is going to leave me at the end of April,' Senator Fersen wrote to his younger son Fabian on 10 March 1785, 'to join his regiment, the Royal-Suédois at Landrecies in Flanders. It is very unclear when I will see him again; if war breaks out, which is probable, his absence will be of long duration.' Senator Fersen's bitterness may be gauged from a letter in which Axel's aunt declared: 'I am truly sorry for his father; he had placed all the consolation of his old age in enjoying the company of his son, and now he looks on him as lost to him for ever.' By this time Senator Fersen surely knew he had to compete with Marie-Antoinette for Axel's affection, for on 13 June 1785 he wrote curtly to Fabian: 'Your brother has been in Paris since 10 May, very busy either with his military or frivolous arrangements.'[12]

Three days before departing from Stockholm on 18 April, Axel told Marie-Antoinette he had finally settled affairs with his father relating to the purchase of the Royal-Suédois, and that he was 'very happy'. Very happy he was soon going to see her again. Very happy to learn of her safe delivery of a son? He arrived in Paris on 10 May 1785, and five days later went to Versailles to pay his court and present the King and Queen with letters from Gustav III. Axel wrote to Sophie (with no indication of the year) from Versailles 'this 15 May Saturday at 10 p.m.': 'I arrived at Versailles this evening at 6 p.m. I'm staying here until tomorrow evening in order to pay my court tomorrow morning.'

Staying where and with whom? It is quite probable that Axel paid several secret visits to Marie-Antoinette during May 1785, for in another fragment of a letter to Sophie, again lacking a date, he wrote: 'But it's 8 p.m., I must close. I've been at Versailles since yesterday. Don't say I'm writing to you from here, because I date my other letters from Paris. Adieu, I must go to the Queen's card-table. Adieu. *At 9 p.m. the same evening*: I've just this minute left the Queen's card-table and I've only got time to finish my letter, because in a moment I have to go and have supper at Mme d'Ossun's. She's a lady-in-waiting; the Queen will be there. When supper is over at one o'clock I'm returning to Paris, and this letter will go tomorrow morning at eight. Adieu. . . .'[13]

Axel was probably scrawling his adieux to Sophie in Marie-Antionette's private *cabinets*. His public appearances at the card-table and at Mme d'Ossun's supper party were part of his smokescreen, to fool courtiers by his formal behaviour that his relationship with the Queen was above reproach. The Comtesse d'Ossun had won the Queen's friendship during the Court's residence at Fontainebleau in 1783, a constant friendship, according to Bombelles, which even alarmed Mme de Polignac. Marie-Antoinette avoided meeting Axel too often *chez* Polignac; had he been a known member of the Polignac set, however formal his manner, rumours would inevitably have arisen about his liaison with the Queen. It is likely that in 1785, as in later years, he stayed with Marie-Antoinette in her private apartments, in a small love-nest she had prepared for him on the top floor of the palace.

Love nevertheless had to take second place to duty. Axel left Paris for Landrecies, probably in June, and remained on full alert with his regiment for the whole summer. Given his visits to the capital from the northern border when he was on duty there with the Royal-Suédois in 1789 he doubtless still managed to make a few trips to Versailles.

The Queen certainly needed someone sympathetic to talk to in August, when the Diamond Necklace Scandal broke.[14] This byzantine plot, hatched by a scheming adventuress, Jeanne de La Motte, involved the Court jeweller Boehmer, the Queen and Cardinal Rohan. Boehmer's famous 1,600,000 *livres* diamond necklace, which Marie-Antoinette had repeatedly refused to buy, was purchased in January 1785 by the cardinal (who claimed to be convinced he was acting on her behalf), with a contract on which La Motte's accomplice had forged the Queen's signature. The cardinal handed the necklace to La Motte to give to the Queen, but was amazed when Her Majesty did not appear wearing it in public. It had, of course, already been broken up; the stones were sold by La Motte's husband in Paris, London and elsewhere in Europe. This audacious theft was not discovered until a distraught Boehmer went to see Marie-Antoinette to demand payment as promised under the terms of the contract. She did not know what he was talking about. Boehmer then implicated the cardinal, the Queen turned to the King for help and Rohan was arrested in the Hall of Mirrors on 15 August 1785. La Motte and various accomplices were also detained a few days later, and sent to the Bastille. 'I hope this business will soon be concluded,' Marie-Antoinette wrote to Emperor Joseph on 22 August, 'but I don't know yet whether it will go to trial at the Parlement or if the accused and his family will rely on the King's clemency. But in either case, I want this horrid affair and all the details to be properly cleared up in everyone's eyes.'[15]

Marie-Antoinette believed the truth would absolve her of involvement in this sordid plot, and hoped Rohan would be punished for having falsely used her name. She was to be cruelly deceived. Rohan opted to be tried by the Parlement of Paris, the French equivalent of the High Court; Mercy drew up a list of the judges for Joseph, detailing any obligations they might be expected to repay the Rohans. There was a slim hope indeed of a fair trial or verdict. The powerful princely Rohan family, still smarting over the bankruptcy of the Prince de Guéméné and his subsequent disgrace, united behind the cardinal. One very easy way to win him support (despite his notoriously bad reputation) was to spread rumours implicating the Queen – no difficult task, since the cardinal's faithful secretary, the Abbé Georgel, destroyed much of the evidence which would have inculpated him and exonerated her, while his co-defendants offered so many contradictory accusations that the truth was only ever half revealed.

Marie-Antoinette was cast as a vicious Queen wreaking revenge on Cardinal Rohan, with whom it was assumed she had enjoyed a love-affair. The necklace theft, according to this scenario, was devised by Marie-Antoinette with Jeanne de La Motte solely to ruin Rohan and destroy his political ambitions. The Queen's unpopularity plumbed new depths. The purchase of Saint-Cloud, the Necklace Affair, Joseph's disastrous foreign policy objectives, all contributed towards her public image as the hated, frivolous, extravagant, lascivious and evil foreigner, hell-bent on the destruction of France. She was even blamed for the huge national debt (largely incurred because of the American war) and economic mismanagement by the Controller-General of Finances, Alexandre de Calonne, a man she detested. Nevertheless he was backed by the Polignacs, which was enough for the public to hold Marie-Antoinette responsible for all his actions.

One comfort for the Queen that autumn was a resolution of the dispute between Austria and Holland, and the consequent averting of war between France and Austria. The Treaty of Fontainebleau (1785) marked the end of an inglorious episode for her brother Joseph. Still denied access to the Scheldt, his plan to exchange the Austrian Netherlands for Bavaria was also rejected. The Dutch were allowed to buy Maastricht and some villages from Austria, but had to pay war reparations. The total sum was 10 million florins, of which France paid 4 million to facilitate a settlement.

On 17 October 1785 Marie-Antoinette expressed her relief to Joseph: 'I hope now no one will be able to spread any more clouds over the alliance. I have no need of exhortation to watch over it; it is more precious to me than to anyone. If they had succeeded in breaking it, I should never have known either happiness or tranquillity again.'[16] She would have been far from tranquil had she known that eight years later she was to be found guilty of sending millions of *livres* to Austria under the terms of this treaty, which was in fact negotiated by that arch anti-Austrian, Vergennes.

After all these troubles, Marie-Antoinette must have keenly welcomed Axel's return to Paris on 30 September 1785. Between 26 September 1785 and 2 June 1786 he wrote no letters to 'Josephine', which meant they must have met frequently. Axel rented a third-floor apartment and stabling for his horses in a Paris house belonging to a Madame La Farre, probably in the Faubourg Saint-Germain, but would have been able to make use of a *pied-à-terre* in Marie-Antoinette's own apartments for their lovers' trysts. His younger brother Fabian was also in Paris at this time, but made few mentions of Axel in his letters home. Still under the care of Axel's former tutor, Bolémany, Fabian probably knew nothing of his brother's royal love-affair or his secret visits to Versailles.

Marie-Antoinette doubtless hoped to relax in her lover's company that winter, but soon had to confront fresh domestic trouble. Her daughter's bad behaviour caused grave concern, while Mme de Polignac wanted to resign her position as royal governess. Her friendship for Marie-Antoinette had been severely strained by political disagreements, and she was not in the best of health. In November 1785 she wrote to Louis XVI requesting permission to retire, but the King asked her to stay and continue to keep an open salon for royal visitors. Bombelles was quite convinced that 'today it is certain that between the King and Queen it is the former who most openly likes Mme de Polignac'.[17]

Mme de Polignac had already contracted tuberculosis, which was to kill her – a disease from which the Dauphin also suffered, though none of his doctors could diagnose it. He had a feverish attack in October 1785 and was sent to La Muette for his health while the Court moved to Fontainebleau, but his recovery was short-lived. On 9 December 1785, three weeks after his mother was reunited with him at Versailles, Bombelles wrote in his diary: 'Monseigneur le Dauphin, who was running about quite gaily at two this afternoon, was all of a sudden attacked by a bout of fever.'[18] He was immediately put to bed; his parents rushed to see him, wondering and worrying yet again how serious their son's illness was. Their only consolation, according to Bombelles, was the fact that seven-year-old Madame showed some tender feelings for the very first time, bursting into tears as soon as she heard her brother was ill.

Preoccupied with her private life, Marie-Antoinette failed to take note of developments which had fatal repercussions for her. In November 1785 her erstwhile gambling and racing companion Philippe, Duc de Chartres, became Duc d'Orléans on the death of his father and inherited an enormous fortune. He immediately demanded the right to continue to style himself First Prince of the Blood (which carried financial and political privileges), despite the fact that Louis XVI's two sons, two brothers and two nephews all took precedence over him. The King, anxious to avoid confrontation with the House of Orléans (always known for its rebellious tendencies), foolishly granted the duke's request. In doing so he gave Orléans a platform for his dynastic ambitions even before the Revolution.

Orléans already regarded himself as the King in Paris, and he was to be led into revolutionary crimes and regicide in his pursuit of the French crown. By 1785 his enmity towards Marie-Antoinette was no secret; she was *l'Autrichienne* – the Austrian traitor in the royal family. In spreading libellous rumours about her through pamphlet shops in his Palais Royal, Orléans was indirectly attacking the husband who protected her. It proved to be a diabolically successful strategy. In 1785 Orléans also forged a close friendship with the Duc de Lauzun, who had his own reasons for hating Marie-Antoinette. Her refusal to further his political career must have been made more galling by the knowledge that Axel Ferson was playing the role Lauzun had destined for himself – that of the Queen's lover. Lauzun too became a dangerous enemy of Marie-Antoinette during the Revolution.

Nothing could have been further from the Queen's mind than revolution during the winter of 1785/6. She was more perturbed by the fact she was pregnant for the third time in three years. On 13 November 1785, when the Court was still at Fontainebleau, Bombelles wrote: 'Another item of news, which is still being kept a profound secret, is the Queen's pregnancy. It is said Her Majesty is as vexed by her fertility this time as she was pleased when it was a question of giving birth to the Dauphin, and even to his brother.'[19] Was she vexed because she really did not want another child, or worried it might not resemble Louis XVI? News of a pregnancy at this time puts conception somewhere in the first two weeks of October, and Axel had returned to Paris at the end of September, doubtless feeling very passionate after two months' separation from Marie-Antoinette.

The pregnancy remained a secret for another three months, because the Queen's doctors could not confirm it. She complained to Joseph on 27 December 1785 of various 'worries and indispositions', and misinterpreting this as indicating further political uncertainties, he demanded an explanation from Mercy. The ambassador assured him on 31 January 1786 that: 'These relate only to her physical condition, and although her health is fundamentally good, her menstrual periods have not appeared for four and a half months. After several weeks a pregnancy was presumed, but certain discomforts which contradict it have suspended her doctors' opinion.'[20]

The pregnancy was eventually declared on 17 February 1786, when Marie-Antoinette's doctors correctly predicted a birth in July. Joseph was dissatisfied with the letter his sister sent him confirming the news, and wrote to Mercy on 1 April:

In informing me of her pregnancy, she displayed her annoyance at it, saying she believes she has enough children, which has made me protest a great deal about this remark in the enclosed letter which you will take care to give her. I'm trying to get her to foresee the unfortunate consequences of such a conduct, in not having more children, in case she ever wanted to separate from the King, either for her comfort or convenience. . . . This idea causes me all the more concern because it is now the fashion among young women who believe themselves *à la mode* to separate from their husbands and think they have fulfilled their duty by becoming the mother of one or two children.[21]

Joseph's mention of a possible separation between Louis XVI and Marie-Antoinette was prompted in part by his great uncertainty about the future of the Franco-Austrian alliance. He obviously thought the Queen's two sons insufficient to ensure that a half-Austrian prince ascended the French throne. Another serious bout of the Dauphin's illness in April 1786 seemed to confirm his fears. This time the boy's fever was attributed by his doctor, Brunier, to the infected air rising from the stagnant fountains near his apartment, but although he recommended a change of residence, Louis XVI refused to let his son leave Versailles.

Mercy reassured Joseph by telling him Marie-Antoinette had no intention of separating from her husband: 'She knows how to value the advantages of an intimate union with the King and the disastrous consequences of a contrary system'.[22] The 'disastrous consequences' were, of course, purely political. That Joseph even considered a separation possible meant he knew his sister's marriage was profoundly unhappy. Though not formally separated, she and Louis XVI already lived separate lives, and 'an intimate union' was surely only a pretence by this time. Marie-Antoinette's love-life was centred entirely on Axel Fersen, a surrogate husband who gave her unquestioning devotion and passion. She could talk to him freely in a way she could not to the taciturn Louis XVI. Their correspondence shows a very deep understanding, an easy, open communication of ideas, almost an intuitive grasp of each other's thoughts and feelings. If not a marriage in law, it was certainly one of true minds.

Axel was a man Marie-Antoinette nevertheless had to live without for long periods. Their 1785/6 idyll was brought to an end when he had to return to Sweden to take up his duties as Captain of the King's Bodyguard. He left Paris on 20 June 1786, and sent a letter to her from London on 26 June, before sailing for Helsingborg, where he arrived on 26 July. Soon afterwards Marie-Antoinette must have informed him of the birth of her fourth and last child.

On 9 July 1786 Louis XVI was about to go hunting when he learnt that the Queen's labour was imminent. She tried to ignore her pains for as long as possible to deter a crowd from rushing to her apartments, finally went into labour at 4.30 p.m. and was delivered of a girl at 7.30 p.m. 'The newborn princess is extraordinarily large and strong,' Mercy informed Joseph. 'One can easily imagine the pain it cost the Queen to give birth to such a superb creature,' wrote the Marquis de Bombelles. Louis XVI was as unenthusiastic about this birth as he had been about the Duc de Normandie's. '*9 July 1786.* The Queen delivered of my second daughter at half-past seven,' he wrote in his diary; 'the baptism followed immediately. Archduke Ferdinand and Elisabeth godparents; there were neither congratulations, fireworks, nor *Te Deum*.' Again, on Louis's orders, no festivities were held for the birth of this princess.[23] She was baptized Sophie-Hélène-Béatrice, and was known as Madame Sophie. Axel must have been delighted she was named after his favourite sister, although ostensibly Marie-Antoinette chose the name in remembrance of one of her husband's aunts.

The birth indeed weakened the Queen, and may have had serious implications for her health. Although still only thirty-one she never conceived another child, and six years later suffered dangerous and debilitating haemorrhages. She spent the summer of 1786 quietly at the Petit Trianon, exhausted after childbirth and long visits by two members of her family. Marie-Antoinette's older brother Archduke Ferdinand visited Paris with his wife from 11 May to 17 June 1786, causing considerable consternation at Court when it was learnt that they shared a bed every night. On 28 July, the Governor of the Austrian Netherlands, Archduchess Marie-Christine, arrived for a stay of several weeks, accompanied by her husband Albert, Duke of Teschen.

Marie-Antoinette had put off this visit for as many years as possible, since she rather mistrusted her oldest sister 'Marie'; during the Revolution her suspicions proved well founded. Nevertheless, the Marquis de Bombelles commented: 'The Archduchess has much more success here than people imagined she would. She makes an effort to please and one cannot deny that she has a great deal of wit.'[24]

This reinforcement of the Queen's Austrian connections could not have come at a worse time. On 31 May 1786 Cardinal Rohan had been acquitted by just three votes on all charges in the Necklace Affair, the blame being apportioned instead between Jeanne de La Motte and her accomplices. Marie-Antoinette was outraged. Mme Campan found her crying in her apartments, railing against the injustice of the French legal system. Mercy told the Austrian Chancellor Kaunitz:

> The judgement against Cardinal Rohan has undergone a notable change. The Queen was affected by it, because people tried to make her believe her dignity was not sufficiently avenged. She has finally calmed down on this point; but it's very true that without the help of intrigue and a great deal of money, the Cardinal would have been convicted as the whole public is persuaded he deserved.[25]

Mercy could not afford to be so cavalier. He did not appreciate the damage inflicted on the Queen's reputation by this acquittal. If a cardinal could use her name with impunity in a daring fraud, her vulnerability to all kinds of slander and libel increased enormously. She was right to be angry. Jeanne de La Motte escaped from prison in 1787 (undoubtedly assisted by highly placed contacts), travelled to London, and from there launched a stream of abuse against the Queen. Although she confessed at her trial that she had never at any time spoken to the Queen, La Motte published memoirs which cast Marie-Antoinette as a bisexual nymphomaniac, who had seduced both her and the cardinal before devising the theft of the necklace to amuse herself and get rid of them. The repercussions of the Necklace Affair certainly had a dramatic and detrimental effect on Marie-Antoinette's tarnished public image. Her portrait by Elisabeth Vigée-Lebrun in the 1786 Salon exhibition – in which she was depicted wearing a straw hat and a plain, sleeveless muslin dress – excited highly unfavourable comment. Henceforth not only was she an Austrian meddling in French affairs, almost solely responsible for the ballooning budget deficit, she was also 'the modern Messalina', guilty of heinous sexual crimes.

Political stability and economic prosperity in France might have saved Marie-Antoinette, but 1787 was not fated to improve her position. In February Louis XVI's trusted Foreign Minister, the Comte de Vergennes, died, and Mercy and Joseph immediately asked the Queen to persuade her husband to replace him by the pro-Austrian Comte de Saint-Priest. She disappointed them. 'The Queen was suddenly seized by the scruple that it was not right for the Court of Vienna to nominate ministers at that of Versailles,' an indignant Mercy told Kaunitz on 1 March. He was even more displeased by the offhand way she had informed him of Vergennes's demise: 'M de Vergennes is going to die tonight; it will infallibly be the tiny Montmorin who replaces him.'[26] The very short Comte de Montmorin, a boyhood companion of Louis XVI, duly became Foreign Minister.

The Austrians regrouped, and their second attempt to place a minister was spectacularly successful. When the discredited Finance Minister Alexandre de Calonne was sacked in April 1787, Marie-Antoinette was persuaded to support the Archbishop of Toulouse, Loménie de Brienne, as his successor. Brienne, a close friend of the Abbé de Vermond, was generally regarded as an excellent administrator, but his rival was the former Finance Minister Jacques Necker, the idol of Parisians. When Brienne tried to force through measures to cut the deficit, and was seen to be too closely entwined with '*l'Autrichienne*', he was subjected to attacks which only rebounded on the Queen.

Marie-Antoinette had no control at all over public finances. One of the main reasons they proved impossible to balance was the opposition to a new fiscal regime from the nobility and the legal profession. Exempt from taxes, they strenuously resisted all efforts to make them liable (which would have greatly eased the burden on the overtaxed poor). The forum for discussions on this vexed question was the Assembly of Notables convened by Calonne, which Brienne was eventually obliged to dissolve in May 1787, having achieved none of the reforms he wanted. The Parlement of Paris refused to register decrees to introduce the new taxes, demanding instead the convocation of the States General to devise ways of reducing the deficit. This was indirectly a demand for a permanent legislative assembly, and Bombelles for one had no doubt that the Duc d'Orléans was 'the motor of all this indecent and dangerous opposition'.[27]

Marie-Antoinette tried to set an example by cutting her household budget in 1787 by 3 million *livres* a year. She cancelled a planned trip to see Joseph in Brussels in May because, according to Mercy, 'she wants to avoid all extra expenditure and give in this regard the same good example she is setting by the considerable reductions in her household'.[28] Of course it did her no good at all. Cutbacks at Court only made the King and Queen powerful enemies among displaced courtiers, who had sponged off the royal purse for years. Even suppression of the Duc de Polignac's post as Director-General of the Mail failed to meet with public approval. By now Marie-Antoinette was thoroughly disenchanted with the Polignacs. Their devotion to Calonne, whom they visited in exile in England in the summer of 1787, weakened their position further. 'The illusion has almost totally ceased,' Mercy reported in November, 'there are only occasional momentary returns whose effects are of little consequence; besides, necessity has closed the door to pillage, and the Queen will no longer listen to any excessive demands.'[29]

She nevertheless remained on friendly terms with Mme de Polignac, and there was no question of dismissing her from her post as governess, which would have been too public a humiliation. Indeed, although the Queen had, in Mercy's opinion, long ceased to have either esteem or genuine liking for her friends, she still seemed afraid to risk a complete rupture. One can but assume she feared they might take revenge by exposing her liaison with Axel Fersen.

Marie-Antoinette no longer needed such a dangerous confidante as Mme de Polignac. When Axel returned to France in May 1787, he stayed secretly with the Queen at Versailles. She needed comforting, for she was extremely concerned about the health of her ten-month-old daughter Sophie. During his absence in Sweden, Axel had written more than twenty letters to 'Josephine', but made few notes of their contents. In January 1787 he mentioned Esterhazy, who had a commission in his regiment and was Marie-Antoinette's friend, and in February spoke of plans for his trip to France. In March he had more definite news to give her, noting 'that I expect to leave between the 15th and 20th', while his letters to her in April are extremely interesting. The précis:

April 7. . . . notables, the children, plan to lodge upstairs; that she replies to me at the regiment, that I'll be there on 15 May.

April 20. What she must find for me to lodge upstairs; that I'm leaving on the 29th or 30th, and expect to be at Maubeuge on the 13th and at Paris the 20th or 21st.
April 27. that I'm leaving on the 30th.[30]

Axel's mention of 'the children' is significant; he does not write '*her* children', which could be interpreted as meaning he himself had a very close interest in some of them. His plan 'to lodge upstairs', in an apartment Marie-Antoinette herself had to make habitable for him, can only indicate a covert stay at Versailles. The Queen certainly had access to a small apartment on the top floor of the palace above her private *cabinets*. Described by Mme Campan as consisting of 'a very small antechamber, a bedchamber and a closet . . . it was destined to lodge Her Majesty's lady-in-waiting, in the event of the Queen being ill or in childbirth'. Marie-Antoinette used this little known apartment for a meeting with the Baron de Besenval in 1775 to try to avert a duel between the Comte d'Artois and the Prince de Bourbon, reaching it unobserved by a staircase from her private *cabinets*.[31]

It would have been an ideal retreat for Axel, who reached his regiment at Maubeuge on 15 May 1787, and Paris on 23 May. After retaining his former lodgings at Mme La Farre's, he arrived at Versailles on 24 May, in time to see the closing ceremony of the Assembly of Notables. Axel gave Marie-Antoinette a letter from Gustav III, which she answered with a heavy heart on 21 June: 'I would have replied sooner to the letter Your Majesty sent me by the Comte de Fersen, if I had not been so grieved and occupied by the illness of my younger daughter, whom I have just lost.'[32] The Queen told the Crown Princess of Hesse-Darmstadt she was 'very upset' over Sophie's death, which occurred at 3 p.m. on 19 June 1787, even though she had half expected it, since the baby had never developed properly after her birth.

Axel had had to go to Maubeuge on 13 June, a week before Sophie died, but returned to Paris on 12 July to represent Gustav III at the christening of the Baron de Staël's first child. He must have managed to pay a short visit to Versailles to console Marie-Antoinette, but they had little time together, since war loomed in both Holland and Germany, and the Royal-Suédois was stationed on the French frontier. Axel detested Maubeuge, but found himself garrisoned there the whole summer. The Queen waited very anxiously for his letters and their reunion, for Louis XVI was less able than ever to fill Axel's place. The King, faced by mounting political tensions and deprived of Vergennes's guiding hand, sank into an alarming state of apathetic gluttony. On 14 August 1787 Mercy (who had already predicted a revolution) told Joseph:

> The spirit of licence and independence has reached such a point that it will be very difficult to remedy, particularly under a reign which has already lost all impetus and consideration. The King's moral temperament offers few resources against so great an evil, and his physical habits diminish them even more; his body gets fatter, and when he returns from hunting he eats such excessive meals they cause absences of his reason and a kind of rough carelessness which is very distressing for those who have to endure it.[33]

Louis XVI's nickname 'the fat pig' dates from this period. Marie-Antoinette no longer seemed to care: inured to her husband's brusque manners, she was well aware of the futility of trying to change his ways. The man she truly loved sent a letter to her from Maubeuge on 8 October 1787 telling her: 'that I will leave on the 18th to reach Paris on the 19th, and be with her that evening: that she sends a letter to me at my apartment at three or four o'clock, telling me what I should do'.[34] As he also asked her 'to get some logs ready for the stove' it would seem he was planning another clandestine stay on the top floor at Versailles, and wanted heating for the cold autumn evenings.

As the political situation lurched from bad to worse, the Queen probably felt she had nothing to lose in enjoying Axel's company as much as possible. Even if her love-affair were discovered, it could hardly make her more unpopular than she already was. In a letter to Gustav III on 27 December 1787, Axel gave a fairly accurate picture of the state of affairs in the royal household: 'Mme de Polignac continues to maintain her position: she is still as well [placed] as she was, but since M. de Calonne's departure the individuals in her circle are nothing and have no influence at all. The Queen is almost universally detested.'[35]

Detested by many, but adored by Axel Fersen. Of course, as far as Gustav was concerned, Axel only ever saw the Queen on formal occasions. In reality they had frequent rendezvous that autumn and winter, and Marie-Antoinette made few efforts to cover her tracks. According to the Comte de Saint-Priest, the Queen used to dine with the Comtesse d'Ossun while 'Fersen proceeded on horseback to the park, beside the Trianon, two or three times a week: the Queen, alone, did the same, and these rendezvous caused a public scandal, despite the modesty and reserve of the favourite, who never revealed anything by his outward appearance.'[36]

Love was nevertheless doomed to suffer yet again. Gustav III recalled Axel to Sweden early in 1788, to join him on a disastrous campaign against the Russians, who were trying to seize control of Finland. Axel was all the more distraught as his father was pressing him to spend two whole years at home. On 30 January 1788 he told his old tutor: 'I cannot resolve to spend two years in Sweden as my father proposes.'[37] Two years without Marie-Antoinette was simply more than he could bear. She would find his absence equally intolerable. Lonely and misunderstood, Marie-Antoinette had only the love of the 'Chou d'Amour' to sustain her after Axel kissed her goodbye.

8

'Elle'

If Marie-Antoinette expected her life to improve in 1788 she was sorely disappointed. France was sliding inexorably towards revolution, and the Queen was a prime target for the covert forces conspiring to bring down the *ancien régime*. Her mind, however, was on the six-year-old Dauphin, whose health was now extremely precarious, as she told Joseph on 22 February 1788.

> My eldest son is causing me a great deal of concern, my dear brother. Although he has always been weak and delicate, I wasn't expecting the crisis he is now suffering. His figure has become deformed; one hip is higher than the other, and the vertebrae in his back are slightly out of place and stick out. For some time he has had a fever every day, and has grown very thin and weak. It's certainly the forcing through of his teeth which is the principal cause of his sufferings.[1]

The Queen was clearly utterly ignorant of medicine, but then the Dauphin's many doctors in fact ascribed his condition to teething problems. A baffling and inept diagnosis indeed. The poor child was sent to the château at Meudon, some miles from Versailles, in the hope that the fresher air would restore his health, but it was already too late. Mercy had no illusions about his chances, and told Joseph the royal physicians were deluding the Queen both as to the true nature of her son's disease and his prospects for recovery.

Marie-Antoinette could derive some comfort from the strength and high spirits of her younger son, whom she described as 'a true country boy, big, fresh and fat'. The Marquis de Bombelles considered the bouncy young Duc de Normandie 'one of the most handsome children one could ever see', and he certainly formed a striking contrast to his sickly elder brother.[2] Nine-year-old Madame seldom gave her mother any trouble as far as her health was concerned, although according to Mercy she had grown from a charming and lively toddler into a solemn and sad little girl – an image which stuck for the rest of her life.

Her children were not the Queen's sole preoccupation during 1788. Joseph's war with Russia against the Ottoman Empire greatly concerned her, while acute political tensions in France forced her once more into taking a public role she disliked. The Parlement of Paris continued in its refusal to implement the Prime Minister Brienne's tax reforms, for reasons of self-interest, as Bombelles noted on 21 June 1788: 'All the animosity comes from nobles and magistrates, who under the new regime would have to pay taxes by virtue of a more equitable distribution of duties, which they have always refused to pay to the royal treasury.'[3] Despite their far from laudable motives, they duped the poor into supporting them by demanding democratic reforms, and their vilification of Brienne inevitably included slander of his protector, the Queen. Brienne eventually conceded defeat on 7 July 1788, when he convened the States-General (consisting of deputies from the nobility, clergy and commons) for 1789, to debate the country's financial crisis. This move immediately opened the door to political agitators, who called for massive curbs on royal authority and a written constitution. There were riots in Brittany and the Dauphiné, and Brienne found his position even more untenable.

Marie-Antoinette could not turn to Axel Fersen for sympathy this time, so she confided instead in her loyal old friend, Valentin Esterhazy. On 17 July 1788, 'walking with him at Trianon', she told him:

> . . . how unfortunate she was in having chosen for Prime Minister a man who, spoken of as gifted with eminent merit, had made himself odious to the nation – how cruel it was for her to see herself detested when she only wanted the best for France, to see at the same time her eldest son in the most lamentable state and her brother humiliated in all his projects.[4]

She was truly distressed, as Mercy informed Joseph in a letter the following day: '. . . the Queen grows anxious, she frets; her position is all the more delicate because the public imagines she has a major influence on all the government's actions'.[5] It was, she told her brother, 'a very unfortunate year', her own *annus horribilis*, and she already looked forward to a better 1789.

Fresh political controversy soon confronted Marie-Antoinette. In August 1788 Brienne was offered up as a sacrifice to the opposition, since his authority to enforce new policies was virtually nil. Bowing to popular pressure, Louis XVI recalled the former Finance Minister Jacques Necker to office, entrusting negotiations for this cabinet reshuffle to his wife, because he and Necker did not get on well. Marie-Antoinette, who hoped the popular Swiss banker would perform an economic miracle and inspire public confidence in the government, had to persuade him to overcome his reluctance to deal with the King. Although she was successful, she had grave misgivings, writing to Mercy on 25 August: 'I tremble – forgive me this weakness – that it is I who am getting him to return. My fate is to bring misfortune; and if some infernal machinations make him yet fail, or he reduces the King's authority, I will be detested even more.'[6]

As happened with her so often in politics, she was uncannily prescient. Necker took up his post two days later. Parisians were 'drunk with joy', according to Bombelles, but the Swiss tycoon proved to be as unable to restore French finances as his predecessor. The next minister to fall victim to hostile public opinion was the Keeper of the Seals, Lamoignon, who had resisted the Parlement of Paris's demands to appoint ministers, approve all laws and take control of the army. He was dismissed on 14 September, and these contentious issues were deferred for discussion by the States-General. Marie-Antoinette had been instrumental in persuading Lamoignon to resign, but the appointment of more popular ministers did nothing to increase her own popularity. 'It is inconceivable, and one cannot express the extent of the public's hatred for this august princess,' Mercy told Joseph on 14 September, blaming it on her former protection of Brienne.[7] She was certainly not given any credit for trying to address public concern by reshaping the government.

The year 1788 was not a happy one for Axel Fersen, either. He spent most of it miserably in Finland as Gustav III waged his campaign against Russia. Axel's ancestor Jacob De La Gardie had won Finland for Sweden: Gustav seemed about to lose it. His depression was eased by the companionship of old friends, among them Count Stedingk, his second in command in the Royal-Suédois, who fought a valiant campaign which eventually restored Swedish pride, and Baron Evert Taube, a court chamberlain and lover of Axel's darling sister Sophie. As Captain of Gustav's Bodyguard, Axel accompanied the King when he left Finland in August 1788, and was overjoyed at the prospect of being reunited with Marie-Antoinette. 'I only have time to tell you that everything which is happening pleases me very much,' he wrote to Sophie, 'because all this will be over and you will be relieved. *She* will be too, and I shall see you both again. Ah, God, why can't I see you both together, nothing would make me happier. . . .'[8]

Henceforth in letters to Sophie and in his diary, Axel always referred to Marie-Antoinette as *Elle – She*. She was only 'the Queen' when he had official dealings with her. His private letters to her were still recorded under the name 'Josephine', and he wrote her twenty-two during his absence that year in Sweden, each one in invisible ink.

One wonders if she received them all. Letters were often opened by the French secret police and any interesting correspondence was copied and sent to the King. Bombelles records an extraordinary scene involving Louis XVI and some mysterious letters on 27 September 1788. The King was out hunting when he received a 'packet of letters' from a messenger. 'He went into a copse to read them and soon he was seen sitting on the ground, his face held in his hands and his hands resting on his knees.' An equerry approached and was dumbstruck to see the King crying. Louis told him to go away and sobbed to himself for some time. He then declared he felt ill, and needed help to remount his horse. Nevertheless, by the time he arrived back at Versailles, the King was totally composed, and his retinue had no idea what had so upset him.[9]

The unfortunate destruction of so many royal letters during the Revolution makes the enigma of this upsetting packet of letters impossible to solve, but one can hazard an educated guess as to their contents. It might be stretching credulity too far to suggest that Louis XVI had suffered a romantic disaster of his own, but he may have read intercepted letters from Axel to Marie-Antoinette. He must surely have suspected their liaison, and perhaps received final wounding proof of his wife's love for Axel. As he was so intensely secretive, he kept his grief to himself, but it might explain his double-dealing acceptance of Axel's assistance during the Revolution.

A more sensational possibility was that the King had purchased letters relating to the Queen, claimed to be in the possession of the Diamond Necklace thief Jeanne de La Motte's husband, who was in London. Louis later secretly bought and destroyed Jeanne de La Motte's infamous memoirs, so this is not a far-fetched idea. In 1787, Marie-Antoinette's closest confidants, Mme de Polignac, Mme de Lamballe and the Abbé de Vermond, had all visited London separately, which was highly unusual. Had they attempted to buy the letters from La Motte on the Queen's behalf? If so, how had he got hold of them?

One intermediary in Axel's correspondence with 'Josephine' was a 'Mr. de Valois': Jeanne de La Motte's brother was a respectable naval officer, the Baron de Valois. She may have learnt of Marie-Antoinette's Swedish lover from her brother, and stolen or copied compromising love-letters to blackmail the Queen. One feels sure the mystery letters which made Louis XVI cry were of deep personal concern. A genuine cause of distress for the King at this time was the Dauphin's painful, slow decline. He and the Queen visited their son regularly at Meudon, and now had little hope of his recovery. Louis XVI's despair at losing his son would have been doubly acute had he received conclusive evidence that the Duc de Normandie was fathered by Axel Fersen.

Marie-Antoinette almost certainly heard in August of Axel's forthcoming return to France, since despite all her worries, Bombelles noticed she was 'in very good humour' in September 1788. Gustav III was now fighting on two fronts, for the Danes were marching on Gothenburg. Gustav saw this merely as an opportunity to salvage his lost prestige. Leaving Stedingk in command of the army in Finland, he set off to confront his old Danish rivals with the words 'Now I've been saved!' His theatricality never deserted him.

Europe generally was in a state of high tension, with wars in both the Netherlands and the Balkans drawing in the major powers. Axel had doubtless been granted leave by Gustav solely because he had to take command of his regiment. He left Sweden on 21 October 1788, reaching Paris on 6 November. 'My dear Sophie,' he wrote immediately to his sister, 'I only arrived here at two o'clock this morning. I'm delighted to be here and that my journey is over.'[10] His first task was to get the Royal-Suédois moved from Rennes, where it had been posted after the troubles in Brittany. Rennes was simply too far away

The young Queen Marie-Antoinette, c. 1778 (*pastel drawing by Elisabeth Vigée-Lebrun*)

Count Axel Fersen, aged 27
(*from a miniature by Hall*)

Part of an autograph letter from Marie-Antoinette to Axel Fersen, January 1792. (*Translation*: 'I'm only writing you a note ... [deletion] ... The person who brings you this will speak and inform you of our position such as it is. I have complete confidence in him, and he deserves it for his loyalty and sense. It is essential that the Emp[eror] is truly convinced that there isn't a word in it of ours or of our way of thinking, but that he still writes me an answer, as if he believed that was my way of thinking, and which I may show, because they are so distrustful here they will demand the reply ...')

Marie-Antoinette aged about 28 or 29; the fashionable hat suggests a date of *c.* 1783 (*portrait by Elisabeth Vigée-Lebrun*)

Louis XVI (*portrait by Duplessis, detail*)

(*above*) Louis-Charles, younger son of Marie-Antoinette, *c.* 1791. Born in 1785, he became Dauphin in 1789, and is presumed to have died in prison in 1795 (*portrait by Kucharsky, detail*)
(*below*) The Petit Trianon at Versailles, view from the garden

from the Queen. Axel's regiment was redeployed to Valenciennes on the northern border, from where he could make frequent trips to his beloved. He was in Paris during November and December, when the capital was frozen and full of starving beggars from the provinces which had been cruelly hit by storms that had ravaged crops in the summer. Fashionable Parisians, however, still enjoyed good meals, danced until dawn, and spent hours discussing politics. 'The fermentation of minds is general,' Axel told his father on 10 December 1788, 'nobody speaks of anything but the constitution . . . it's a delirium. . . . We have a very hard winter here. It's been freezing for three weeks . . . there are four inches of snow everywhere on the streets of Paris, and the roofs are covered in it. The river is frozen solid.'[11]

On 12 December the Marquis de Bombelles met Axel at Versailles, leaving the closing ceremony of the second, equally inconclusive Assembly of Notables. 'He spoke to me again about his desire for me to take over as Ambassador to Sweden and of the satisfaction we would give his master [Gustav] in getting rid of M. le Marquis de Pons.' Gustav had clearly given Axel a diplomatic mission relating to the Franco-Swedish alliance, and Marie-Antoinette was required to help. On 8 January 1789 Bombelles heard 'that the Queen had asked M. de Montmorin to give me the Swedish embassy . . . and that the worthy little man . . . told Her Majesty I was still too young, and also too new an ambassador to be entrusted with such an important post as Stockholm'.[12] Marie-Antoinette was shocked by the Foreign Minister Montmorin's refusal, since he was himself younger and far less experienced than Bombelles, who had held several ambassadorial posts with distinction. Her failure in this minor matter is ample proof of her lack of any influence in the government, which muddled along in woeful incompetence under a weak and ineffectual Louis XVI, while the country clamoured for radical reforms.

Hatred of the Queen was nevertheless stronger than ever during 1789, but she had Axel's loving presence to comfort her. He divided his time between his regiment at Valenciennes and Paris, and items in his expense book show he paid frequent visits to Marie-Antoinette. In January 1789 he noted a tip of 24 *livres* to a footman in the Oeuil de Boeuf, 12 *livres* 'to the maid at Versailles', and money for various dinners 'on the road to Versailles'.[13] He also paid for 'heating at Versailles', which may indicate further clandestine stays at the palace.

Political turmoil did not prevent the usual Carnival celebrations in the capital, although entertainments at Court were more muted. There were balls for the royal children, while on 16 February 1789 the Queen spent the evening in Mme de Polignac's salon, singing operatic arias with her friend's daughter, Mme de Guiche. Bombelles, who played the piano, was rather surprised by what happened next. 'From music we proceeded to dance, and the Queen, to the sound of the piano, waltzed with the Chevalier de Roll.'[14] Roll, a German, had probably brought the dance from Vienna. It was extremely daring for anyone to dance the newfangled waltz in 1789, let alone the Queen of France. Had there been no Revolution, the golden age of the waltz might well have begun two or three decades sooner. A Viennese waltz for a Viennese princess . . . she probably yearned for the warmth and security of her childhood home during that bleak winter of 1789, but only sorrow and danger awaited her.

By late February, the Dauphin's condition was deteriorating rapidly. 'There are no longer any means of saving the young prince,' Mercy told Joseph. 'As far as possible the circumstances are concealed from the Queen, but she sees enough not to flatter herself with hope, and she is very affected by it.'[15] To add to her grief, the royal family itself was rent by schisms. Louis XVI was apathetic, his brothers had political disagreements and vied with each other to win the Queen's backing, while Monsieur's unhappy wife had taken refuge in alcoholism. Worse still,the one man who really had the power to help Marie-Antoinette was being slowly killed by tuberculosis like his nephew. Her adored brother Joseph had been ill since mid-1788, and his constant exertions during the war against Turkey had greatly weakened him.

Despite these mounting tribulations, Marie-Antoinette found time to console Axel when political events in Sweden took an ugly turn. Weary of Gustav's expensive military disasters, the leaders of the Senate, in particular Senator Fersen, refused to vote through his decrees and tried to reclaim the power they had lost in 1772. On 20 February 1789 the King had several rebellious noblemen arrested and imprisoned without charge. The illusion of enlightened despotism was shattered; Sweden was plunged anew into political and financial crisis. The King turned to the more biddable clergy and peasantry to vote through the new taxes he wanted. Ultimately his alienation of the nobility was to prove calamitous for Gustav. The situation was more immediately catastrophic for Senator Fersen, who, arrested in the *Riksdag* itself, spent two months in prison before his decision to retire from politics secured his freedom.

'Axel,' his sister Hedda wrote to their younger brother Fabian on 13 April 1789, 'was at Valenciennes when he was sent letters by a courier from Paris, with an order to return to Paris, apparently either to distract or console him.'[16] Axel paid regularly for couriers from the Queen in 1789 and who else but Marie-Antoinette could have consoled him? She evidently took Senator Fersen's part, for Axel kept a copy in her handwriting of a letter his father wrote in prison denouncing arbitrary power and regal injustice. Marie-Antoinette, the supposedly arrogant, ruthless despot of anti-monarchic propaganda, ought to have applauded Gustav. Instead she sympathized with Senator Fersen, and was probably very relieved Axel was safe with her instead of in a Swedish gaol. Gustav was not, however, rash enough to make enemies of all the Fersens. After Senator Fersen's release he asked the rest of the family to retain their Court posts; they were far too important to be disgraced, and besides, at heart the King was rather fond of them all.

Events in Sweden gave Axel little incentive to return home, particularly as he felt himself more urgently needed in France. It was soon his turn to console and support Marie-Antoinette. He returned to Paris from his regiment on 14 March 1789, and witnessed all the early stages of the seismic change which would destroy both the France he knew and the woman he loved.

The States-General opened with a grand ceremony at Versailles on 4 May, with deputies from the Third Estate (or commons) outnumbering the nobility and clergy and determined to press their claims to represent the whole nation. They cheered Louis XVI, but the Queen was insulted as she walked in procession with her husband. Her enemy, the throne-seeking Duc d'Orléans, walked with the Third Estate and received a rapturous welcome, as did the Marquis de Lafayette, hero of the American war, idol of the Parisians, and a closet republican. An independent American spectator, Gouverneur Morris, wrote: 'I cannot help feeling the Mortification which the poor Queen meets with for I see only the Woman and it seems unmanly to break a Woman with Unkindness.'[17]

Marie-Antoinette's life itself would soon be at risk. As the deliberations of the States-General got under way, propaganda against her poured out of Orléans's headquarters in the Palais Royal. Mercy described her position on 10 May as 'overwhelming': 'All eyes are turned towards her because of the supposed inactivity of her august spouse; there follows a responsibility all the more unjust because everything the Queen thinks or suggests for the best is seldom acted upon and is always incompletely executed.'[18] Her fate, like Cassandra's, was to have her predictions continually disbelieved and her advice ignored. Both she and the King were preoccupied by the Dauphin, who was nearing his end. On 31 May 1789, Bombelles wrote:

Mgr le Dauphin is still fighting against death, but the swelling is such that it disfigures him and water is seeping into his lungs. . . . Nevertheless he has suffered less in the last few days, and he has never been so amiable, especially to the Queen. Yesterday he wanted her to dine next to him; he took care to see she was served dishes he knew she most liked. He paid the same attention to Mme de Polignac.[19]

Four days later he was dead. His parents were deeply distressed, but even so a deputation from the States-General tried to force its way into the King's apartments with a petition. Axel was preparing to spend the summer with his regiment at Valenciennes, but drove post-haste to Versailles on 6 June to comfort Marie-Antoinette. Royal deaths were formal occasions like royal births in *ancien régime* France. On 7 June the Queen had to endure a mourning visit from the cream of the aristocracy. 'Nothing was more dismal or more moving than seeing Her Majesty, leaning against the balustrade in her chamber, accompanied by all her household in black, trying to stop herself choking as she saw her whole Court walk past her in single file, curtsying to her.'[20]

Protocol dictated that neither King nor Queen attended their son's burial. His funeral cortège, watched by a large crowd, left Meudon for Saint-Denis at 8 p.m. on 13 June, led by the Prince de Condé. The Dauphin's heart had been buried in the Paris church of Val-de-Grâce the previous day. As First Prince of the Blood the Duc d'Orléans was supposed to witness the ceremony, but he refused, and was represented by his son, the future King Louis-Philippe. Marie-Antoinette was so upset she could no longer bear to look at the 1787 portrait by

Vigée-Lebrun of her with her children and ordered it to be put into storage.

Axel paid another visit to the grieving Queen on 11 June, and on the 13th left for a long, worrying stay at Valenciennes. A revolution occurred during his absence. On 17 June the Third Estate declared itself a permanent representative body in the famous Tennis Court Oath; on the 23rd and 27th Louis XVI ordered the nobility and clergy to join them, and a National Assembly was formed. This was an enormous leap forward politically, but it divided the country as never before. The Comte d'Artois led diehard aristocrats who wanted the Prime Minister Necker arrested for what they regarded as a violation of their rights (Marie-Antoinette opposed this idea), while Orléanists and republicans in Paris scented the King's weakness and planned acts of terror to undermine his authority.

At this time Marie-Antoinette received a call from Austria and Russia to commit France to their alliance against the Turks. She flatly refused to consider the idea, giving her reasons to Mercy in a letter of 27 May:

> Given the current state of our affairs, we would be unable to supply help, either in men or money; and in that case we would not be acting in good faith by making any new defensive alliance. Besides, I find that even in the interests of the peace which the Emperor [Joseph] desires, this notice of alliance would render us incapable of acting as mediators for the Turks. . . . And as for me . . . you know the prejudices against my brother; you know how half the people have been persuaded I sent millions to Germany. This treaty would without fail be attributed to me, and the ministers would excuse themselves to the States-General by the appearance of my influence. Think of the odious role I would be made to play.[21]

This letter, with its unmistakable echoes of Maria-Theresa, in itself refutes the accusations flying about in 1789 that the Queen made all important decisions and intended to put down the Revolution with Austrian troops, but she remained the personification of evil despotism for most French people. The Duc d'Orléans certainly masterminded the virulent attacks on Marie-Antoinette and the constant uproar in Paris. Arthur Young, an Englishman visiting the French capital, described Orléans's Palais Royal as a meeting-place for malcontents when he went there on 27 June 1789. Celebrations over the formation of the National Assembly were then in full swing. 'At night the fire-works, and illuminations, and mob, and noise, at the Palais Royal increased; the expense must be enormous. . . . There is no doubt of its being the Duc d'Orléans's money: the people are thus kept in a continual ferment.[22]

This 'continual ferment' had a sinister purpose. Orléans, the richest man in France, had millions to spend in his pursuit of liberty for the people and a crown for himself. He had already staged a serious riot in Paris in April 1789, and the government could no longer rely on troops stationed in the capital, who could easily be bought with Orléans's gold.

The next *coup de théâtre* offered by Paris was the fall of the Bastille on 14 July 1789, an event which sent shock waves through the whole of Europe and finally convinced Louis XVI he was facing a revolu-tion. The excuse for the attack on the Bastille was Necker's dis-missal on 11 July. It was, however, a well-organized attempt to destroy any remnant of royal authority in Paris. The King reacted with charac-teristic and fatal indecision. A council was held at Court on 16 July, to decide whether Louis XVI should leave Versailles with loyal troops and regain control of the country from a royalist stronghold, or go to Paris as the self-appointed municipality demanded and acknowl-edge defeat. According to Mme Campan: 'The Queen wanted to leave. On the evening of the 16th she made me take all her diamond jewels from their cases and put them in a small box which she was going to carry in her own coach. She burnt a large quantity of papers with me, for, from that moment, Versailles was menaced by an invasion of armed people from Paris.'[23]

Doubtless many of Axel's letters were consumed by the flames. But Marie-Antoinette's preparations were in vain. Louis XVI was persuaded by his ministers, generals and his brother Monsieur to recall Necker, and on 17 July he went to Paris with the National Assembly to eat humble pie at the Hôtel de Ville. Lafayette later boasted that he could have imprisoned the King, so great was his power over the newly formed Garde Nationale. The Queen spent the whole day dreading that her husband would be killed.

The brutal murders of De Launay, Governor of the Bastille, and De Flesselles, Provost of Paris, were enough to persuade the Comte d'Artois, the Princes de Conti, de Condé and several ministers to emigrate. With them left the Polignacs, at midnight on 16 July. Marie-Antoinette would have dearly liked to leave Versailles with her old friend, whom she was never to see again. 'Nothing was more moving than the farewells of the Queen and her friend,' wrote Mme Campan. 'Overwhelming unhappiness had made them completely forget their differences which were caused by political opinions alone.'[24] Marie-Antoinette also said a last goodbye to the Abbé de Vermond, fearing he might fall victim to a mob who regarded him as the power behind the throne, though his influence over the Queen was long dead. She sent him to Valenciennes before he travelled on to Vienna, so he probably took a letter from her to Axel.

From 14 July onwards, Marie-Antoinette was in constant fear of her life. She told Mme Campan she had no doubt at all that the Duc d'Orléans had ordered the murder of Joseph-François Foulon, a cabinet minister whose crime was to have advised the King to arrest Orléans and several deputies, and lead the Revolution himself by addressing his subjects' demands. The Queen rightly suspected she too was a target for Orléans's hired assassins. Propaganda against her reached fever pitch after the emigration of the Bourbon princes and the Polignacs, as Mercy informed Emperor Joseph on 23 July 1789:

> One cannot divine the causes of the frenzy against the Queen which on this occasion took possession of people's minds. The gift she is imputed to have made to Your Majesty of several hundred millions, the demand for an Imperial army to oppose the nation and other similar absurdities, have made a profound impression, not only on ordinary people, but on a class of persons who should blush to believe them.[25]

Mercy told Kaunitz he was convinced 'some secret cabal' was at work against Marie-Antoinette, and gave details he was afraid to tell Joseph: '. . . the fury against her has reached the point of horror of publicly putting a price on the Queen's head and that of M. le Comte d'Artois at the Palais Royal'.[26] A sample of the 'absurdities' circulating about Marie-Antoinette that July even reached Arthur Young, who was by then in Nancy. On 31 July he noted incredulously: 'the current report . . . is that the queen has been convicted of a plot to poison the King and Monsieur, and give the regency to the Count d'Artois; to set fire to Paris, and blow up the Palais Royal by a mine!'[27]

How did Marie-Antoinette bear these dangerous slanders? With 'great patience and courage', according to Mercy and many courtiers. Her immediate concern was to find a new governess for her children. Given public fury against her, the choice was not easy. The King and Queen eventually decided on the Marquise de Tourzel, a respectable widow with five children whose husband had been killed in a riding accident when out hunting with Louis XVI in 1786. The Queen wrote a detailed and very objective report on her four-year-old son for the new governess, instructing her 'not to lose sight of him for an instant'. She probably feared a kidnapping. The little Dauphin, the erstwhile Duc de Normandie, whom Mme de Tourzel came to love like her own child, though very lively and tempestuous in character, 'had a charming face and was astonishingly intelligent', and showed signs of possessing all the decisiveness and flair Louis XVI so sadly lacked.[28] He was a great consolation to his mother during the summer of 1789, as she told Mme de Polignac on 12 August: 'My children are my only resource; I have them with me as much as possible.'[29]

It was the summer of 'the Great Fear', when revolutionary agents spread rumours throughout France that Austrian troops had invaded the country; discipline in the army collapsed, châteaux were pillaged and burnt, and their owners either killed or forced to flee. A summer for Marie-Antoinette without letters from Axel. His last recorded letter to 'Josephine' was dated 11 July. It was probably she who ordered him to suspend their correspondence, for she told Mme de Polignac: 'I don't write, nor do I want anybody to write to me through the post. . . . I don't want it to be said that I receive letters, because then they will invent some.'[30] Her fears were justified. Several letters from and to members of the royal family had been opened and published, and even diplomats were not spared illegal visits by the all-powerful Parisian authorities. In August, Mercy's house was broken into by the municipality and many of his papers were seized. Undoubtedly Orléanist agents were looking for incriminating material against the Queen, but they were disappointed. No 'Austrian plot' was discovered, for the simple reason that none existed.

Axel watched with growing horror France's rapid descent into chaos, and told his father on 15 August:

> Paris is the home of all the troubles, and nearly everybody is in a
> hurry to leave the city. Only vagabonds and deserters take refuge

there. . . . They are being enrolled in the new militia which is being
raised under the command of M. de Lafayette. They are better paid
than in our regiments, and every means possible is employed to cor-
rupt them. . . . The King's authority is completely destroyed, as is
that of the *parlements* and magistrates; the States-General themselves
tremble before Paris, and this fear has much influence on their deliberations. There is no longer any law, order, justice, discipline or religion in the kingdom.

On 3 September, Axel told his father of riots and looting by drunken
soldiers near Valenciennes, although his own regiment was still reason-
ably well behaved. All this unrest was nevertheless far from spontaneous. 'There are secret agents who distribute money, they are known
almost everywhere,' Axel wrote; but although 'M. le duc d'Orléans
is strongly suspected of being the leader and motor of it all', no
action was taken against him.[31]

Axel's great anxiety for Marie-Antoinette during this violent period
was conveyed to Sophie, although he now had to be even more careful in expressing himself, lest his letters were intercepted. On 24
August he noted in his correspondence book that he had told Sophie
'to be prudent when speaking to me about the affairs of this country
and of *Her*'.[32] When his service at Valenciennes ended on 14 September, he returned to Paris, but only in order to pack and move to
an apartment he had rented in Versailles. He had made arrangements
for this move in July, unquestionably in order to watch over his beloved Queen. On 30 September 1789 he wrote to Baron Taube from
Versailles: 'I have been here for five days and I'm settling here for
the winter.'[33]

In the event, Axel's sojourn at Versailles lasted only ten days. Ten
days in which he and Marie-Antoinette enjoyed a brief, happy res-
pite from worry and danger; still very much in love, they looked
forward to a long winter together. The Duc d'Orléans, however,
wrecked their plans. On 5 October 1789 several thousand citizens
from the slums of Paris marched on Versailles with cannons, vowing
to avenge an alleged 'insult to the nation' which supposedly occurred
when royalist cockades were distributed at a regimental banquet held
at the palace and attended by the King and Queen.

Marie-Antoinette was at the Petit Trianon on 5 October when she
received a note from the Minister for the King's Household, the Comte

de Saint-Priest, begging her to return instantly to the palace. Louis XVI was recalled from a hunting trip at Meudon and shut himself up with his ministers to decide on a course of action. The plan favoured by Saint-Priest and several others was for the royal family to leave at once for Rambouillet, escorted by their loyal guards, while the Régiment de Flandres (whose banquet had so outraged Parisians) deployed its artillery from the heights of Meudon to cut off the approaching citizens' army. Louis XVI refused to fire on his own subjects, but had agreed to leave for Rambouillet when the Prime Minister Necker threw cold water on the idea. Saint-Priest had to take his pregnant wife to safety, and 'M. Necker profited from his absence to sow so many doubts in the King's mind about the consequences of this decision, and on the impossibility of finding money for the subsistence of his troops and household, that he made him change his mind.'[34]

There is no doubt Marie-Antoinette wanted to leave; the Parisians had come for her head, and she knew it. She may have persuaded the King to rethink his decision to stay, for according to Mme Campan the royal carriages were eventually ordered for departure. By then it was too late. The vanguard of the Parisian mob was already at the palace gates, and their supporters from the town of Versailles seized the carriages in the courtyard.

Where was Axel during all these fruitless delays and discussions? Probably with the Queen, since he later told his father: 'I was a witness to everything.' He never ceased to regret the King's fatal weakness and the utterly stupid decision to stay and let the mob into the palace precincts. On 5 October 1798 he wrote in his diary: 'I vividly recall this day, nine years ago, and all our anguish at Versailles. If only we had gone everything would have been saved.'[35]

Louis XVI thought he had saved the situation by meeting a deputation of Parisian *poissardes* (the lowest form of female life in the capital, who later constituted the audience of raucous knitters at revolutionary trials and executions), and promising to see they were supplied with food. The tardy arrival of Lafayette with the Garde Nationale and the King's acceptance of the Declaration of the Rights of Man appeared to have defused a very ugly situation. Most of the *poissardes* dispersed to bars and cafés, while others went to frighten deputies in the National Assembly with lewd drinking songs. Lafayette, having inspected all entrances to the palace and posted his guards, assured the King there was nothing to fear.

The apprehensive occupants of the palace sat about in nervous silence, unsure if it were safe to go to bed. 'The Queen,' recorded Mme de Tourzel, 'showed that day the grandeur of her soul and that courage which always characterized her. . . . She reassured everybody, thought of everything, and took much more care of those who were dear to her than of herself.'[36] Finally at 2 a.m., when all was silent outside, the royal family retired. Was Axel hidden in Marie-Antoinette's apartments that fatal night? He was most definitely inside the palace, for had he been at his own lodgings, he would not have been 'a witness to everything' – witness to an attempt to murder the woman he loved. At 6 a.m. an armed band of men, notorious for committing atrocities in Paris, somehow got into the locked palace courtyards, butchered two guards, and made straight for the Queen's apartments. Several people later swore they saw the Duc d'Orléans, dressed in a riding-cape and slouch hat, directing this murderous gang to their quarry. She was saved by the sentry outside her apartments, who held the assassins off long enough for her to escape to the King's apartments, where she was reunited with her children and husband.

The royal family's fate was sealed that very day. Early on 6 October a crowd swarmed into the palace courtyards and demanded that they leave Versailles for Paris, fifteen miles away. The mob was well armed, while the royal bodyguards were outnumbered, disarmed and lucky to be alive. Any thoughts of resistance were surely nullified by the sight of the heads of their murdered comrades paraded on pikes. Louis XVI appeared twice on a balcony overlooking the teeming *cour de marbre* to announce his decision to go to Paris; then his heavily armed subjects below demanded to see the Queen. She stepped out to face her enemies holding her children by the hand. 'The crowd looked at her with fury, and roared: "Send in the children!" The Queen made them go inside and showed herself alone. Her air of grandeur and heroic courage in the face of a danger which made everybody tremble, so impressed the mob that it instantly abandoned its sinister plans, and, struck with admiration, cried 'Long live the Queen!"'[37]

Axel could breathe again. She was still alive, but for how much longer? A 1 p.m. on 6 October the royal family, the entire Court, the government and the National Assembly left Versailles for Paris. 'I returned to Paris in one of the coaches which followed the King's,'

Axel told his father on 9 October. 'We were $6\frac{1}{2}$ hours on the road. God preserve me from ever seeing another spectacle as distressing as that of those two days!'[38]

It was a delightful spectacle for the Duc d'Orléans, who gloated as the royal prisoners passed his house at Passy. Marie-Antoinette knew full well what this atrocious journey meant. She accompanied Louis XVI to the capital only out of a sense of duty which with hindsight begins to seem very misguided. She could, after all, have left Versailles with her children and gone to Rambouillet without the King; but she obeyed her husband, who listened to ministers with questionable motives. Two of them, Montmorin and Saint-Priest, had actually prevented Mercy from seeing the Queen that day at Versailles, probably afraid the Austrian ambassador would convince her of the need to escape while she still had a chance.

Paris was triumphant. The mayor, the astronomer Sylvain Bailly, welcomed the royal family at the Hôtel de Ville before they were escorted to their new home, the palace of the Tuileries. It was guarded solely by the suspect Garde Nationale, for Louis XVI was weak enough to agree to Lafayette's demand that he dismiss his loyal Bodyguard. Marie-Antoinette wrote to reassure Mercy about her position the following day:

> I'm well, don't worry. If we forget where we are and how we got here, we have every reason to be satisfied with the mood of the people, especially this morning. I hope, if there is no shortage of bread, that many things will recover. I speak to the people: the militia, the *poissardes*, they all offer me their hands and I give them mine. Inside the Hôtel de Ville I was personally very well received. This morning the people asked us to stay. I told them on behalf of the King, who was beside me, that it depended on them if we stayed, that we asked for nothing better, that all hatred must cease; that the slightest bloodshed would make us flee in horror. Those closest to us swore that it was all over.[39]

Marie-Antoinette was never more majestic and impressive than during those early days at the Tuileries, and Parisians reacted to her with a warmth which was certainly not in Orléans's script. They crowded into the palace gardens and courtyards for several days to cheer the royal family, who had to keep showing themselves at the windows of Marie-Antoinette's ground-floor apartment.

Axel was probably somewhere in the crowd, for on 9 October he wrote to his father: 'The Queen is greatly applauded, and she cannot fail to be when they get to know her and give her credit for her desire to do good and the kindness of her heart.'[40] He relished every word of praise he heard about her, a small consolation for the fact they were now separated. The Queen was as yet very unsure of her new guards, and could receive no visitors in the small apartment she shared with her son and daughter.

Eventually some semblance of normality was brought to life at the Tuileries. Furniture was moved from Versailles to make the place more habitable. Marie-Antoinette had three rooms on the ground floor and a little library-cum-office upstairs next to her daughter's bedroom. Louis XVI and the Dauphin shared an apartment immediately above the Queen's, connected to it by a small private staircase. They became, because of this unaccustomed proximity, a very close-knit family. Marie-Antoinette spent the morning with her children, dined *en famille* with her husband, daughter and sister-in-law Madame Elisabeth, then played billiards with Elisabeth and the King to give him a limited form of exercise. She then did needlework or wrote letters in her room until supper, which Monsieur and his wife also attended.

During that long, dreary autumn Marie-Antoinette maintained an outward appearance of serenity, but she was deeply unhappy inside, as she confided in a letter to Mme de Polignac on 29 December 1789:

> You speak of my courage; I assure you that I needed much less in the dreadful circumstances I faced than to bear our position continually and every day. One's own troubles, those of one's friends, and those of everyone around us, make a load too heavy to bear; and if my heart were not held fast by strong links to my children, to you and to two friends I have [probably the Duchesse de Fitz-James and Comtesse d'Ossun], often I would wish to die. . . . You should have received a letter from my daughter. The poor little soul is still wonderful to me. In truth, if I could be happy, these two little beings would make me so. The *Chou d'Amour* [the Dauphin] is charming, and I love him to distraction. He loves me very much too, in his fashion, and makes himself at home. I like calling him that to remind him of you and yours. . . . He's very well, growing strong and no longer throws tantrums. He goes out every day, which does him a great deal of good.

I shan't write to you of affairs here; I find one either has to say nothing or write volumes. My husband sends you his best regards; I believe he wrote to you not long ago. I've recently twisted my bad leg again, which meant I had to spend twelve days in my room. But when one cannot be where and with whom one wants, one could spend a year in the same place without thinking of moving. . . .[41]

One glaring omission in the Queen's list of those who had a place in her heart is Louis XVI, and the reason can be found in a cryptic paragraph inserted in this very letter: 'I have seen him: for, after three months of grief and separation, although we were in the same place, the person and I managed to see each other safely once. You know us both, so you can imagine our happiness. He's going to make a trip to your brother's house. . . .[42]

As Marie-Antoinette had already spoken of Mme de Polignac's 'brother at Valenciennes', and Axel actually left Paris for his regiment at Valenciennes on 29 December, the day she wrote this letter, there is no doubt he was 'the person' who made her so happy. Proof is found in a letter Axel sent to Sophie on 27 December, which dates this blissful lovers' reunion to Christmas Eve: 'My dear friend. . . . At last on the 24th I spent the whole day with *Her*. It was the first: imagine my joy – only you can feel it.'[43]

Axel had told Sophie several times how miserable he was during his separation from Marie-Antoinette in October and November. Revolution had certainly not dimmed the flame of their love. Soon he was to be given the opportunity to demonstrate his deep devotion to the Queen.

9

Her Majesty's Secret Agent

January 1790 saw the beginning of a new phase in Axel Fersen's career, where love and duty were entwined more intricately than ever before. After his happy reunion with Marie-Antoinette on Christmas Eve 1789 he went as planned to Valenciennes, then on to Aachen to see his old friend Baron Evert Taube. Taube was still in pain from a shoulder wound received during the Russo-Swedish war and was at Aachen ostensibly for a cure. In fact, as one of Gustav III's most loyal aides, he had been sent to negotiate a renewal of the Franco-Swedish alliance with Louis XVI and to offer Swedish help to the beleaguered French King. Gustav could no longer trust his ambassador in Paris, the Baron de Staël, whose celebrated wife, the daughter of the Prime Minister, was deeply involved with the revolutionaries holding the royal family hostage at the Tuileries. Both Taube and Gustav considered Axel the very man they now needed in Paris to open discussions with Louis XVI.

Axel was overjoyed by this chance to serve not only Sweden but also the woman he adored, and wrote a warm letter thanking Gustav for his commission on 7 January 1790, telling him: 'In order to carry out Your Majesty's intentions, I believe it would be better not to bring my return to Paris too far forward. It could give rise to conjecture, especially at a time when all actions, even the most simple, are watched and have interpretations put on them. Baron Taube agreed with me; besides it will only be a delay of ten days and I'll be in Paris on the 17th or 18th.'[1]

During those ten days at Aachen, Axel and Taube pondered the political situation in France and the unenviable position of the royal

143

family, and made arrangements for the transmission of coded dispatches. They also had time to talk of love – in this case, Taube's
love for Sophie. Axel's favourite sister, though married with three
children, was deeply distressed by her lover's absence. During 1790
Axel wrote often to console her. He had also commiserated with Taube
in August 1789 when the baron had had to leave Sophie for 'that
accursed Finland'. Who better than Axel to sympathize? He clearly
knew all about the pain of a lovers' parting. 'Nobody,' he wrote to
Taube, 'knows better than I all it cost you to leave her. I feel all that
you felt, and I would have given everything in the world to have
been there to alleviate the horror of that moment.'[2] These two sen-
tences give some indication of how bitter Axel always found his many
enforced separations from Marie-Antoinette. Sophie, of course, had
long known of his love for the Queen, but he was extremely reticent
with Taube. He could not afford to let news of his liaison with the
Queen of France reach Gustav III, and although he always praised
her in his correspondence with the King, it was with diplomatic formality and circumspection.

Axel lost no time in commencing his work when he returned to
Paris in mid-January 1790. At the beginning of February he told his
father why he was remaining in France. Judging by his letter, he
must already have had several confidential meetings with both Marie-
Antoinette and Louis XVI.

> I am attached to the King and the Queen, and so I should be because
> of the very kind way they have always treated me, when they were
> able to; I would be vile and ungrateful if I abandoned them now they
> can do nothing for me and while I hope to be of service to them. To
> all the kindnesses they have always bestowed on me, they have just
> added yet another flattering distinction. It is that of giving me their
> confidence. This is all the more [valuable] since it is very limited and
> restricted to three or four people, of whom I am the youngest. If we
> can serve them, what a pleasure it will be to me to repay some of the
> obligations I owe them – what sweet enjoyment for my heart to be
> able to contribute to their happiness![3]

How delighted he was to be able to show Marie-Antoinette he
loved her, to rescue her from distress. Despite his mention of the
King, it was certainly not Louis XVI Axel was speaking of with such

tender concern, but the Queen. Senator Fersen, however, like Taube never knew (officially at any rate) of his son's intimate relationship with her. Marie-Antoinette had given Axel her heart and her entire confidence many years before; but how did he get on with Louis XVI? A watchful amity seems to have developed between them. The King implicitly trusted Axel's loyalty and devotion, while Axel respected Louis's integrity and the goodness of his heart, though he criticized his lack of political judgement. According to the Comte de Saint-Priest, a minister with whom Axel was on very good terms ('his house is mine, he overwhelms me with kindness,' Axel told his father, adding, 'despite all that, I tell him only what I want to, and I'm prudent'), Marie-Antoinette had used feminine wiles to convince her husband that her relationship with the handsome thirty-four-year-old Swede was entirely innocent: 'She had found a way of making him [Louis XVI] accept her liaison with the Comte de Fersen; she repeated to her husband all the public gossip she learnt was circulating about this affair, and offered to stop seeing him, which the King refused. Doubtless she insinuated to him . . . that this foreigner was the only man they could count on.'[4]

It is inconceivable that Louis XVI could have been hoodwinked by such a stratagem, even if he appeared to be taken in. He was by now probably well aware of his wife's love for Axel Fersen, although he never gave any overt sign that he either suspected an affair or was troubled by it. Certainly Marie-Antoinette and Axel never flaunted their love, and went to elaborate lengths to keep it secret from the King. Louis had too few friends left to refuse the assistance of a man whose love for the Queen only increased his desire to be of service, a man moreover well known for his honesty, zeal and discretion. The idea lurks that the unfathomable King concealed his jealousy for many years and made use of Axel Fersen's talent for organization with the intention of sidelining him at an opportune moment.

Marie-Antoinette needed Axel now more than ever before. The events of October 1789 had left her acutely aware of her perilous position. The National Assembly had usurped all power in the country, but retained an impotent King as a scapegoat for repeated policy disasters. At the end of 1789 it had decreed the suppression of the old *parlements*, thus destroying the French legal system at a single blow. Thenceforth, the Assembly not only made laws but policed them, ordering the summary arrest of those deemed guilty of political crimes. Although this was institutional despotism of the worst kind, the captive Louis XVI was now unfailingly described as a tyrannical oppressor of the people.

Powerless in her imprisonment, Marie-Antoinette turned to Axel for consolation; from his letters to Sophie, she would seem to have spent a lot of time crying in his arms. Her greatest grief in 1790 was the death of her brother Joseph. The Emperor had been declining in health for several months, but had still offered to do everything possible to help Marie-Antoinette. When he received a note from her through Mercy after the march on Versailles on 6 October 1789, Joseph wrote: 'I'm so cruelly tormented about her fate, it was really consoling to me to see her handwriting . . . the dangers the Queen faced and still faces make me shudder.'[5]

In November 1789, at Louis XVI's request, Joseph prevented an armed incursion into Provence by the Comte d'Artois and a force of émigré army officers, and had he lived would unquestionably have moved heaven and earth to save his beloved sister. His loss was truly calamitous for her. Joseph died on 20 February, a week after receiving the last rites and sending his last letter to Marie-Antoinette. 'He had always tenderly loved the Queen,' wrote the royal governess, Mme de Tourzel. 'During the final days of his life he wrote her the most tender and most touching letter. He told her that one of his most bitter regrets in dying was leaving her in such a cruel position, and not being able to give her real proof of the love he had always borne her.'[6]

Marie-Antoinette shut herself away to weep for several days. Gustav III's offers to assist the French royal family must have been doubly welcome at this time, for Austria could no longer be considered a staunch ally. Joseph was succeeded by his brother Leopold, Grand Duke of Tuscany, whom Marie-Antoinette had not seen since she was ten years old, and although he immediately promised his sister friendship and support, events proved him to be utterly insincere. Mercy told the Austrian Chancellor Kaunitz that in its troubled state France was no longer of interest to Austria, and asked to be relieved of his post. So much for his loyalty to the Queen! Not suspecting his duplicity, she still trusted him and firmly believed he had her interests at heart.

Axel Fersen's task in 1790 was to persuade Louis XVI that he could hope to regain his authority only by leaving Paris. Axel told Gustav III on 7 January that when the National Assembly finally lost all credibility it would be time for the King to reassert his position as Head of State.

> But how can it be done as long as the King is a prisoner in Paris? He made a mistake in allowing himself to be taken there; now it is necessary to get him out, and the declaration made last October that he was free, and that to prove it he could go and visit the provinces in the spring, this declaration is a good pretext for getting him out.[7]

Axel's arguments appear to have fallen on deaf ears. Louis XVI made no attempt to escape his confinement at the Tuileries during 1790, despite (or perhaps because of) violent unrest both in Paris and the provinces. Instead he meekly accepted Jacobin ministers nominated by Lafayette into his cabinet and hoped secret negotiations to buy the services of Mirabeau, an ally of the Duc d'Orléans and the most powerful orator in the Assembly, would yet save the monarchy.

The deeply unhappy Marie-Antoinette became a hapless spectator watching her own tragedy unfold. 'We must inspire confidence in these unhappy people,' she told Leopold on 29 May, 'they try so hard to stir them up and turn them against us! Only excessive patience and the purity of our intentions can bring them back to our side.' The same day she wrote with desperate bravado to her sister Marie-Christine:

> . . . all my wishes and all my actions are intended firstly for the happiness of the King, for whom I would give my blood, but in truth also for everybody's happiness; for I desire only an order of things which will restore calm and tranquillity to this unhappy country and prepare a happier future for my poor child – as for us, we have seen too many horrors and too much blood ever to be truly happy again.[8]

The Queen was unfortunately prophetic yet again. She never knew another moment's true happiness to the end of her life, and she did indeed have to give her blood for Louis XVI. The Revolution brought out the underlying strength in their peculiar marriage – a fierce loyalty to each other which grew ever stronger in adversity. The King turned to his wife for support, and received complete devotion. Marie-Antoinette was, however, totally unable to influence his actions, and thereby doomed to share his horrible fate. In 1792 she complained to Mme Campan about the King's timidity and failure to rally his guards but felt herself in too weak a position to act unilaterally: 'As for me, I could certainly take action and ride a horse if it were needed. But if I were to act, I would be giving weapons to the King's enemies. . . . A queen who is not a regent must, in these circumstances, remain inactive and prepare to die.'[9]

In 1790, though desperately miserable, the Queen nursed hopes of escaping the net closing in on her, and she could draw strength from Axel's love. He was making the most of his new role as a secret agent, which gave him many more opportunities to see her privately. On 4 April 1790 he thanked Sophie for her warm support for the Queen of France: 'Believe me, my dear Sophie, *she* deserves all the feelings you have for her; she's the most perfect creature I know, and her conduct, which is perfect too, has won over everyone, and everywhere I hear her praised – imagine how I enjoy it.'[10]

A week later he gave his sister more details about the parlous state of France and his frequent rendezvous with Marie-Antoinette.

> There is a constant fear of riots; every scourge desolates this country at the same time and we live under the despotism of the mob, which is the worst of all. . . . I'm beginning to feel a little happier because from time to time I see my love freely in her apartments, and that consoles us a little for all the sorrows she's enduring, poor woman. *She* is an angel for her conduct, courage and sensibility; never has anyone known how to love like her. She greatly appreciates everything you wrote about her; she cried a lot over it and asks me to tell you how touched she was. She would be so happy if she could see you sometimes. She thinks that if our plan succeeds you could then come here and the idea makes her very happy. . . .[11]

The 'plan' Axel refers to was presumably an escape from Paris and the re-establishment of law and order in France under the King's authority. From this letter one may deduce that Marie-Antoinette favoured an escape more than Louis XVI; several more months of anarchy were to pass before the King belatedly decided to flee. Axel sent weekly diplomatic reports to Gustav III, a task he found rather onerous, as he confessed to Taube on 11 April. 'Think to yourself, that being all alone, not even able to employ a secretary, and being obliged to show myself in society to avert any suspicion, I am over-whelmed with business.'[12]

Axel was never so overwhelmed he could not find time to make love to Marie-Antoinette or write sympathetic letters to Sophie. There was now no attempt at all to disguise the nature of his liaison with the Queen. A real sisterly feeling sprang up between her and the Swedish countess, and they frequently exchanged messages through Axel. His intimacy with Marie-Antoinette is revealed in a letter to Sophie of 7 May 1790. 'We never stop wishing for your happiness, my dear friend,' he wrote, 'and *She* thinks often about you.'[13] The *We* says it all. Axel Fersen and the Queen of France were without doubt a couple.

Axel was nevertheless compelled to be very secretive about his new diplomatic role. He quite untruthfully told Sophie she need not worry: 'I'm in no danger, being removed from affairs here because I'm a foreigner. I take no part in them and consequently I'm not at all at risk.' On 31 May he wrote:

> Everything continues the same here, my dear friend, that is to say badly, and you will read in the gazettes about the horrid and cruel acts being perpetrated in the provinces and in Paris. . . . *She* is ex-tremely unhappy, but very courageous. She's an angel. I told her everything you asked me to tell her and it pleased her. I try to con-sole her as much as I can, I owe it to her, she's so perfect for me.[14]

In late May 1790 Axel feared he might have to leave the Queen and his work for Gustav III to join his regiment, but chaos in the army meant the end of his career as Colonel of the Royal-Suédois. The royal family were allowed to move to Marie-Antoinette's château at Saint-Cloud for the summer and Axel soon followed them. By the summer of 1790, many people genuinely believed the Revolution was over. The King had been stripped of power, the National Assembly was preparing the constitution, the Declaration of the Rights of Man had been accepted, and nobody was paying any taxes. That, of course, was the problem. The deficit, which the States-General had origi-nally been convened to discuss, spiralled out of control. One reason for the relative calm in Paris might have been the Duc d'Orléans's absence in London. He returned to France in June 1790, in time to witness the last triumph of the royal family. Already Bastille Day, 14 July, had replaced St Louis as the national holiday. It was celebrated in Paris by a 'federation' – an assembly of detachments of the Garde Nationale from the whole country.

The royal family moved back to Paris for the 'Fête de la Fédération', and although the ceremony took place on the Champ de Mars in a downpour, they received rapturous applause. Guardsmen crowded into the Tuileries for two weeks afterwards, asked the King to visit their provinces, and queued to see the Dauphin, who was, according to his governess, 'adored by all those who approached him'. Many courtiers urged Louis XVI to accept the offer of these loyal *fédérés* to escort him safely from the capital, but as usual he baulked at so bold an action, saying he feared starting a civil war. So the *fédérés* left Paris, Louis and his family returned to Saint-Cloud, and the revolutionary leaders plotted the downfall of the monarchy. 'If the King had known how to profit from the occasion,' Antoine Barnave, the National Assembly president, told him a year later, 'we would have all been lost.'[15]

Louis XVI never learnt to turn circumstances to good account. According to both Mme de Tourzel and Mme Campan, cabinet ministers begged him to escape from Saint-Cloud. The château, guarded by 400 Parisian *gardes nationales*, was also garrisoned by loyal Swiss Guards, and located at a convenient distance from the Paris mob. Again, Louis XVI refused to leave: ' . . . the fear of a civil war which would spill the blood of his subjects was so firmly imprinted on his brain, that he could not make up his mind to leave, always hoping the nation would open its eyes to the misfortunes brought about by the Assembly's decrees'.[16]

The King, underestimating republican strength and violence, may well have hoped for tangible results from his secret negotiations with Mirabeau, for the fiery democrat was adored by Parisians. Marie-Antoinette held a clandestine meeting with Mirabeau in the gardens at Saint-Cloud, but was shocked by his brutal advice. 'How can M ____, or any other thinking man,' she wrote to Mercy on 15 August 1790, 'believe that ever, but especially now, the moment has come for us, *us* to provoke a civil war?'[17] If only she and Louis XVI had heeded his advice, they might have survived to a comfortable old age. Mirabeau was privy to all the schemes of the Duc d'Orléans and the opposition, and was certain the King and Queen would perish unless they took military action to regain control of the country.

They were possibly unsure who their worst enemies were. At Saint-Cloud life was made miserable by Lafayette's zealous and intrusive policing, and at that time they probably feared him most. Marie-Antoinette detested Lafayette, holding him responsible for what was her house arrest in all but name. Although she enjoyed much greater freedom at Saint-Cloud than at the Tuileries, being able to see her friends and take her children out for country walks, she was never free from the unwelcome company of Lafayette's officers. According to the Comte de Saint-Priest, one of Lafayette's aides-de-camp even 'slept in the Queen's antechamber' and 'when she went out either on foot or on horseback, he followed her constantly'. But, Saint-Priest adds:

> This did not stop Fersen's visits from being always admitted. He was staying with one of his friends in the village of Auteuil, and used to arrive at Saint-Cloud at dusk. I was informed that one of the guards . . . who encountered Fersen leaving the château at three o'clock in the morning, almost arrested him. I thought I ought to speak to the Queen about it, and warned her that the presence of the Comte de Fersen and his visits to the château could pose a danger. 'Speak to him about it,' she replied, 'if you think it necessary. As for me, I'm not concerned.' And, in effect, the visits continued as usual.[18]

Marie-Antoinette would certainly not give up her lover and loyal friend to appease a public who hated her and ministers she mistrusted. Axel was staying with her old friend Valentin Esterhazy at Auteuil. His visits to the Queen seem to have been quite frequent in June and early July; he even wrote a letter to Sophie from her salon at Saint-Cloud. At the end of July he left Esterhazy to spend a few days in the country with the Duchesse de Fitz-James, and returned to Paris on 6 August. Two days later he wrote to Sophie, lamenting his separation from Marie-Antoinette.

> I've been staying with the Duchesse de Fitz-James. . . . She's the best woman in the world, very unhappy at everything that's happening, both on her own account, because she's been ruined, and also because of her attachment to the Queen. She's her lady-in-waiting, and I like her very much. There were only seven of us there . . . but *She* was not there to make me happy, and without *her* nothing is right for me.[19]

Nevertheless Axel was soon able to enjoy the Queen's love again. In August Esterhazy took his wife and children to England for safety, lending Axel his house at Auteuil for the duration of the Court's stay at Saint-Cloud. On 15 October 1790 Axel congratulated Sophie on Taube's return to Sweden, then added: 'What Taube told you about *Her* gave me great pleasure. *She* deserves it, her conduct is angelic. She astonishes me and I want everyone to love her as much as she deserves and to do her justice. I'm still staying at Auteuil and I'm very content and very happy here.'[20]

He must have seen Marie-Antoinette almost every day to feel so elated, and was far from pleased when he had to return to the capital on 28 October. 'Now I'm confined in this vile cesspit,' he wrote to Sophie from his house in Paris on 30 October. 'The Court is still at Saint-Cloud and they say it will stay there until 15 November.'[21]

When the royal family returned to the Tuileries Louis XVI finally decided he would have to take decisive measures to reassert his authority. The Assembly had decreed the abolition of the nobility, and nationalized all crown property. Church lands were already being sequestrated and sold off to speculators, yet the deficit still rose inexorably – a fact which probably led the now discredited financial 'genius' Jacques Necker to tender his resignation in September 1790. The ministers who replaced him were equally unable to govern, the Assembly issued countless unworkable decrees, and there were violent disturbances throughout the country. More dangerous still was the army of bitter, reactionary noble émigrés, led by the Comte d'Artois and the Prince de Condé, who threatened to march into France from the German border and restore the *ancien régime* by force; whether the hostage royal family perished as a result was immaterial to them.

Louis XVI did not even want to reinstate the *ancien régime* and remained resolutely opposed to any action liable to precipitate the civil war he so dreaded. Through the Foreign Minister Montmorin and the Comte de La Marck, he continued his secret talks with Mirabeau, though evidently with little hope of achieving anything, since he was simultaneously hatching an escape plan with Axel Fersen.

Axel was indispensable to the execution of this plan, and made all necessary preparations in Paris. Also pivotal to the enterprise were the Marquis de Bouillé, a royalist general in command of troops at Metz on the northern frontier, and the Baron de Breteuil and Mercy, who were both based in Brussels. Mercy had been sent by Emperor Leopold to govern the Austrian Netherlands in October 1790 but continued to advise Marie-Antoinette by post, while the former minister Breteuil conducted Louis XVI's secret negotiations with all foreign countries.

The escape plan and counter-revolutionary *coup* were revealed to Mercy by Marie-Antoinette in a letter of 3 February 1791, when she sent a box to him at Brussels containing all her diamonds. The royal family were to leave Paris secretly at night and drive post-haste to Montmédy, a fortified town in Lorraine on the north-eastern border which Bouillé would garrison with loyal troops. The King would then issue a proclamation pardoning all but the most violent revolutionaries, ordering the surrender of all weapons, and setting out his own political agenda. He would promise 'to re-establish the *parlements* as courts of justice only without letting them meddle in the administration or finances', and would propose his own democratic constitution for France. 'We have decided to take the declaration of 23 June [1789] as the basis for the constitution, with such modifications as circumstances and events have dictated. Religion will be one of the key points to bring forward.' Marie-Antoinette was already asking for Mercy's ideas about the choice of prime minister, but she realized the whole scheme might fail without the support of neighbouring countries. The royal family needed assurances of protection by Swiss and Austrian troops should Louis XVI fail to rally enough French supporters – which Mercy seemed to think quite likely. Caution was the Queen's watchword: 'We shall not act in haste,' she told Mercy. 'It would be better to spend another year in prison and be sure of getting out, than to risk being brought back.'[22]

Discussions and preparations for this momentous journey meant that Axel continued to see a great deal of Marie-Antoinette at the Tuileries that winter. In December 1790 Sophie asked for a lock of the Queen's hair which she wanted to set in a ring, and Axel duly enclosed it in a letter to his sister on 3 January 1791: 'Here is the hair you asked for; if there isn't enough I'll send you some more. It is *She* who gives it to you, and she was deeply touched by your request. She is so good and so perfect, and I seem to love her even more now she loves you. She asks me to tell you how much she feels and shares your sorrows.'[23]

Sophie was evidently going through difficult times; in his next letter on 17 January, Axel revealed the warm, sympathetic side of his nature which so many women found irresistible.

. . . your sorrows pierce my soul. My dear friend, speak to me often about them, speak to me always, tell me everything you are suffering and all you feel. You need to, it's a consolation to open one's heart to a friend, and you know you have no truer or more tender friend than I. Tell me you are desperate, that you are really unhappy; you could never tell me as much as I know and feel it, but it will console you for a moment, and that means everything to me. . . . Adieu, adieu. *She* sends her warmest wishes and tenderly shares your sorrows. She often cries about them with me – imagine how I must love her. If you think it easier to have the ring you want made here, tell me so and how you want it made. It's *she* who wants to do it and to give it to you.[24]

This shows a very different Axel indeed, a feeling and compassionate man who seems a stranger to the cool practical diplomat who wrote brisk letters to Bouillé, Mercy and Breteuil and methodically arranged every aspect of the royal family's departure from Paris. He now found his old Russian friends Mme de Korff and Mme Stegelmann of enormous help. Marie-Antoinette told Mercy: 'We have a coach which doesn't belong to us and which none of our servants knows about' – a berline with room for seven people, ordered by Mme de Korff on 22 December 1790, which cost 5,944 *livres* (about 180 guineas) and was paid for by Axel. It was always described as a fantastically luxurious vehicle, hardly likely at such a moderate price, although it was of necessity much larger and slower than a chaise for only two or three passengers. Mme de Tourzel declared 'there was nothing extraordinary about it', and Axel certainly did not intend to attract attention. 'Everything depends on speed and secrecy,' he wrote to Bouillé on 26 May, 'and if you are not quite sure of your troops, it would be much better not to deploy any. . . . The King will then pass quite easily.'[25]

Bouillé and Axel had to fix a route for the royal party. Axel suggested they go to Montmédy via Meaux, Châlons, Reims, Île-Réthel and Pauvre, but Bouillé proposed an alternative which Louis XVI accepted. The staging posts were Meaux, La Ferté-sous-Jarre, Montmirail, Châlons-sur-Marne, Sainte-Menehould, Varennes, Dun and Stenay – a distance of 61 leagues or 183 miles. 'From Sainte-Menehould to Stenay there will be good troops stationed as an escort,' Bouillé assured Axel on 9 May 1791.[26]

Much diplomacy was required before the escape could be attempted. Bouillé demanded that Austrian troops fake manoeuvres on the border to give him a pretext to assemble his own forces, but it took several months, numerous letters and the dispatch of the Marquis de Bombelles to Vienna to negotiate personally with the new Emperor Leopold before the Austrians agreed even to this modest request. Marie-Antoinette intervened directly with her brother on 22 May to press him for 'a corps of eight to ten thousand men at Luxembourg, available on our demand', and begged for a speedy response, since the émigré princes were threatening an invasion which would wreck her own plan. Although Louis XVI was nominally in command of the whole enterprise, he left the detailed work to Marie-Antoinette, and without her it is unlikely it would ever have been undertaken. Gouverneur Morris was told in April 1791 by the Foreign Minister Montmorin that 'the King is absolutely good for nothing; that at present he always asks when he is to work with the King, that the Queen be present'.[27]

Although the Queen eventually overcame Austrian tergiversation, there remained the pressing problem of money. Paying for the necessary troops and for an interim government once Louis XVI was established at Montmédy would demand vast resources. The King managed to raise 2 million *livres* from his civil list, but much more was needed. Axel Fersen undertook to find it, and wrote to Taube in Sweden on 1 April 1791 asking him to borrow 'two or three millions in your name, my name and those of several other people. I will stand surety for this sum'.[28] He sent Bouillé 1 million *livres* in banknotes at the end of May, telling him the royal family had 3 million more 'outside the Kingdom'. Bouillé's reiterated demands for money ought to have alerted Axel to the unworthy motive for his interest in aiding the royal family.

The 1 million *livres* used to pay for Bouillé's men and horses at Montmédy, and all the preparations in Paris, was raised by Axel and his royalist friends. Axel paid interest on the loans for years and was eventually also obliged to repay the capital. His devotion to Marie-Antoinette proved very expensive indeed. Mmes de Korff and Stegelmann put up 300,000 *livres*, and even Axel's porter, Louvet, lent him 3,000 *livres*. Another 300,000 *livres* came from a woman who was to play a very important part in Axel's life for several years to come – Eleonore Sullivan.

Born in Milan to a theatre stage-hand, Eleonore joined a travelling acting company at the age of twelve. She was very attractive,
and by the time she met Axel Fersen in Paris in 1789, had already
had a chequered career. She was married young to a fellow-actor,
but left him for Duke Karl-Ernst of Württemberg, by whom she had
two daughters and a son. This liaison did not last long. The beautiful, dangerous Eleonore left Duke Karl-Ernst and her children and
went to Vienna, where she became the mistress of none other than
Marie-Antoinette's brother Joseph. According to Emperor Leopold,
Joseph was completely smitten with Eleonore, but Empress Maria-
Theresa was not, and ordered her son's mistress to leave Austria.
Next stop for Eleonore was Paris, where she married a Mr Sullivan.
He took her to Manila, which is where she met an exceedingly rich
Scotsman, Quentin Crawford. When Crawford offered to take her
back to Europe in 1780, Eleonore abandoned her husband and began
her most durable incarnation as the wealthy Mme Sullivan, who kept
a good table and entertained the best company both at Crawford's
Paris mansion and his house in London.

Eleonore was devoted to the French royal family and particularly
to Marie-Antoinette – possibly she felt a loyalty to the captive Queen
because of her previous affair with Joseph. When Axel was planning
the escape to Montmédy, she persuaded him to confide in Crawford,
who had extensive diplomatic and financial connections, and was eager
to serve Louis XVI. This committee of three – Axel, Eleonore and
Crawford – held its meetings at Crawford's house, which Axel visited frequently from the spring of 1791 onwards. Crawford offered
him know-how and useful contacts, while Eleonore offered money,
dinners and her body. Exactly when she and Axel became lovers is
unclear, but it was evidently before 20 June 1791, when the escape
took place.

In his diary, Axel used to make a note in Swedish after the names
of certain women he visited: '*stayed there*'. This has been assumed to
mean he was on intimate terms with the woman concerned. Between
12 and 20 June 1791 he either dined '*chez Sullivan*' or visited her
every day except 18 June, and wrote '*stayed there*' three times, on 15,
17 and 19 June.[29] He also noted visits to Marie-Antoinette – '*chez
elle*' – on 12, 13, 16, 18, 19 and 20 June; some of their meetings
lasted several hours, but Axel gives no indication of what went on.
As he claimed to have found these diary entries some years later and

copied them, he possibly felt it imprudent to reproduce *'stayed there'* against his meetings with Marie-Antoinette, as it seems he tried to obliterate a similar note made in 1792 (see Chapter 10). One may also suspect editorial alterations to his diary; since Crawford lived with Eleonore and was a very suspicious man, how did Axel manage to spent two nights with her undiscovered? And why are there no *'stayed there'*s later in the diary when Axel saw Eleonore more frequently? His editors may have hoped to divert attention from his affair with Marie-Antoinette by implying a greater intimacy with Eleonore than actually existed at this period.

The Queen surely never suspected Axel's liaison with Eleonore Sullivan at this critical time. Perhaps he did not intend this long on-off affair to develop; perhaps sleeping with Eleonore (who appears to have liked him far more than he did her) was only his way of thanking her and saying goodbye. She left Paris with Crawford for Brussels the day Axel drove the royal family out of the Tuileries, and he had no intention of joining them; he asked Bouillé on 14 June to prepare a room for him at Montmédy, so he could be with Marie-Antoinette.

Axel later found Eleonore a very poor substitute indeed for the Queen, the woman upon whom he had centred his whole life for more than a decade. But 20 June 1791 nevertheless marked the virtual end of his relationship with Marie-Antoinette, although he did not know it at the time. It is distinctly possible that Louis XVI intervened in the affair during 1791, having decided to reclaim his wife. Axel had always intended to accompany the royal family along the whole route to Montmédy. On 4 April he wrote to Taube: 'It would be right for me to wear a Swedish uniform to accompany the King of France. Ask His Majesty [Gustav III] if he will permit me to wear on this occasion the uniform of his dragoons. . . . I don't have the Bodyguard uniform with me, and I dare not order one at the moment.'[30]

In the event, no uniform was needed. On 29 May Axel informed Bouillé: 'I shall not accompany the King, he didn't want me to. I shall pass through Le Quesnoy and leave for Mons via Bavay.'[31]

Why did Louis XVI refuse the one loyal, cool-headed man who knew most about the route he was to travel, who alone was entrusted with escorting the royal family out of Paris, permission to accompany them the whole way to Montmédy? Was it because he could no longer bear to be upstaged by Axel? What greater humiliation than to have the whole of Europe know he owed his deliverance to his wife's lover? Had Axel Fersen driven Louis into Montmédy, it would have been tantamount to sticking horns on the King's head.

This is one explanation for Louis XVI's uncharacteristically decisive behaviour at this time. The King gave the Queen public marks of his love as they left Paris, which was highly unusual, and she was extremely upset at parting from Axel. When he left her after making final preparations for the departure on 20 June 'she cried a lot'. Why, if she hoped the escape would succeed and they would be soon reunited? The King may well have told her that once they reached Montmédy, her almost daily meetings with Axel Fersen had to cease. Unfortunately Louis could never even hope to equal Axel for Marie-Antoinette. Her feelings never once wavered. She loved her Swedish count to her dying day, and had real reason to regret bitterly her incompetent husband's short-lived pose as a masterful monarch.

Louis XVI was not a man for grand gestures and bold deeds, which is why he had hesitated so long before deciding to flee Paris. Events early in 1791, however, had finally galvanized him into action. In February his elderly aunts, Mmes Adélaide and Victoire, emigrated to Italy, and tension around the Tuileries immediately increased. Fearing the palace was about to be stormed by a wrathful mob, on 28 February several hundred gentlemen armed with pistols and daggers rushed to defend the King. They were promptly accused by Lafayette of attempting to help the royal family escape; an ugly stand-off between them and the Garde Nationale was ended only when Louis ordered his gallant defenders to disarm. Several were arrested and imprisoned. It was but one of his many unwise betrayals of those who tried to assist him.

More alarming, however, was the *journée* of 18 April 1791, when the royal family tried to leave the Tuileries to spend Easter at Saint-Cloud. Religion was already dying under sustained attacks by the Jacobins, and priests and nuns refusing to accept the Civil Constitution of the Clergy were often subjected to brutal physical assault. The pious Louis XVI's strong opposition to dismemberment of the Church was excuse enough for the Garde Nationale to prevent him leaving the palace. A large, angry mob was baying for blood outside the gates, but the King was determined to leave. Lafayette tried to get his men to clear a passage for the royal coach, but was only insulted, as was the King: 'They employed the most insulting terms against the King: that he was a f____ aristocrat, a b____ aristocrat, a fat pig; that he was incapable of reigning; that he should be deposed and replaced by the Duc d'Orléans. . . .'[32]

Worse was to come. The guards threatened to shoot Louis if he tried to force his way out, and after two and a half hours the royal family were obliged to return to their apartments. The Queen snatched up her son and ran indoors with him, afraid of the guards pressing close around her. It was an inglorious day for Lafayette, who immediately resigned, but was reinstated as commander-in-chief of the Garde Nationale four days later. 'The Duc d'Orléans's faction is believed to have been behind what happened,' Axel told Taube, 'because the leaders of the Jacobins are rightly very angry about it.' He was convinced the palace guards were paid to mutiny, and that night came across a man outside the Tuileries 'reading, by the light of a torch, a paper full of horrors against the King, in which he exhorted the people to storm the château, to throw everything out of the windows, and above all not to let slip the chance they had missed at Versailles on 6 October'.[33]

Orléans had clearly intended a fresh assassination attempt on Louis XVI and Marie-Antoinette. He certainly had reason to rejoice at Mirabeau's sudden death on 2 April 1791, which many people attributed to poison. The great democrat had already made a couple of pro-monarchist speeches in the Assembly, not without effect, and his untimely demise ended the King's chances of restoring order (and, more importantly, regaining his liberty) through peaceful means.

Against this backdrop of mounting violence and treachery, there seemed little alternative to Louis XVI but to escape. If he thought his plan to establish an alternative royal government at Montmédy a closely guarded secret, he was, however, sadly mistaken. Gustav III of Sweden had been sent only the vaguest details by Axel Fersen, who feared his indiscretion. Although the Swedish King never let fall any compromising information, he travelled to Aachen in May 1791, where his presence alone was enough to spark off intense speculation that something was about to move in France. The Austrians, of course, were privy to the plan, since it required their co-operation, and in London rumours were rife that the royal family intended to leave Paris.

Axel received several letters during June 1791 from the Comtesse de Saint-Priest, whose husband had resigned in late 1790 and taken her to London. Evidently madly in love with Axel, she had been forced to accept that his heart belonged to Marie-Antoinette, and promised that she regarded him simply 'as a brother whom I cherish. I have no other feeling for you now. I've made this painful effort to obey you'. She was in touch with Mme de Korff from whom she doubtless learnt of Axel's efforts to help the royal family, which worried her greatly. Mme de Saint-Priest sent Axel interesting snippets of gossip from high-society London drawing-rooms, which show that many people knew both of his liaison with the Queen and his plan to rescue her. The Prince of Wales, she told Axel, was devoted to 'his bosom friend' the Duc d'Orléans, and 'seems to have inherited the hatred he bears *Her* [Marie-Antoinette]', while the Duke of Dorset, a friend of both the Queen and Axel 'assured me that [the Abbé de Vermond] alone had influence over her mind and governed her despotically in everything, that even you have no power over her, but that you cared only about your interests and your regiment'. Mme de Saint-Priest was at pains to rebut these accusations, both for Axel's sake and the Queen's, but she had an argument with her husband about it.

> My husband told me you were much blamed for your conduct, and that you had greatly wronged and continued to wrong a certain person [Marie-Antoinette], whom you were sacrificing to general scorn; that all those who had spoken to him about it expressed their astonishment at your lack of consideration for her reputation, and that you would lose *Her* entirely in the eyes of those who might take some interest in *Her*, without thinking that you were even risking her life. I quarrelled about that with my husband, because I see things very differently. I find that at this moment you could not prove your affection for her too much, by not leaving her and by giving her all the tokens [of love] you ought. And what people censure and find improper on your part, I find sublime, and I can only hold you in greater esteem. I am too fond of both you and *Her* to think differently.[34]

No wonder Louis XVI did not want to enter Montmédy with Axel Fersen! Nevertheless he accepted his money, used his brains, and magnanimously let him undertake the most hazardous part of the escape plan, which was getting the royal family out of Paris. The escape had been scheduled originally for the end of May 1791; it was postponed until 12 June so the King could get a 2 million *livres* instalment from the civil list, and then delayed yet again because of 'a bad *femme de chambre* of the Dauphin's, whom we could not get rid of'.[35] The royal family had been forced to sack most of their former retainers and take on new staff who spied on them for the Jacobins. Many suspected the royal prisoners were planning a journey – the Queen had been seen sorting through her possessions, destroying letters and packing up clothes – but none took any action to prevent a departure, which was finally fixed for midnight on Monday 20 June 1791.

Everybody involved in the plan left Paris at the same time. Mme de Korff (who had obtained Russian passports for the travellers), and Mme Stegelmann were gone by 17 June, while Crawford and Eleonore Sullivan left the same day as the royal party. Louis XVI was not, however, entirely confident of success. On the afternoon of 20 June Axel held a final meeting with him and the Queen at which contingency plans were discussed in the event of failure. Axel's terse diary entry for 20 June reads: 'We agreed . . . that if they were arrested I should go to Brussels and get something done for them, etc. etc. As he left me the King said: "Mr. de F., whatever may happen to me I shan't forget everything you're doing for me."'

Then came a farewell alone with Marie-Antoinette. 'The Queen cried a lot. I left her at 6 o'clock; she went for a walk with the children as an extra precaution.'[36] The royal governess Mme de Tourzel records this evening walk, made to delude the Garde Nationale, who were told to be ready to accompany the Queen on a similar outing the next day. The Dauphin was even put to bed, but at 10 p.m. his mother woke him up and told him he was going to command his regiment. Unlike Louis XVI, the Dauphin adored everything to do with the army, and cried: 'Quick, quick, let's hurry. Give me my sabre and my boots, and let's go!'[37] He was surely mortified to find he was to travel as a girl. Using Russian passports, Mme de Tourzel became Mme de Korff, Marie-Antoinette became a governess named Mme Rochet, Louis XVI a valet named Durand, his sister Madame Elisabeth was 'a young lady', while the royal children became Amélie and Aglaé de Korff.

Axel had found 'an old and antique carriage, resembling a fiacre' which he drove into the Cour des Princes at 10.15 p.m. Mme de Tourzel and the children were his first passengers, having left the palace through 'a little used door' shown them by Marie-Antoinette.

To avert suspicion, the fiacre set off on a journey along the banks of the Seine, returning by the rue St Honoré to pick up the others. Madame Elisabeth came out next at 11.15 p.m., and then there was a long wait for the King and Queen. 'M. de Fersen,' recalled Mme de Tourzel, 'played the part of fiacre coachman to perfection; whistling, and chatting to a so-called comrade who happened to be there, even offering him some snuff from his snuff-box'.[38] Axel's youthful performances on the royal stage at Drottningholm were not entirely useless after all.

The occupants of the fiacre received a nasty shock when Lafayette and the Mayor of Paris, Sylvain Bailly, rode past. They delayed the King, who was forced to admit them to his *coucher*, chat to them, and then get up and dress when they had gone. After midnight he eventually slipped past guards who mistook him for the Chevalier de Coigny, and joined his sister and children. But where was the Queen? Apparently she could not find the fiacre, and came across a sentry unexpectedly blocking her path. The King grew so anxious he was going to look for her, and when she finally arrived 'he clasped her in his arms, kissed her and said "How glad I am to see you!"'

The fiacre moved off. A fresh alarm awaited the fugitives at the Porte Saint-Martin, where a wedding party was in full swing, but they passed through the checkpoint without incident. They transferred to their berline at 1.30 a.m. on Tuesday, 21 June and Axel drove it to the first staging post at Bondy. Here he reluctantly bade farewell to the royal family, who were to be driven the rest of the way by his coachman. Louis XVI had ordered Axel to go to Mons and join his brother Monsieur, who left his own imprisonment at the Palais de Luxembourg the same night. 'The King, in saying goodbye to him,' wrote Mme de Tourzel, 'expressed his gratitude in the most affectionate manner, saying he hoped to be able to do so other than in words, and that he expected to see him again soon.'[39]

Axel disappeared into the night, doubtless watched very closely by an emotional Marie-Antoinette. The berline set off on its long journey. Axel travelled alone from Bondy to Le Bourget, and arrived safely at Mons at 6 a.m. on 22 June 1791. At 11 a.m. that day he wrote a short note to Baron Taube: 'My dear friend, the King, the Queen, Mme Elisabeth, the Dauphin and Madame left Paris at midnight; I accompanied them as far as Bondy, without incident. I'm leaving this instant to join them.'[40]

10

Adieu, My Love

While Axel Fersen journeyed to Mons, where he duly encountered Louis XVI's brother, Monsieur, who crossed the frontier unhindered in a post-chaise, the royal berline trundled on through the Champagne countryside. At Claye it was joined by a cabriolet containing four *femmes de chambre*, and all was going remarkably smoothly. According to Mme de Tourzel, Louis XVI was in a buoyant mood, and on the morning of Tuesday, 21 June 1791 chuckled at the thought of Lafayette's confusion when he discovered his prisoners had escaped. It was a chuckle too soon. Not long afterwards the berline hit an obstacle on the road, and the travellers were delayed for over an hour while repairs were carried out. Progress thereafter was slow and they were several hours behind schedule by the time they reached Châlons, where their troubles escalated.

Piecing together the sequence of events which followed is not easy, since the various eyewitness accounts conflict. Axel questioned all the key participants later. His findings present a picture of incompetence and sheer bad luck, compounded by Louis XVI's fatal indecision and weakness. The royal party were recognized at Châlons, but no action was taken to stop them until one of Lafayette's aides-de-camp, M. de Romoeuf, galloped into the town an hour after their departure carrying a warrant for their arrest. The question is inevitable: how could Lafayette have known their route unless the King had been imprudent enough to indicate it in the proclamation he had left behind at the Tuileries? Many servants at the palace were questioned by Lafayette, and Axel's part in the escape was soon discovered, but none appeared to know where the royal family had gone.

The only other possible source of this leak was one of the body-guards who accompanied the berline, M. de Valory, who told his mistress he was leaving that day.

Romoeuf was exhausted when he reached Châlons, so the post-master rode on to the next staging post at Sainte-Menehould to warn its postmaster, a six-foot former cavalryman named Drouet, that the royal family were escaping and at all costs had to be stopped. According to Drouet's own testimony, he immediately saddled a horse and rode hard, reaching the next staging post at Varennes three-quarters of an hour before the berline. Much has been made of Drouet's supposed recognition of Louis XVI at Sainte-Menehould. According to Mme de Tourzel, Drouet 'looked into the carriage for a moment', while other versions described Louis XVI poking his head out of the window to ask directions. Tourzel's account tallies with Drouet's, clearing the King of recklessness. It does not, however, exonerate him from blame for what followed.

The young Duc de Choiseul (about whom Axel always had strong misgivings) commanded a detachment of forty hussars detailed to join the berline just beyond Châlons, but they failed to make the rendezvous. The coach was so late it became impolitic for the escort to wait. Local peasants suspected the hussars were about to enforce tax collection, and sounded the alarm. After waiting as long as prac-ticable, Choiseul assumed the escape had been aborted, split his forces, and sent them to Varennes on back roads. The berline reached the town at 11 p.m., by which time Drouet had blocked a vital bridge with a cart. Without their expected escort, the royal fugitives were lost. They did not know where to find their fresh horses, and while they were looking Drouet alerted the town's mayor, a spicer who gloried in the name of Monsieur Sauce, that they were in Varennes.

A detachment of Choiseul's hussars, commanded by one of Marie-Antoinette's most trusted officers, M. Goguelat (who also served as her secretary), arrived just as the occupants of the berline were be-ing arrested. Goguelat asked Louis XVI for permission to force a passage through the town, but the King as usual refused to author-ize violent action. The royal family went into M. Sauce's shop, and while the mayor promised he would let them continue their journey he simultaneously raised the alarm. When Choiseul arrived half an hour later he found three to four hundred poorly armed citizens outside Sauce's house. General Bouillé's son, who was supposed to have an escort ready at Varennes, was actually asleep, and his soldiers scattered in various hostelries in the town.

Louis XVI tried to convince the people of his good intentions, but the mayor told them they would be massacred if they let him pass. Choiseul went into the house to speak to the King. 'The King was told he could get through with the hussars,' the duke later told Axel Fersen, 'that M. de Bouillé was surely on his way and they would meet him; but the advice was difficult to follow, because they would all have had to have gone on horseback, and could not be sure they would not be shot. The King preferred to stay and wait for M. de Bouillé, because at that time there was no talk of making him go back to Paris'.[1]

Louis XVI possibly hoped he could yet reach Montmédy safely; his aunts had been arrested twice when they left France, but still crossed the Italian border. Between 3 a.m and 4 a.m., however, Lafayette's aides-de-camp Baillon and Romeouf arrived at Varennes bearing the Assembly's decree ordering the arrest of the royal family and their return to Paris. The Queen seized the decree and was about to tear it up when the King stopped her. 'She had to be satisfied with throwing it scornfully to the floor', from where it was retrieved by her law-abiding husband.[2]

Louis XVI's unutterable weakness at Varennes must have made Marie-Antoinette profoundly regret Axel's absence. She tried everything possible to delay their departure for Paris, getting one of the *femmes de chambre* to feign an illness and complaining herself of fatigue, in the hope that General Bouillé would still arrive with his troops and rescue them. Had the King possessed an ounce of initiative he would have seized Baillon and Romoeuf as hostages and forced his way out with Choiseul's hussars, but he remained, as always, inert, completely incapable of taking effective action. Lafayette's officers would brook no delay. Fearing Bouillé was about to march on the town, they ordered the arrest of all the King's guards, bundled their royal prisoners back into the berline, and accompanied by a motley army of townsfolk and *gardes nationales*, set off on the ignominious return to Paris between five and six o'clock on the morning of Wednesday, 22 June 1791.

Bouillé and his men arrived on the outskirts of Varennes as the royal captives were leaving, but took no action. They were heavily outnumbered, and Bouillé feared an attack would simply endanger the lives of the royal family. He fled acrosss the frontier that very day. Axel, on his way to Montmédy, found him at Arlon in the Austrian Netherlands late in the evening of 23 June: '*23 June 1791* . . . Arrived at Arlon at 11 p.m. Found Bouillé. Learnt that the King was captured. Details not very clear; the troops didn't do their duty, the King lacked firmness and will.'[3] There was now no reason for Axel to continue his journey to Montmédy. At midnight he wrote a poignant note to Senator Fersen: 'Everything is lost, my dear father, and I am desperate. The King was arrested at Varennes, 16 leagues from the frontier. Think of my misery and pity me. . . .'[4]

Varennes was the graveyard of all his hopes. Axel now had to deliver the letter Louis XVI had given him for Mercy in the event of an arrest, and, feeling 'dreadfully miserable', he left Arlon at 4.30 a.m. on 24 June for Brussels.

By 24 June the royal family were approaching Meaux, now accompanied by three deputies from the National Assembly, sent to meet them near Épernay. Two of them – Jérôme Pétion and Antoine Barnave – joined the prisoners in the berline, and opened Marie-Antoinette's eyes to the splits in the Jacobin party. Barnave impressed her by his good manners, attentiveness and sensible conversation, while Pétion behaved disgustingly; he also amused himself by telling Madame Elisabeth how the Assembly would set about appointing a Council of Regency, assuring her that France would soon be a republic. When he sat the six-year-old Dauphin on his knee and began pulling his hair, he went too far. The Queen snatched back her son and berated his tormentor. Axel later recorded what Marie-Antoinette told him about this republican deputy: 'Pétion said they knew everything, that they had seized a hired carriage near the château [the Tuileries] driven by a Swede. He pretended not to know my name and asked the Queen if she knew it. She replied: "I'm not in the habit of knowing the names of hackney coachmen."'[5]

It was truly a long and dreadful journey. Royalist sympathizers greeted the King and Queen at Châlons and La Ferté-sous-Jarre, but were cowed by a Jacobin mob who arrived as an escort from Reims. Though the heat was intolerable, the deputies would not allow the berline's blinds to be drawn. Its occupants, according to Mme de Tourzel, were covered in dust and drenched with sweat, but that was the least of their worries. Near Épernay a loyal but unpopular subject of the King, the Comte de Dampierre, rode up to offer his greetings.

He gave his arm to one of the Dauphin's women to help her into the carriage. She warned him to go away, that the people had a grudge against him. He said no. He mounted his horse and at fifty paces they shot him down on the plain like a rabbit. When he fell off his horse they massacred him and returned to the carriage, their hands dripping blood, carrying his head.[6]

Barnave's horror at this murder and his brave defiance of the mob, whom he bitterly harangued for their brutality, gave the Queen and Madame Elisabeth a favourable idea of his character. Marie-Antoinette's efforts to keep calm after this atrocity nevertheless demanded super-human self-control. Just days after returning to an even closer con-finement at the Tuileries on 25 June 1791, her hair turned white. 'The first time I saw Her Majesty, after the dreadful catastrophe of the flight to Varennes,' wrote Mme Campan, 'I found her getting out of bed. Her features were not greatly altered, but . . . she took off her nightcap and told me to see the effect grief had had on her hair. In a single night it had turned as white as that of a woman of seventy.'[7] This unhappy transformation was noted by Gouverneur Morris as having taken place before 4 July, so the Queen's state of shock must have been severe.

The royal family's entry into Paris was stage-managed by Lafayette to be as unpleasant as possible. Huge, silent crowds lined the streets, their hats on their heads as a mark of disrespect for a monarch now deemed to have forfeited his crown. Lafayette, according to Mme de Tourzel, wanted a republic declared immediately and openly expressed disappointment that the royal fugitives had not been murdered. It would have saved him the trouble of making their lives hell at the Tuileries. They were guarded night and day, and had not a single moment's privacy. A kind-hearted actor from the Comédie-Française, M. Saint-Prix, who served in the Garde Nationale, allowed the King and Queen to hold brief private conversations in the small corridor linking their apartments, but their other movements were constantly observed.

Marie-Antoinette later told Axel that Lafayette's officers would shut her bedroom doors only 'for a moment, while she changed her shift', and even wanted to sleep in her room.

All she could manage was that they remained between the two doors.

Two or three times they came in at night to see if she were in her bed. One night when she couldn't sleep and she lit her lantern, the officer came in and settled down to talk to her. There was a camp outside the windows which made an infernal noise all night, and the officers in her room were relieved every two hours.[8]

Marie-Antoinette nevertheless forbore all public complaint. According to Mme Campan she never once displayed the slightest bad temper at her humiliating treatment, which probably infuriated Lafayette all the more. The Queen had her reasons for keeping quiet. The Assembly was finding it virtually impossible to name a regent, since both Louis XVI's brothers were émigrés and the next available contender, the Duc d'Orléans, was by now held in almost universal contempt. Marie-Antoinette capitalized on this impasse to open secret negotiations with Barnave over the constitution. She was playing for time, for her life, for her family and for the crown, which explains the reassuring tone of a note she scrawled to Axel on 29 June 1791:

I exist . . . [deletion] How worried I have been about you, and how I feel all you must be suffering at having no news of us! May Heaven let this reach you. Don't write to me, you would be exposing us, and above all don't come back here on any pretext. They know it was you who got us out of here; everything would be lost if you appeared. We are guarded and watched night and day; it doesn't matter to me . . . [deletion] Don't worry, nothing will happen to me. The Assembly wants to treat us leniently. Adieu . . . [deletion] I can't write any more . . . [deletion][9]

The deletions which crop up so frequently in Marie-Antoinette's letters to Axel were made by Axel's great-nephew, Baron Klinckowström, who edited the letters for publication and then destroyed the originals. He always staunchly denied that the Queen and Axel were lovers, but another coded letter she wrote after Varennes, received by Axel from Mercy on 4 July, escaped Klinckowström's censorship and tells a quite different story.

I can tell you I love you and I have only time for that. I'm well. Don't worry about me. I wish I could know you were too. Write to me in code through the post: address it to M. de Browne . . . with a

second envelope to M. de Gougens. Get your valet to write the ad-
dresses. Let me know to whom I should send those I'm able to write
to you, because I can't go on living without that. Adieu, most loved
and loving of men. I embrace you with all my heart.[10]

The use of a code and two intermediaries suggests that Marie-
Antoinette had to be sure Louis XVI knew nothing of her correspondence with Axel; following the failure of their escape she doubtless
felt any promise made to her husband to end her love-affair was invalid.

After hearing news of the disastrous capture at Varennes, Axel
went as instructed to open diplomatic negotiations with Mercy at
Brussels, where he was joined by Louis XVI's brothers, Monsieur
and the Comte d'Artois. No one seemed to know exactly how to
react to news of the King's arrest. Artois wanted the émigrés and
Austrians to invade France forthwith. Monsieur was 'reserved and
embarrassed', while Marie-Antoinette's sister, Archduchess Marie-
Christine, treated Axel kindly but promised no help, and suggested
he go to Vienna to negotiate with Emperor Leopold. Axel had to
brief Gustav III, who was at Aachen, before further fruitless talks
with the Bourbon princes. He found himself the object of much attention in Brussels when people discovered his role in the ill-fated
escape, but had a poor opinion of both the French and Austrians he
had to deal with. Axel was later disgusted to find that against orders
Bouillé had given 600,000 *livres* left from the escape fund to the princes.
On 27 June he wrote to Marie-Antoinette and Louis XVI asking them
whether they wanted to give powers of regency to Monsieur, or to
negotiate with foreign countries for help. 'I am well,' he added at
the end to the Queen, 'and I live only to serve you.'[11]

Letters to Paris were exceedingly difficult to get through, and after
27 June Marie-Antoinette lacked news of her lover for many weeks.
He sent a Swedish officer, Reuterswaerd, to Paris early in July with
a letter, but Reuterswaerd was arrested in Picardy and the letter taken.
Axel himself was prevented from returning to France; in July a warrant was issued for his arrest, and his house in Paris was broken into
and documents were seized. (It was then that Eleonore Sullivan's
major-domo Franz decided to burn Axel's diaries from 1780, left
with him for safe-keeping). Others involved in the escape, including
Goguelat and Choiseul, were imprisoned.

After taking soundings in Brussels, Axel went to Aachen on 30 June to see Gustav III, who had his own ideas on how to organize an 'armed congress' to rescue the French royal family and crush the Revolution. 'The King wanted me to go to England. Suggested Crawford for that and myself for Vienna. Accepted. Sensibility of all the French for me; I was touched. Boredom and estrangement I felt for Sweden when I saw all those faces.'[12]

Axel returned to Brussels on 2 July, to discuss his mission to Vienna with Mercy, and only five days later did he find time to write to Sophie.

> My dear, kind, feeling and very tender friend, this is the first mo-
> ment of peace I've been able to give you, and my heart has real need
> of it; your own must feel all the heart-break I'm suffering, and I feel
> at this moment more than ever the need for friends. But I won't be
> discouraged and I've decided to sacrifice myself for them and to serve
> them [Louis XVI and Marie-Antoinette] as long as any hope remains.
> This idea is all that sustains me and helps me to bear patiently all my
> sorrows.[13]

He was horrified by the attitude of some French émigrés in Brussels, who were overjoyed at Louis XVI's arrest. The dangerous split in the royalist cause was fast becoming a chasm. The reactionary Comte d'Artois, supported by diehard aristocrats and the former Finance Minister Alexandre de Calonne (Marie-Antoinette's enemy), advocated force at all costs and seemed completely unconcerned by the captive King's plight. Indeed, Artois demanded that the regency be given to Monsieur, with or without Louis XVI's consent.

Axel and Quentin Crawford received their final instructions from Gustav III at Aachen on 21 July 1791. Crawford set off for England on 23 July with letters for George III and the Prime Minister, William Pitt, hoping to secure a promise of British neutrality. Axel left for Vienna the following day, arriving in the Austrian capital on 2 August after stopping at Coblenz for further dispiriting meetings with Monsieur and the Comte d'Artois. His mission was to gain Emperor Leopold's consent to an offensive alliance with Sweden against France should the Assembly fail to restore Louis XVI to power. This involved the use of Ostend to disembark Swedish troops, the provision of food and forage, and the loan of Austrian artillery. Gustav's plan was to rally royalist French troops in Normandy and then march on Paris to liberate the royal family.

Given Emperor Leopold's duplicitous character, the intrigues of the princes, and Russian and Prussian counter-proposals, Axel's task was doomed. For him, the safety of the French royal family was paramount, but he found it counted for nothing in political terms. Leopold originally promised all manner of support for his sister but steadily retreated from translating his words into deeds. While negotiating with Sweden, he simultaneously talked with the princes, signing the Declaration of Pillnitz with the Comte d'Artois and King Frederick William of Prussia. Issued on 27 August 1791 it threatened military action by all foreign power unless the French monarchy was respected. This was merely window dressing. As Leopold slyly informed the aged Austrian Chancellor, Kaunitz, 'this act commits us to absolutely nothing, and contains only general declarations without meaning'.[14] If Leopold led the Swedes on, he was no less two-faced with the princes. 'Don't do anything the French ask of you,' he ordered his sister Marie-Christine in Brussels, 'neither troops nor money. I pity their situation: but they think only of their romantic ideas and their personal interests and vendettas.'[15]

This political brinkmanship was bad news for Marie-Antoinette. By 16 September Axel was convinced the Austrians were merely prolonging his negotiations to prevent Sweden launching a campaign in 1791. 'This is shameful and dreadful for the Queen,' he noted. Baron Taube rightly suspected the Austrians wanted to cut out Sweden so they could themselves take action the following spring – to seize French territory rather than help Louis XVI. Axel thought Leopold was simply fearful of a war, though he called him 'a complete Italian', not a compliment! When he received a formal refusal to allow Swedish troops to use Ostend on 26 September 1791, he packed and left Vienna. 'Delighted to be leaving' was his comment.[16]

It was without regret that Axel also left two people who had once been very close both to him and Marie-Antoinette: the Duc and Duchesse de Polignac. When he first met the duchess at her house in Vienna on 14 August he noted that 'she cried when she saw me. I felt both pleasure and pain at seeing her'. He was hoping to talk about Marie-Antoinette but Mme de Polignac 'spoke of a thousand other things'. The Polignacs were far happier to see the Comte d'Artois and Calonne, and Axel recorded another disappointing conversation with the duchess on 24 August: '. . . she always talks of politics and very little about her friend'.[17] Determined to safeguard their own future, the Polignacs had joined the princes' camp, abandoning their old friend and benefactress the Queen to her fate.

If anything could have made Marie-Antoinette truly appreciate Axel's devotion, it must have been this betrayal. He never abandoned her and never asked anything of her, and she sorely missed him during his absence in Vienna. When their correspondence came to an abrupt halt, she was desperate to discover his whereabouts. On 12 September she asked Mercy: 'Tell me if you passed on to M. de F. a short letter I sent you for him, by a traveller, at the beginning of August. I have no news of him. What country is he in?'[18] Mercy, who favoured the Queen's negotiations with Barnave, had strong reasons for keeping her in ignorance of Axel's mission to Vienna, for Axel was opposed to any compromise with the revolutionaries. Marie-Antoinette also asked Valentin Esterhazy, now in St Petersburg, what had become of Axel, enclosing a token of her love. 'Our friend sent me a ring for you,' Esterhazy informed Axel in November, when the latter had returned to Brussels. 'I'm sending it in a box to my wife by this courier, and have told her to keep it until you ask for it.'[19]

Axel in fact received a letter from Mercy on 20 August, writing in his diary: '. . . there was also a note from the Queen in code. I was very pleased to have a means of writing to her'.[20] It must have been his reply which prompted her letter to him of 26 September 1791.

Your letter of the 28th reached me. For two months I had no news of you; nobody could tell me where you were. If I had known her address I was on the point of writing to Sophie; she would have told me where you were . . . [eight lines deleted] Here we are in a new situation since the King's acceptance [of the constitution]. It would have been nobler to have refused, but that was impossible in our circumstances. I would have preferred the acceptance to have been simple and shorter, but that's the misfortune of being surrounded only by scoundrels. Still, I assure you, it is the least evil bill to have been passed. You will judge them one day, because I'm keeping for you all that . . . [deletion] be there, I was happy to find again, since there are some papers of yours.

The follies of the princes and émigrés forced us in our actions. It was essential, in accepting it [the constitution], to remove all doubt that it was not in good faith. I believe the best way to disenchant people with all this is to seem to embrace it entirely; that will soon make them see that none of it can work. Besides, despite the letter my [Louis XVI's] brothers wrote to the King (and which, by the by, has certainly not produced the effect here they hoped for), I don't see that foreign help is that imminent, particularly by the Declaration of Pillnitz. Perhaps it's fortunate, because the more we proceed the more these wretches here will recognize their misfortune; they may even come to want foreign intervention themselves. . . .

As soon as you reach Brussels, let me know; I can write to you quite easily, as I have a safe method always available. You wouldn't believe how much everything I'm doing at the moment pains me, and that vile race of men, who say they are attached to us and have only ever done us harm, are still *enragés* at the moment. . . . I've had only one happiness, that was seeing again all those gentlemen who were imprisoned on our account, especially M. Goguelat.[21]

The mysterious item the Queen was 'happy to find again', containing some of Axel's papers, was a portfolio of correspondence entrusted to Mme Campan before the flight to Varennes.

Marie-Antoinette's summary of the French political situation in this letter displays her customary acumen and foresight. In politics she greatly resembled her mother, Empress Maria-Theresa, having inherited an instinctive grasp of political realities which seemed to elude most of the men with whom she had dealings. She had been far from idle while the rest of Europe busied itself with unproductive conferences. Seeing that the only way the royal family could survive was by reaching an agreement with their captors, she began a long correspondence with leaders of the *constitutionnel* or *enragé* faction in the Assembly – Antoine Barnave, Alexandre de Lameth and Adrien Duport – who promised freedom for Louis XVI if he accepted the constitution.

Marie-Antoinette disliked the high-handed tone this 'triumvirate' adopted towards her, complaining to Axel that they thought her 'very frivolous, incapable of undertaking anything serious, incapable even of thinking logically'. But she told Mercy she had to give them credit for 'their great frankness, strength and a real desire to restore order and consequently royal authority'.[22] Barnave wrung a decree from the Assembly on 15 July 1791 which granted the King immunity from prosecution over the flight to Varennes (it is difficult to see what crime Louis XVI had committed) and promised his restoration to power once the constitution was accepted. In return the Queen was asked to prevent foreign powers from invading France, to persuade the émigrés and Bourbon princes to return home, and to ask the Vatican to accept the Civil Constitution of the Clergy – a very tall order indeed. She was also instructed to disband the royal Bodyguard and enlist fresh 'patriotic'guards (i.e. Jacobins), which she refused to do. She had seen too many patriotic guards at the Tuileries already.

Barnave's decree of 15 July sparked off a violent republican demonstration in Paris on 17 July which was put down by force. It was hardly auspicious for the constitution, which, the Queen told Mercy, was 'a tissue of impractical absurdities.' On 16 August she informed him: 'We have reached the point where this constitution will be accepted. It is in itself so monstrous, that it's impossible for it to last long. But can we risk refusing it in our position?'[23]

Many people urged Louis XVI to reject the constitution, among them Gouverneur Morris, who was to be appointed American ambassador to France in January 1792. Although a liberal who helped draft the American constitution, he considered the model proposed for France 'such that the Almighty himself could not make it succeed without creating a new Species of Men'. After Louis XVI's formal acceptance of this 'absurdity' in the Assembly on 14 September 1791, Morris told George Washington: 'It is a general and almost universal conviction that this Constitution is inexecutable. The Makers to a Man condemn it. Judge what must be the Opinion of others.'[24]

Following the King's formal acceptance, in a long, rambling speech written by the 'triumvirate' which Marie-Antoinette trenchantly criticized, events unfolded very much as she had forecast. Former members such as Barnave were barred from sitting in the new Legislative Assembly, and the pro-republican deputies who replaced them did their utmost to overturn the constitution, which gave them, rather than the government, sweeping powers. Louis XVI obediently played by the rules, appointed *constitutionnel* ministers and tried to persuade the émigrés to return to France, but was forced to sign decrees which grew ever more illiberal and extreme. If he vetoed them he could expect a riot at the Tuileries.

This political nightmare was exacerbated by what was virtually a civil war between republicans and royalists in Provence, as well as hyper-inflation. The economy had collapsed. Some idea of the scale of France's financial ruin (to which ministerial corruption undoubtedly contributed) may be gleaned from Morris's letter to Washington: '. . . after consuming Church property to the Amount of one Hundred Millions Sterling they [the outgoing Assembly] leave this Department much worse than they found it'.[25] The Queen also proved accurate in her prediction to Axel that Barnave and his friends would themselves eventually welcome foreign intervention. Reduced to inactivity as their incompetent constitution was wrecked and France slid further into chaos, they too ended up believing only foreign troops could save them.

Axel Fersen retained a lifelong hatred for Barnave, Lameth, Duport and Lafayette, the early *constitutionnel* leaders of the French Revolution he never forgave for imprisoning Marie-Antoinette and destroying the monarchy. Their alternative name, *enragés* (literally: 'madmen'), was not inappropriate. All had applauded and even contributed to the violent destruction of the *ancien régime*, without thinking what political institutions could best replace it.

Barnave had responded to the brutal murders of Foulon and de Launay in July 1789 by casually asking, 'Is their blood then so pure?' – a remark he lived to regret. In February 1791 he had sponsored a bill which demoted Louis XVI from King to the status of 'first public functionary' and he always seemed to flirt with republicanism. The degrading captivity of the royal family, the destruction of the Church, economic disaster and unchecked savagery throughout France were hardly advertisements for the *enragés*' attempts to run the country since 1789. By mid-1791, when they finally perceived the dangers they themselves had unleashed and attempted a *rapprochement* with the monarchy to stabilize the situation, it was far too late.

Antoine Barnave, a thirty-year-old lawyer from Grenoble who in 1790 became one of the National Assembly's most gifted orators and its President, opposed Lafayette, who after Varennes proposed the immediate declaration of a republic. A mutual appraisal between the Queen and Barnave during their miserable journey back to Paris in the berline seems to have convinced them they could do business. Barnave felt he could use Marie-Antoinette to cement the Revolution: she used him to gain time, safety and to prove his political principles (in the form of the 'inexecutable constitution') unrealistic. As she pointed out to the 'triumvirate', a constitution without the necessary legal safeguards could be destroyed at will: laws with no law enforcement were useless.

Marie-Antoinette's dealings with the *enragés*, and in particular Barnave, were anathema to Axel. His outrage was fuelled not only by his diametrically opposed political views, but also, one senses, by personal and professional jealousy. After all, from July 1791 it was not he, but Barnave, who had secret meetings with the Queen at the Tuileries. Perhaps, horror of horrors, she was even attracted to the young deputy from Grenoble, whose manners and attentiveness she praised to Mme Campan. Axel must surely have agonized over Marie-Antoinette's motives in negotiating with a man hitherto her sworn enemy, and clearly regarded these discussions as a betrayal. His bitterness over the failure of Varennes intensified; after all his efforts and huge financial sacrifice, he found himself effectively marginalized, no longer the most important man in the Queen's life.

Axel vented his hurt pride and feelings repeatedly in letters to her during the autumn of 1791. 'Don't let your heart be swayed by the *enragés*,' he pleaded on 13 October, 'they are scoundrels who will never do anything for you.' His mention of the Queen's heart, rather than her mind, is highly significant. Marie-Antoinette reassured him by return of post, and again on 2 November: 'Rest assured, I shall never go over to the *enragés*; they must be used to prevent even greater ills.' Further reassurances came in subsequent letters, but it was not until she had finally spoken to him that Axel was convinced her dealings with Barnave had been both necessary and innocent. Marie-Antoinette explained that she had to appease all factions in the Revolution: 'The French are atrocious on all sides: we must be very careful that if those here have the upper hand and we have to live with them, they should have nothing to reproach us with. But one must bear in mind that if those abroad become masters once more, one must not displease them.'[26]

Acceptance of the flawed constitution nevertheless brought the royal family some semblance of liberty. They were released from twenty-four-hour surveillance, Court life resumed, and they were even cheered when they viewed illuminations in Paris to celebrate the constitution. The Queen, obeying her 'triumvirate', made several appearances at the theatre, where she was well received, but nurtured no illusions about her popularity. 'The people are still, as they were, ready to commit atrocities,' she told Axel. 'We are told they support us; I don't believe a word of it, at least not as far as I'm concerned.'[27] The affections of a paid mob were, as she well knew, volatile. One real comfort was the amnesty granted to all those imprisoned after the flight to Varennes. Marie-Antoinette was delighted to see her trusted secretary Goguelat again, and he was indispensable in the extensive and continuous correspondence she undertook to get foreign powers to come to the rescue of the royal family.

Two days after his return to Brussels on 8 October 1791, Axel wrote a long letter to Marie-Antoinette which contains frustrating deletions. After giving her a résumé of his negotiations in Vienna, he asked what she and Louis XVI wanted to be done. He also informed the Queen that Crawford had obtained assurances of British neutrality, adding: 'As M. Crawford eagerly accepted this mission, won't you send me some kind words for him which you can say better than anyone else?' Axel's next letter to her on 13 October, logged as 'No. 60', is much more personal in tone, and evidently formed part of his long private correspondence with the Queen. 'It was the fear of compromising us which prevented me from writing to you,' he declared. 'At the moment I'm drowning in paperwork. I can't return to Sweden because I'm entrusted with the King's [Gustav's] correspondence.' It would appear that Marie-Antoinette feared for Axel's safety in Brussels, where Jacobin agents were known to operate, but he had no intention of being further sidelined by returning home, even though both his father and his beloved were pressing him to do just that. Axel restated his position to Marie-Antoinette on 25 November:

> As for my departure from Brussels, despite my desire to satisfy you about it and set your mind at rest it's impossible. I'm here on the King's orders, and cannot leave. . . . He has instructed all his ministers and ambassadors to correspond with me here and to rely on what I send them. You see therefore that I cannot move. Besides, you mustn't worry, I run no risk here.[28]

Marie-Antoinette's unusual wish that Axel should go as far away as Sweden may well have increased his suspicions about her dealings with the *enragés*, and added to his determination to watch over her as closely as possible. His fear of compromising them both suggests that the deleted passages in his letters to the Queen, as in hers to him, were of an intimate nature. These deletions occur most frequently at the beginning and end of their letters, where one might expect personal messages, and also whenever Marie-Antoinette asked about Axel's health or gave details of her own. They both expressed their political views freely, so the secret must have been their love-affair. From the letters which survived and were published by Klinckowström, it seems they maintained a double correspondence, one far more private than the other.

Louis wanted the foreign powers to establish a congress without the émigrés and princes, which would decide unanimously on action to guarantee his freedom and re-establish order in France; a congress which became ever more vital in his opinion as the much-vaunted constitution delivered only increased political instability. Axel, working closely with the Baron de Breteuil, was involved in trying to set up this congress, transmitting letters and dispatches, holding discussions with foreign diplomats, and sending envoys to brief Louis and the Queen in Paris. He invariably addressed his political letters to the Queen, who seems to have assumed many of her husband's responsibilities. She certainly wrote more expressive letters than Louis.

Some letters were purely political, to be read by the King and Breteuil. If she were sure of delivery, she wrote them in her own handwriting; otherwise they could be in code (the code-book used was *Paul et Virginie*, Bernardin de Saint-Pierre's novel of 1788, a suitably romantic choice), in invisible ink, or both encoded and in invisible ink. Marie-Antoinette and Axel also used to write in pamphlets, beneath prints, on the blank pages of books, or smuggle letters through in newspapers and parcels. Mercy proved an untrustworthy intermediary; Axel warned the Queen in October 1791 that Mercy had already decoded part of a letter she had written him. He and the Austrian ambassador were on bad terms. Mercy blamed Axel for turning the Queen against her brother, Emperor Leopold, while Axel denounced Mercy as a hypocrite who promised help for the Queen but continually advised Leopold to do nothing. Couriers such as Goguelat and the Queen's faithful hairdresser Léonard were very reliable, and Eleonore Sullivan's housekeeper in Paris, Mme Toscani, was also an invaluable intermediary.

That some of these letters were strictly personal may be deduced from a few scattered remarks. On 25 November Marie-Antoinette wrote to Axel: 'There is no [deletion] for you inside, so let B[reteuil] decode it', and after a long letter on 7 December told him: 'Again today M. de Laporte, who takes everything to the King, gave him your packet [1½ lines deleted]. I shall see about the Brabant Journal, and it will surely get to me, so you will then be able to say what you want. Adieu . . . [deletion].'[29]

Axel, however, was far from satisfied with mere correspondence. He had been in Brussels only two weeks when he told Baron Taube he wanted to go to Paris for discussions with Marie-Antoinette and Louis XVI about a possible congress of foreign powers, and wrote them a 24-page report on 25 November, detailing the attitudes of other countries and warning them that if they failed to decide on a plan, they would be abandoned in favour of the émigrés. Gustav III already seemed to be listening more sympathetically to counsels from Louis XVI's brothers in Coblenz. As for Emperor Leopold, 'he is deceiving you,' Axel informed Marie-Antoinette. 'He will do nothing for you . . . he will abandon you to your fate and let the whole kingdom fall to complete ruin.' By late November, Leopold had been forced to reveal his hand. He refused point blank to take part in a congress 'on the pretext that it would be useless' now Louis XVI had accepted the constitution. This rather removed the need for Axel to venture a journey to Paris, but nothing could quench his desire to see the Queen. Knowing she would strongly oppose such a trip, he tried to forestall her objections, and perhaps Louis XVI's suspicions, by claiming it was the King of Sweden's idea: 'Answer me about the possibility of coming to see you, quite alone and without a servant, in case I receive an order from the King. He has already hinted to me his wishes on the subject.'[30]

While awaiting a reply, Axel sent the Bishop of Pamiers (a trusted aide of the Baron de Breteuil) to Paris to speak to the Queen. She was delighted to see him, and on 7 December told Axel:

> You wouldn't believe how pleased I was to see the bishop; I couldn't leave him; I would have very much liked to have written to you by him, even if only a note . . . [1½ lines deleted] He will tell you many things from me, especially about my new acquaintances and connections. I found him very harsh: I thought I'd already done a lot, and that he would admire me. Not at all. He told me quite plainly I could never do too much. But, joking apart, I'm keeping for you, for the happy time when we see each other again, a very curious volume of correspondence. . . . It's absolutely impossible for you to come here at the moment; you would be risking our happiness, and when I say it, you can believe me, because I have an extreme desire to see you.

Marie-Antoinette went on to give Axel news of the latest cabinet changes, including the appointment of Mme de Staël's lover, the Comte de Narbonne, as War Minister – 'what glory for Mme de Staël,' she added wickedly, 'and what a pleasure for her to have the whole army . . . to herself!' The Queen also told Axel how much she detested Lafayette (whom she mockingly nicknamed '*sans torts*'), and justified her dealings with the *enragés* yet again.

Can you conceive [2$\frac{1}{2}$ lines deleted] my position and the role I'm obliged to play all day? Sometimes I don't even understand myself, and I have to stop and think to see if it's really me speaking; but what can you expect? It's all necessary, and believe me, we would have been in an even worse position than we are if I hadn't immediately taken this course of action; at least we are gaining time by it, and that's all we need. . . . I haven't a moment to myself, between the people I have to see, writing, and the time I spend with my children. This last occupation, which is not the least, is my only happiness . . . [deletion] and when I'm really sad, I take my little boy in my arms, I kiss him with all my heart and that consoles me for a moment.[31]

This last sentence may well have had special significance for Axel. The six-year-old Dauphin, Marie-Antoinette's *Chou d'Amour*, adored his mother, according to Mme de Tourzel, who also records the hours the Queen spent writing letters that winter. She was often up until 2 a.m., writing to the various courts of Europe, pressing for action to resolve the crisis in France – a crisis which she warned Axel was worsening by the day. Her republican enemy Pétion was appointed Mayor of Paris on 15 November 1791, which did not promise tranquillity for the capital.

Help, however, seemed as far away as ever. Reluctantly obeying Marie-Antoinette's orders, Axel remained in Brussels, but in late December 1791 he sent Crawford (accompanied by Eleonore Sullivan) to Paris to speak to the Queen. Crawford was led to Marie-Antoinette's apartments by Goguelat for a private audience the day after his arrival. Many further meetings with her followed, and he left an interesting description of the Queen, now aged thirty-six and with white hair.

Marie-Antoinette had more brilliance than beauty. Taken separately, her features were not at all striking, but together they had the greatest charm; and the expression, so often used, 'full of charms', is that which suited her in all its accuracy, and best described her whole person. All her movements were graceful.[32]

Much to his disappointment Axel was continually denied the opportunity to be reunited with the Queen. She feared for his safety if he returned to France, and the Assembly's new decrees over passports made such a journey even more hazardous. While waiting discontentedly in Brussels, he received a letter from Sophie, warning him that a Swedish friend had told her he was on several occasions seen talking to a young Englishwoman at the theatre. Sophie could think only of the distress this might cause Marie-Antoinette: 'I'm warning you, my dear Axel, for the love of *Her*; if this news is carried to her it could cause her mortal grief. Everybody watches you, and talks about you. Think of *Her* unhappiness, and spare *Her* the most mortal of all pains. . . .'[33]

Love surely played a large part in Axel's desire to see Marie-Antoinette. He had actually made arrangements to leave for Paris when he received yet another letter on 3 February 1792. 'Letter from *Her*,' he noted dejectedly, 'telling me that because of individual passports it's impossible for me to come and I must give it up. This is bad for me and for business.'[34] The 'business' was a fresh escape plan proposed by Gustav III, which Taube sent to Axel on 16 December 1791:

His Majesty [Gustav] wants the King of France and the Queen to leave France. He thinks that if they don't succeed in getting out of France, efforts to deliver them from the hands of their assassins may perhaps be in vain. . . . Only the English must be employed in this: they alone are bold and generous enough.

Gustav suggested that Louis XVI should escape alone, but if the whole royal family wanted to leave, they should split up and, heavily disguised, take different routes to the Channel coast. They would then embark on an English ship and sail for the Netherlands. 'Your situation is violent,' he told Marie-Antoinette, 'and violent means must be used to extract you from it.'[35] Gustav nevertheless fully appreciated that Louis XVI might refuse to separate from his family, or dislike relying on his traditional enemies, the British. Marie-Antoinette, however, had many English friends.

Axel was sworn to secrecy on this plan, making a meeting with the Queen even more imperative, since he could not ask Crawford to discuss it with her. On 6 February 1792 he decided to make his much-postponed trip to Paris after receiving a letter from her saying Louis XVI would veto the decree on passports. Three days later Axel was visited by the Russian ambassador to France, Baron Simolin, who had been sent by Marie-Antoinette to persuade Russia and Austria to agree to a congress. 'I fear nothing', she had told Simolin, 'and I would rather face every possible danger than continue to live in the state of degradation and unhappiness I am in.'[36]

Axel surely thought his new escape plan most apropos after hearing this. His journey, however, was still extremely risky, and he took great precautions to avoid detection. He and his aide Reuterswaerd set off from Brussels on Saturday, 11 February, using 'couriers' passports for Portugal under false names'. Gustav III's letters for Louis XVI were concealed in an envelope addressed to the Queen of Portugal, and Axel carried a forged letter to her from Gustav for added authenticity. At Gournay, where the two Swedes spent a night, they were told by the local commandant they would never get to Paris in less than a fortnight and were in constant danger of arrest, but he fortunately proved to be mistaken. 'I kept myself well hidden and I had a wig,' Axel wrote in his diary. 'People were very polite everywhere, especially at Peronne, even the *gardes nationales*.' He and Reuterswaerd arrived without incident in the French capital at 5.30 p.m. on Monday, 13 February 1792.

In an official account of his journey to Taube, Axel stated that he saw both Louis XVI and Marie-Antoinette that evening,

> . . . and again the following evening, at midnight. I left again and to avert suspicion I was obliged to go as far as Tours, and came back by Fontainebleau. I returned to Paris on the 19th. . . . I didn't dare risk going to the château [Tuileries]. I wrote to see if they had any orders to give me, and I left at midnight on the 21st. . . . It is impossible that my journey will ever be discovered.[37]

Most of this letter was a fabrication. Axel's diary reveals what he had to keep secret at all costs: his final reunion with Marie-Antoinette.

M[onday] 13. Very fine and mild. . . . Arrived without incident at

Paris at 5.30 p.m. without anyone saying anything to us. Left my officer [Reuterswaerd] at the Hôtel des Princes, rue de Richelieu. Took a fiacre to go to Gog[uelat]'s house, rue Pelletier. The driver didn't know the street. Afraid he wouldn't find it. Another driver pointed it out to us. Gog. wasn't there; waited in the street until 6.30 p.m. He didn't come, that worried me. Wanted to go and pick up Reuters. – he hadn't found a room at the Hôtel des Princes, nobody knew where he had gone. Returned to Gog's. He hadn't come in. Decided to wait in the street. At last he came at 7 p.m. My letter didn't arrive until midday today and they couldn't find him before. Went to see *Her*; passed through my usual way. Afraid of the *gard nat*.] Marvellous relief. Didn't see the King [*stayed there*].

T[uesday] 14. Very fine and mild. Saw the King at six in the evening. . . .[38]

Axel and Marie-Antoinette therefore spent a whole night and day together before his meeting with Louis XVI. The '*stayed there*' (not sufficiently smudged out either by Axel himself or Klinckowström) suggests that they made love. Marie-Antoinette had been afraid to let Axel come to Paris earlier lest he 'risked their happiness', despite her 'extreme desire' to see him. She had to be sure of absolute privacy for this rendezvous. After so many frustrating delays, it must have been, as he noted, marvellous to know he was still the Queen's 'most loved and loving of men', her one true and lasting passion. Perhaps it was more than mere coincidence that their night together was St Valentine's.

The deception Axel always employed when referring to his liaison with Marie-Antoinette is strikingly illustrated in the diary entry for his official meeting with her and Louis XVI at 6 p.m. on 14 February. On 13 February she is *Elle*, the woman he adored, whom he visited in secret through his 'usual way'. The next day, when she and Louis XVI tell him what happened at Varennes and give details of their current position, she is 'the Queen'. This meeting could be recorded unambiguously. Her *affaire de coeur* could not. Axel's total silence about what they said in those twenty-three hours alone together after their long separation in itself speaks volumes. Doubtless many lovers' secrets were exchanged. One thing is apparent: Marie-Antoinette allayed Axel's suspicions about her negotiations with the *enragés*, not only by making love to him but by suppressing some details which would still have made him furiously jealous. She told him she was

seeing Alexandre de Lameth and Adrien Duport, studiously avoid-
ing all mention of Barnave, whom Axel so hated. She also gave him
the 'volume of curious correspondence' she had saved for him – all
the letters between her and the *enragés*, accompanied by her own
commentary. The Queen wanted to be sure her lover could reproach
her with nothing, even in politics. Axel took great care of this 'portfolio', which eventually ended up in his family archives in Sweden.

Discussing business with Louis XVI must have been a real anti-
climax after this long-awaited lovers' reunion. Even more so when
the King flatly rejected Gustav III's plan of escape. Never was his
weakness, lack of initiative and self-apologetic ingratitude more apparent than in the conversation Axel recorded on 14 February 1792.

> Saw the King at six in the evening. He doesn't want to leave, and he
> cannot because of the extreme surveillance; but in truth he has scruples
> about it, having so often promised to stay, because he's an honour-
> able man. He has nevertheless consented that when the armies arrive
> he will go with smugglers through the forests to meet a squadron of
> light troops. He wants the congress at first to make only demands,
> and if they are granted, to insist then that he is allowed out of Paris
> to go to a specified place for the ratification. If there is a refusal he
> agrees to let the Powers take [military] action, and will undergo all
> dangers. He doesn't believe he will run any risk, since the rebels need
> him to obtain a capitulation. . . . Then he said to me: 'Ah, well, we
> are amongst ourselves and can speak openly. I know I'm charged with
> weakness and indecision, but nobody has ever been in my position. I
> know I've lost my chance, I lost it. It was 14 July [1789]. It was
> necessary to go then and I wanted to, but what could I do when
> Monsieur himself begged me not to leave, and the Maréchal de Broglie,
> who commanded the army, replied: 'Yes, we could go to Metz, but
> what are we going to do when we get there?' I lost my chance then
> and I've never found another since. I've been abandoned by every-
> one. . . .' The Queen told me she was seeing Alex. Lameth and Duport,
> that they constantly told her there was no other remedy but foreign
> troops; without them all would be lost. . . .[39]

Louis XVI's dismissive forgetfulness of the chance he threw away
at Varennes must have been truly galling for Axel and the Queen.
Those who tried to assist him shared the dreadful consequences of
his inertia. His country too suffered calamitous bloodshed; Louis XVI

continually claimed he did not want a civil war, but his failure to take an iron grip on France gave rise to the Terror, civil war and foreign wars in which hundreds of thousands of his innocent subjects perished. Marie-Antoinette may well have favoured Gustav's plan. Axel reported to his King on 29 February that 'The Queen especially recognizes all the advantages [of an escape], and assures me the failure of their first attempt would never stop them from a second.'[40] He may even have begged her to leave France alone. She told Mme de Tourzel she had been offered 'a safe means of escape', but only for herself, which she could not possibly accept, since it meant leaving behind her children.

At 9.30 p.m. on 14 February Axel left the Queen, telling her he was going to Tours as though he really were a courier, and would return to Paris the following week. He told Taube the same story, but it was quite untrue. Axel was afraid of being recognized anywhere in France, and instead he spent the next six days holed up in the attic of Crawford's Paris house. Crawford, however, did not know, which probably explains why Axel lied to the Queen, since she was seeing Crawford quite regularly at the Tuileries. The gossip of royal servants after Varennes may well have made Axel conclude that the fewer people who knew his whereabouts the better.

Eleonore Sullivan got her servants to smuggle Axel food and firewood (by 20 February the streets were covered with a foot of snow), and he whiled away the time by reading five novels and Bligh's story of the *Bounty* mutiny. When Crawford and Eleonore were out, Axel sent for Reuterswaerd, who had to obtain their return passports for Brussels from the Swedish chargé d'affaires, Bergstadt. Axel's excessive caution was justified. Reuterswaerd told him 'that he had been obliged to give his name to the police, and decided to give the real one'. On 18 February Axel learnt that 'twenty-one people were arrested at Senlis. That worried me, but I should be able to get through somewhere else'. Bergstadt nevertheless insisted on seeing him before handing over the passports (Axel was to travel as Reuterswaerd's lackey). At a nocturnal meeting in the snow-filled street, Bergstadt released the passports, seemingly 'terrified' of the whole business.

On Tuesday, 21 February, Axel slipped out of his hiding place at 6 p.m. to make final preparations to leave with Reuterswaerd. He then returned openly to Crawford's house, where he received a visit from Goguelat and a letter from Marie-Antoinette. There was no call to return to the Tuileries. He had supper with Crawford and Eleonore, and left them at midnight. Reuterswaerd was fifteen minutes late for their rendezvous, and after going to his inn to pick up Axel's 'little dog Odin', who must have been staying with the Queen at the Tuileries, they finally set off. 'At 1 a.m. we got into the carriage. I had nothing in my pockets which could betray me, nor did he; nevertheless I was not very reassured, and as it was Mardi Gras there were a lot of drunken *gardes nationales* about. It was because of this that I didn't leave yesterday as I wanted to.'

The two Swedish 'couriers', chilled to the bone, eventually reached Brussels at 3 a.m. on 23 February, after being stopped once at a little village near Cambrai and having their passports examined. 'I was overjoyed at having succeeded so well,' wrote Axel, 'and of finding myself at home.'[41] His longed-for reunion with Marie-Antoinette had passed off beautifully, and remained a total secret. Little did he realize he had kissed her for the last time.

11

The Death of Kings

Back in Brussels, Axel continued to prod foreign powers to intervene in French affairs. Austria and Prussia formed an alliance on 7 February 1793 which promised at least a united response to the French Revolution, but Sweden's calls for military intervention went unheeded. Like Marie-Antoinette, Axel realized the situation in France was swiftly reaching crisis-point, and he was desperate for action. Whilst awaiting reactions to the congress suggested by Louis XVI, he received some surprising news: '*8 March*. The Bishop [of Pamiers] came at half-past seven to tell me the Emperor had suddenly died.'[1]

Leopold's unexpected demise produced immediate political change. He was succeeded by his son Francis, known as the King of Hungary until the German states elected him Emperor Francis II. Greatly influenced by his uncle Joseph II, Francis was far more warlike than his father. Axel now entertained real hopes that decisive steps to help Marie-Antoinette were imminent, but another royal death in March 1792 was destined to reduce his own role in affairs considerably: Gustav III was assassinated.

Gustav died as he had lived – dramatically. On 16 March 1792 he received an unsigned note warning him not to attend a masked ball at the opera-house in Stockholm. Gustav ignored it, and, dressed with his usual flair, made a conspicuous entrance. He mingled with guests for several minutes before one of them, Count Horn, touched his arm and cried out: '*Bonjour, beau masque!*' It was the prearranged signal for Gustav's assassin, Jakob Anckarström, who fired a shot at the King before fleeing into the crowd. Gustav fell, seriously wounded but still conscious, and terrified guests tried to leave. Anckarström might have avoided detection had Baron Armfelt, Gustav's quick-thinking equerry, not ordered the opera-house to be sealed off and everyone present to unmask and be searched as they left. Despite these precautions, Anckarström and his fellow-conspirators succeeded in getting out, but their behaviour aroused suspicion. Anckarström was arrested the following day with Counts Liliehorn (who had written the warning note), Horn and Ribbing. Other conspirators were rounded up later, although one, Baron Bielke, took poison before he could be caught.

It was rumoured that Gustav too may have been poisoned, since he showed signs of recovering before dying suddenly on 29 March 1792. He bowed out in style, asking that the conspirators be treated leniently, and summoning his children and his estranged wife for a tearful farewell. He also said a fond goodbye to Senator Fersen, who was now an invalid, and gave him a message for Axel. Gustav's affection for the Fersens was shared by his son, King Gustav IV Adolf. Sweden, however, was now ruled by a regent, Gustav III's brother Karl, Duke of Södermanland, who was suspected of involvement in the King's assassination.

Duke Karl and his intimate friend Baron Reuterholm (whom he immediately appointed to a high cabinet post) were adepts of the Illuminati, a secret society established in 1776 which also boasted the Duc d'Orléans's sister as a member. The Illuminati, closely linked to both freemasonry and the Jacobins, zealously preached the doctrines of liberty and equality. Their founder Adam Weishaupt, believing that property was a barrier to equality and political institutions a bar to liberty, advocated the abolition of all religious and civil laws which underpinned existing social and political structures. The connection with rabidly anticlerical and republican Jacobin tenets was obvious. It was highly alarming for monarchists like Axel Fersen to find Baron Reuterholm in charge of Swedish policy. Reuterholm was initiated into the Illuminati in Avignon in 1789, had several 'illuminated' friends in the French National Assembly, and seemed willing to recognize the new regime in France. Gustav's plans for another escape attempt by the royal family and a Swedish invasion of Normandy were abandoned.

Axel was overwhelmed when he received news of Gustav's death. On 17 April, having mastered his grief a little, he told Marie-Antoinette: 'You will have heard the sad and devastating news of the King's death. You have lost in him a firm support, a good ally, and I have lost a protector and friend. This death is cruel.'[2] Gustav would have been consoled to know that tears were shed for him in the Tuileries. When Marie-Antoinette told her daughter of his death, young Madame, who remembered him with great affection, 'threw herself into her [mother's] arms and then into the King's in the most touching manner'. Mme de Tourzel, who noted with disgust Jacobin rejoicing over Gustav's murder, wrote: 'The Queen burst into tears as she told me of the death of this prince.'[3]

Swedish support for the French royal family had now officially evaporated, and Axel was apprehensive he might be recalled home. He was, however, determined to remain in Brussels to help Marie-Antoinette, since he alone was in charge of her foreign correspondence. On 24 April 1792 he told the Queen:

> I still have no news concerning my position, and I don't know if I will be kept on or not. My father is pressing me to go home and abandon everything, which is what I shall never do, even were I reduced to poverty. I have enough possessions to live for some time yet by selling them. . . . I have made up my mind; nothing in the world could make me abandon everything at this moment.[4]

Axel thought his father might persuade Duke Karl to abolish his post and stop his salary, but his fears were unfounded. Despite his lukewarm interest in the survival of the French monarchy, Duke Karl hedged his bets by keeping Axel in place in the event of a successful counter-revolution. In April 1792 this seemed a definite possibility, for Austria and Prussia were now committed to military action after a French declaration of war. Without active Swedish participation in the 'armed congress', Axel nevertheless found his usefulness and influence severely limited, and his ability to assist Marie-Antoinette was undermined.

At the Tuileries, the royal family feared they might be killed before foreign help arrived. Gouverneur Morris heard that Emperor Leopold's sudden death was 'attributed to poison'. This rumour emanated from no lesser source than the Austrian Chancellor Kaunitz, and after Gustav's assassination royalists everywhere trembled. On 6 April 1792 Morris informed George Washington: 'Those who conceive the French Jacobins to be at the bottom of a great King-killing Project, approach the Deaths of the Emperor, the King of Sweden, and the Movements making against France, from whence they infer that the King of Prussia should take care of himself and be cautious of his cooks and Companions.'[5]

Louis XVI also took extreme care. His loyal Minister of the Household, Arnaud de Laporte, suspected a plot to poison the entire royal family, for Jacobins had successfully ousted 'aristocratic' cooks from the Tuileries' kitchens. For several weeks Louis XVI, Madame Elisabeth and Marie-Antoinette pretended to eat what was put before them. As soon as the footmen had withdrawn, the meals were thrown away. Mme Campan and the King's valets then brought in fresh food they had bought outside. Louis XVI seemed happy enough as long as he received a plentiful supply of his favourite pastries, but the Queen was far from calm. Not long after his return to Brussels, she wrote to Axel complaining she had not heard from him. His letters were being intercepted. Marie-Antoinette asked him to get Eleonore Sullivan to instruct her Paris housekeeper, Mme Toscani, to transmit letters. This had to be done without Crawford's knowledge, since he did not like Eleonore meeting the Queen's messenger, the Chevalier de Jarjayes. Eleonore was only too happy to help, and letters packed in shirts and biscuits started travelling between Brussels and Paris.

Marie-Antoinette was in an exceedingly perilous position in March 1792. On 13 March Axel heard of the arrest of the *constitutionnel* Foreign Minister M. de Lessart, who was wrongly suspected of being a member of an inner 'Austrian' cabinet controlled by the Queen. A letter from Crawford in Paris on 18 March worried him even more: 'The Jacobins plan to put the Queen in a convent or take her to Orléans to be confronted with M. de Lessart . . . on 10 March M. Vergniaud said in the Assembly: "Terror must now enter that palace from whence it has issued so many times; everybody inside must tremble; there is only a single person [the King] who is inviolable."'[6]

Marie-Antoinette took these threats seriously enough to burn many more of her papers, but her planned arrest failed to materialize. The Assembly turned its fire instead on the Dauphin, claiming the right to appoint his governor and dictate his education. Goguelat, on his way to Vienna to speak to Francis II on Marie-Antoinette's behalf, arrived at Axel's house in Brussels on 23 March and told him the royal family's situation was 'horrifying'.

Marie-Antoinette still maintained a brave public face, and in her letters to Axel always sounded optimistic; but when she said goodbye to Quentin Crawford on 14 April 1792, her guard slipped a little.

As war seemed imminent, Crawford and Eleonore were leaving for Brussels before they became trapped in Paris. 'I went to take my leave of the Queen in the evening,' he later wrote: 'She received me in her little mezzanine room. At about nine o'clock I left her. She led me out through a narrow room, full of books, which opened into a dimly lit corridor. She opened the door for me herself, and stopped awhile to speak to me; but, hearing someone in the corridor, she went back in.'

'I have no illusions,' she told Crawford, 'there is no more happiness for me.' Axel would have been distraught had he heard her then calmly assert that although she thought her husband in no danger, she herself would most certainly be killed by the Jacobins.[7] The day after parting from Crawford, Marie-Antoinette informed Axel that Goguelat had received assurances from Francis II that Austrian help was at last forthcoming; 'they are absolutely insisting on war here,' she added. 'So much the better if it makes everybody make up their minds, because our position is no longer bearable.'[8]

The war he had so long avoided was in fact thrust upon Louis XVI by his own government. On 20 April 1792 he went reluctantly to the National Assembly to declare war on Austria for failing to disarm and sustaining armed émigrés on French borders. The panic generated by this declaration caused most people to overlook the appearance of another instrument of destruction which received its first public trial five days later. At 3.30 p.m. on 25 April the guillotine claimed its first victim on the Place de Grève – a thief named Pelletier was the unfortunate man who initiated this 'humane' form of execution.

The die was cast. The fortunes of war would decide whether *constitutionnels* or Jacobins ruled France. Both factions were hated by the royal family. The *constitutionnels* who were responsible for their parlous position would probably abandon them if the war went badly, while the Jacobins, having all but destroyed the constitution, made no secret of their desire to overthrow the monarchy. Marie-Antoinette and Axel hoped a swift victory by Austrian and Prussian forces would deliver the royal family from imprisonment at the Tuileries. Correspondence was now exceptionally difficult, since letters to Brussels had to cross battle lines, but Marie-Antoinette still managed to write to Axel, and even, very unwisely, sent him details of French military preparations on the northern frontier.

Gouverneur Morris was assured by Prussian and Austrian diplomats on 20 May 1792 that the Prussian army commanded by the Duke of Brunswick would undoubtedly reach Paris by the middle of June, and their early successes against disorganized French troops seemed to make this a realistic date. Many people left Paris for safety, among them Antoine Barnave, who asked for a final audience with the Queen. Mme Campan recorded that he kissed Marie-Antoinette's hand and wished her well, but predicted she would be lost before help arrived. He offered her an escape plan, but the *enragés* recommended to carry it out were not deemed trustworthy. The Queen never forgot who was responsible for her predicament.

If Marie-Antoinette still spent most of her nights occupied with correspondence, Louis XVI probably slept soundly enough. During the spring of 1792 he sank back into total apathy. 'The King,' wrote Mme Campan, 'lapsed into a despondency which extended even to physical prostration. For ten consecutive days he didn't utter a word, not even to his family, except at the games of *tric-trac* he played with Madame Elisabeth after dinner, when he was obliged to pronounce words necessary to this game.'[9] The Queen eventually begged him on her knees to speak. He responded by embracing her and then bursting into tears. His mind was full of tragedy and gloom; his habitual reading, according to Bertrand de Moleville, the only minister he trusted, was a history of the English Civil War containing a detailed account of Charles I's trial and execution. Certainly no one could expect Louis XVI to take a grip on a desperate situation. He was merely studying how to die with dignity.

A Jacobin triumph in France was by no means a foregone conclusion that spring. Though the Jacobins could call on the support of a murderous army of 'patriotic' citizens from the poorest sections of Paris, many ordinary Parisians were now heartily sick of a revolution which had failed to deliver promised liberty and prosperity. On 25 May 1792, Gouverneur Morris had a long conversation with his tailor, Roubet, who was an officer in the Garde Nationale: 'He speaks of the present Administration as a Set of Scoundrels and the Jacobin Club as being the most abominable Tyranny. The ancien Régime so much complained of never, he says, affected him or others in his Line of Life, but the present System renders the whole Community miserable.'[10]

Such disaffection in the Garde Nationale was dangerous. The

Assembly, evidently fearing a successful royalist *coup* in Paris now foreign troops were ready to advance into northern France, ordered Louis XVI to disband his Bodyguard and replace it with a new 'patriotic' guard. Compliant as ever, he yielded to his enemies. M. d'Hervilly, an officer in the Bodyguard, suggested that instead of dismissing his 1800 loyal men the King use them to surround the Assembly and arrest Jacobin deputies. The Queen, Mme de Tourzel noted, seemed to favour the idea, but left the decision to Louis XVI, who refused d'Hervilly's offer. Gouverneur Morris, who presented his credentials as American ambassador at the Tuileries on 3 June 1792, paints a picture of a hopeless King – 'his Tone of Voice and his Embarrassment mark well the Feebleness of his Disposition'.[11]

Louis XVI was not, however, blind to the danger of allowing an armed camp of 20,000 '*fédérés*' to be established in Paris to celebrate 14 July. The Jacobins planned to draft in supporters from the Midi to deliver the final blow against the constitution and monarchy. Failing that, Morris informed Thomas Jefferson, the entire Assembly would leave Paris before the enemy armies arrived, taking the royal family with them as hostages. Louis XVI made one last futile stand against this onslaught. He vetoed the decree summoning the *fédérés*, and another banishing priests who refused to accept the constitution. On 15 June 1792 he also sacked three Jacobin ministers, and on 17 June the Assembly received a Jacobin petition demanding the abolition of the monarchy. It was the prelude to another serious riot in Paris.

Watching events from afar, a desperately anxious Axel monitored the slow build-up of Austrian and Prussian forces, and devoured any newspaper reports he could get from Paris. Letters from Marie-Antoinette were now little more than paragraphs in invisible ink inserted in innocuous decoy letters written by Goguelat. Axel was exceedingly sceptical about Austrian motives in the war and made use of *carte blanche* from Louis XVI and Marie-Antoinette to negotiate with Prussia to prevent the Austrians seizing French territory. He was also terrified the royal family would be taken off as hostages by the Jacobins. 'Prussia is good, it's the only country you can count on,' he told Marie-Antoinette on 2 June. 'Vienna still plans to dismember [France] and to negotiate with the *constitutionnels*. . . . Try to keep the war going, and don't leave Paris.' On 11 June he sounded very alarmed. 'My God! How your situation pains me; my soul is deeply and grievously affected. Just try to stay in Paris and help will come.'[12]

Undoubtedly the Austrians' double-game slowed the advance of Prussian forces. The Jacobins capitalized on the delay to strengthen their hand. Overruling Louis XVI's veto, they summoned *fédérés* to Paris, and also staged a terrifying demonstration of their power. At 4 p.m. on a cool, wet 20 June 1792 the Tuileries was invaded by a 30,000-strong mob screaming for the blood of 'Monsieur and Madame Veto'. They wore tricolour sashes and cockades, Jacobin *bonnets rouges*, and were armed with axes, pikes, swords and pistols. The Paris Municipality had organized the whole event. Two municipal officials ordered the Garde Nationale to open the palace gates to prevent the mob from being crushed, and locked doors inside the Tuileries were then smashed open with axes.

Louis XVI was defended by two loyal battalions of the Garde Nationale. As the first 'patriots' stormed the King's apartment, his guards shoved him into a window embrasure and parried axe blows aimed directly at his head. Madame Elisabeth, who ran in to see what was happening, was almost mistaken for the Queen and attacked. She was saved by guards who formed a defensive hedge around her. The Queen, playing with her children in the Dauphin's room, was rescued just as the mob broke in and was hauled off to the cabinet room where she was defended by 200 guardsmen who made a rampart out of the cabinet table. She sat there for two hours as *sans-culottes* and *poissardes* filed past, hurling abuse at her and threatening to kill her. Not until it was clear that the assassination attempt on the royal family had failed did Mayor Pétion turn up and send his loyal citizens home after thanking them for their brave demonstration. When Marie-Antoinette was reunited with Louis XVI at 8 p.m. his powdered hair was still crowned by the *bonnet rouge* given him by a *sans-culotte*. His diary entry for this momentous day was laconic in the extreme: 'Affair at the Tuileries'.

The *journée* of 20 June was by no means an unqualified success for the Jacobins. A petition supporting the King was signed by 20,000 people in Paris, Pétion's arrest was demanded, and the whole of Picardy sent offers of assistance to Louis XVI. As usual, he failed to take advantage of this favourable popular mood. Bertrand de Moleville suggested he ride out openly from Paris with his guards; public indignation over 20 June would guarantee the royal family's safety, but Louis would not budge. 'I could see very clearly they wanted to kill me,' the King told Bertrand on 21 June, 'and I don't know how they didn't manage it. But I shan't escape them another day, so I'm no further forward. It doesn't matter whether one is assassinated two months sooner or later.' Bertrand insisted that escape was the only course of action. 'Oh! I don't want to flee a second time,' exclaimed the King. 'I found myself in too bad a position over it.' When Bertrand suggested he ought at least to ensure his family's safety, Louis XVI displayed astonishing insensitivity. Despite constant threats against the Queen and several attempts to murder her, he declared he thought she and her children would be in no danger if he were killed. 'Yes, I believe so,' he insisted. 'I hope so at least. And if it happens otherwise, I shan't have to reproach myself with being the cause.'[13]

This was unforgivable. Louis clearly blamed the flight to Varennes for his precarious position. Was it to punish Marie-Antoinette that he now insisted she expose herself and the children to the death his inertia would surely bring on them?

Axel received an account of 20 June from the Swedish chargé d'affaires in Paris, which made him shudder. On 30 June 1792 he wrote to Marie-Antoinette:

> Your position torments me ceaselessly. . . . Try not to leave Paris . . . then it will be easy to reach you and that's the Duke of Brunswick's plan. His entry will be preceded by a strong manifesto, in the name of the allies, which will hold the whole of France and Paris in particular responsible for the royal family. Then he will march straight on Paris.[14]

Brunswick's troops, however, were still awaiting orders. Staying in Paris without protection was hardly a sensible idea, but Axel feared the Jacobins would carry off his Queen and kill her if she proved to be a useless bargaining counter. She replied to his letter on 3 July: 'Our position is dreadful but don't worry too much. I have courage, and something in me tells me we will soon be happy and safe. Only this idea sustains me. . . . Adieu. When shall we see each other again in peace?'

Four days later she reassured him again. 'Don't torment yourself too much about me,' she wrote in code, and added: 'Hasten, if you can, the help which is promised for our deliverance.' A footnote in invisible ink was less comforting. 'I still exist, but it's a miracle. The *journée* of the 20th was terrible. It's no longer me they hate the most, they want even my husband's life. They conceal it no longer.'[15]

Axel, trembling for Marie-Antoinette but still hopeful the Prussians would reach Paris in time, busied himself with Mercy and the Marquis de Limon in drawing up Brunswick's manifesto. In the interim, Lafayette dashed to the French capital from his new military command on the northern frontier, hoping to resuscitate the constitution and save the very monarchy he had done so much to undermine. Success would have brought him glory and the applause he always thirsted for, but his reproaches to the Assembly fell on deaf ears, and the Garde Nationale did not give their former commander-in-chief the welcome he expected. Lafayette planned to take the royal family to Compiègne, but 'the King was very reluctant and the Queen even more so, although she told the Duc de Choiseul and others she had no opinion and it was for the King to decide'.[16] This idea in any case proved impracticable; Lafayette found 'he could not even assemble 400 [guards] to chase the Jacobins', so he returned inglorious to his army.

Early in July Marie-Antoinette wrote to press Mercy for the publication of the Brunswick manifesto, and also asked his advice on a possible escape from Paris. Mercy informed Axel he had told her to go to Compiègne and summon help from royalist troops in Amiens and Soissons. Axel also received definite news of an escape plan from the Queen, and wrote to her on 10 July: 'M. Lasserez and M. Léonard have arrived and given me your letters. I have no need to tell you that they gave me great pleasure.' He went on to warn her 'to be very careful that you are certain, before you attempt it, of the courage and fidelity of those who must protect your route, because if it fails you will be lost without resource, and I cannot think of it without trembling'.[17] This escape was devised by the Interior Minister, Terier de Monciel, and the American ambassador Gouverneur Morris, whom Marie-Antoinette had always trusted. 'The measures were so well arranged,' Morris later informed the Queen's daughter, 'that success was almost certain, but the King (for reasons which it is pointless to detail here) gave up the plan on the very morning fixed for his departure, when the Swiss Guards had already left Courbevoie to cover his retreat. His ministers, who found themselves gravely compromised, all tendered their resignation.'[18] Since the resignations took place on 10 July, it was probably the '*baiser Lamourette*', a false show of unity by opposite wings of the Assembly on 7 July, which deluded Louis XVI into believing he was now safe in Paris.

Events quickly proved him wrong. Hordes of heavily armed *fédérés* descended on Paris for the 14 July celebrations, and Lafayette made another unsuccessful attempt to revive his own escape plan for the royal family. On 30 July, when 600 Jacobin *fédérés* arrived from Marseilles, nobody had any doubt as to what would follow, least of all the King. 'A band of Marseillais has arrived in Paris,' he noted in his diary. 'An insurrection is planned for 10 August which will definitely topple the monarchy.'[19] Louis XVI was resigned to his fate. Nobody could now persuade him to take either defensive or evasive action. He was quite entitled to prepare his own destruction, but surrendering his family and supporters to their murderers was thoroughly reprehensible.

Brunswick's manifesto was eventually published at the beginning of August, and the Prussians were finally ready to march into France. It was far too late. Axel was clearly quite out of step with events, despite desperate bulletins from Goguelat warning of imminent danger to Marie-Antoinette and Louis XVI. On 3 August 1792 Axel (who had just been appointed special Swedish envoy to France) confidently expected Brunswick to rescue the royal family, and wrote to the Queen about the establishment of a new government, suggesting necessary diplomatic negotiations with foreign powers. In Paris, however, demands were made in the Assembly for the overthrow of the monarchy, the Marseillais fought the Garde Nationale in the streets, and the Tuileries gardens were opened to the mob.

The Jacobin plan for 10 August was set out in detail in a pamphlet which Louis XVI and many courtiers had read by 31 July. The Queen already slept with a little dog in her room to alert her to danger, but on Mme de Tourzel's insistence, moved upstairs to share the Dauphin's bedroom. The *Chou d'Amour* was delighted; unaware of impending doom, he joyfully bounced up and down on 'Maman's bed' and woke her up every morning with hugs and kisses.

In Brussels, Eleonore Sullivan, though ignorant of the attack on the Tuileries planned for 10 August, read enough newspapers from Paris to convince her that Axel's view of the situation was far too optimistic. On 7 August, after reading of calls for the royal family's annihilation, she was 'sick with worry', and suggested that Axel 'send someone to England to ask the King [George III] to do something to save their lives; to get him to say he would not tolerate any attempt on their lives and would wreak a terrible vengeance'. Axel foresaw many obstacles to this scheme, not least British neutrality and known British sympathy for certain revolutionaries. 'She replied that even with all that it should at least be tried, that one could not regret any troubles one took. . . . I had nothing to say to that and decided to speak to the Baron de Breteuil.'[20] Breteuil was very sceptical, but the following day changed his mind. The Bishop of Pamiers was immediately dispatched to London with letters for Pitt, several government ministers, and the Duke of Dorset, former ambassador in Paris.

Long before Pamiers reached the English capital, the French monarchy had fallen. The *journée* of 10 August 1792 was a resounding success for the Jacobins, not least because Louis XVI played his part in their script to perfection. In his last letter to Marie-Antoinette, on 10 August, which she could not have received, Axel wrote: 'My torment over you is extreme, I haven't a moment's peace of mind.' His anxiety increased tenfold when he received full details of that murderous day at the Tuileries.

Without doubt Louis XVI could still have saved both himself and the monarchy had he acted resolutely and been prepared to employ force against his enemies. On 8 August his ministers begged him to leave Paris for Compiègne; the Swiss Guards and several hundred gentlemen were prepared to escort him, but 'the King refused everything'. On 9 August, as the mob and the Marseillais assembled, guards were posted all around the Tuileries. The Mayor of Paris, Pétion, arrived, and disturbed to find them disposed to defend the King, sent 'patriotic' reinforcements. At 6 a.m. on 10 August Louis XVI, accompanied by the Queen, inspected the Garde Nationale, but silent and awkward, he failed to inspire them with confidence. Marie-Antoinette spoke to the men and encouraged them, as did their commandant, M. Mandat, who was summoned to the Municipality an hour later and promptly murdered.

It was all to no avail. Louis XVI had no intention of defending the Tuileries. He said he would seek shelter in the Assembly (housed in the Tuileries' riding school), although his ministers 'warned him that this was part of the plan'. At 8 a.m. the *procureur-syndic* of the Department of Paris, M. Roederer, duly arrived with an ingratiating smile.

He asked to speak to the King alone. He went with him, the Queen and the ministers into his apartment. M. Roederer asked him to go to the Assembly, as the only decision to take. The Queen strongly opposed him. M. Roederer then asked her if she would take responsibility for events, for the massacre which might take place, for the King, her children and all the gentlemen?[21]

Marie-Antoinette, recorded Mme de Tourzel, protested that the royal family could not abandon their servants, courtiers and all the people who had come to defend them, but the King was determined to surrender. When the Queen heard her husband following Roederer's advice she almost fainted. Mme de Tourzel had to leave behind her teenage daughter Pauline (whom the Dauphin adored), to accompany the royal family to the Assembly, where they were immediately taken prisoner. As usual, Louis XVI blundered even in defeat. His garbled message telling the Swiss Guards and the Garde Nationale to surrender was not properly delivered. They fired on the mob and the Marseillais who were just storming into the palace courtyards. A dreadful massacre ensued in the heat of that fine August day. Hundreds of Swiss Guards were slaughtered, as were some *gardes nationales* who had the misfortune to wear similar uniforms, and many loyal gentlemen inside the Tuileries were also butchered. Mme Campan, her sister and two other maids of the Queen were saved only by a group of Marseillais, who, to prove they were still gallant, escorted them past the bodies of two of Marie-Antoinette's footmen, and out of the palace to a small tavern.

News of this calamitous *journée* reached Brussels on 13 August. 'Terrible news from Paris,' Axel wrote tersely in his diary, then put down some gory details. 'My God, how horrible!' Two days later he sent a short letter to Baron Taube.

Silversparre [attaché at the Swedish embassy in Paris] will send you details of the execrable *journée* of the 10th; they will horrify you. The royal family exists, but how. As for me, the state I'm in is frightful. It's not living to have these continual torments. What an abominable and cowardly nation! My God, if only I could save this unfortunate family with my blood![22]

Now more than ever he bitterly reflected on the failure of the flight to Varennes. The Bishop of Pamiers's return on 21 August with assurances of British support for the French royal family (a threat against the Jacobins was instantly dispatched to Lord Gower, British ambassador in Paris) was no comfort now.

Marie-Antoinette was a prisoner in the tower of the Temple, which, she confided to Mme de Tourzel, she had repeatedly begged the Comte d'Artois to pull down. She, her children, husband, sister-in-law Madame Elisabeth and a handful of retainers spent three stifling days in the Assembly, waiting to know their fate. The few deputies there had no authority now. Paris had been taken over by an unelected Commune, headed by Danton and Robespierre, who first declared Louis XVI dethroned and then ordered his detention.

On 11 August Mme Campan and her sister managed to argue their way into the monks' cells at the Feuillants where the royal family were guarded. They found Marie-Antoinette on a bed, 'in a state of grief which cannot be described'. She held out her arms to embrace them, before bursting into tears. When she regained her composure, she sent for her children, and complained that Louis XVI's gluttony and lethargy were making a very bad impression on the Assembly. It was the last time Mme Campan saw the Queen she had served for twenty-two years. Pétion refused her permission to join the royal prisoners in the Temple on 13 August. 'I can still see that little cell in the Feuillants,' she wrote many years later, 'with its green wallpaper and miserable little bed, where our dethroned sovereign held out her arms to us.'[23]

In Brussels, Axel still hoped the advancing Prussians would reach Paris in time to crush the new regime in France. The Commune, however, acted swiftly and ruthlessly to exterminate its enemies. From 11 August 1792 Paris was a closed city. No one could leave or enter without a passport from the new authorities. On 29 August a curfew was declared and suspect houses were searched; weapons and papers were seized, and anyone important with *constitutionnel* or royalist affiliations was arrested. Mme de Tourzel, her daughter and the Princesse de Lamballe had already been carried off to the prison of La Force from the Temple on 18 August. The Queen was distraught at parting from the princess. She had begged her old friend to leave the Feuillants when she had the chance, but Mme de Lamballe insisted on sharing Marie-Antoinette's imprisonment. Her devotion cost her her life. She was one of the first victims of the September massacres, in which almost 2,000 inmates of all Paris prisons were systematically butchered – aristocrats, priests, nuns, common criminals and even juvenile delinquents. The Commune's justification for this bloodbath was that 'the *patrie* was in danger'. Prussian forces had captured several towns in northern France and were marching on Châlons; it was asserted that all these 'aristocratic' prisoners would destroy Paris unless they were killed. The Terror had begun.

Only the efforts of an official from the Commune, M. Hardy, whom she did not know, saved the royal governess Mme de Tourzel. He smuggled her daughter Pauline out of La Force on the morning of 3 September; about two hours later the Princesse de Lamballe was taken from the same cell. When, much later still, Mme de Tourzel herself was fetched by Hardy to face a kangeroo court of 'patriots', he assured her Pauline was safe, but his silence about the Princesse de Lamballe told her the Queen's oldest friend was dead. 'Mme la princesse de Lamballe was tortured for four hours in the most horrible manner,' Axel informed the Duke of Södermanland in an official dispatch. 'The pen refuses to write the details. . . .'[24] His agony was extreme. He had known the Princesse de Lamballe very well; she had even spent an evening chatting and joking with him in Brussels in October 1791 before she returned (much against Marie-Antoinette's advice) to Paris after the failure of Varennes. Now she was dead, murdered solely because she was Marie-Antoinette's friend.

On 7 September Axel received fresh news from Paris. 'All is calm at the moment,' he wrote, 'but I'm not.'[25] His grief and anxiety increased daily as it became clear that the Austrians and Prussians had no intention of marching on the French capital. Mercy, a disgraceful turncoat, even tried to dissuade Axel from urging Britain to issue another demand for the royal family's liberty (the British ambassador in Brussels, Lord Elgin, assured Axel of British goodwill). Threats and entreaties were, however, quite useless. France was declared a republic on 22 September 1792, all public symbols of the monarchy were destroyed (statues of Louis XIV suffered in particular) and Brunswick's army began to retreat. This was the final blow. Axel blamed the Austrians for the Prussian withdrawal, convinced they wanted to launch a fresh campaign the following spring to seize large swathes of French territory. The fate of Marie-Antoinette, former Austrian archduchess and deposed Queen of France, was immaterial. Immaterial except to one man who could never stop loving her, who now clung to every slender hope to stop himself sliding into despair.

12

Love Lies Bleeding

Life in the Temple for the royal family during the autumn of 1792 followed an eerily calm domestic pattern. The King and Queen gave lessons to their children every morning, and dined *en famille* after strolling in the prison garden, where Louis XVI's faithful valet Jean-Baptiste Cléry played ball with the children. In the afternoons Marie-Antoinette and Madame Elisabeth sewed, read and played with the children while the King pored over books from the prison library. The royal prisoners were denied both letters and newspapers, possibly a blessing in disguise. They had had to mourn far too many murdered friends already. News of daily atrocities in Paris and the retreat of the Prussian army supposed to rescue them would have been intolerable.

The Duke of Brunswick's evacuation of northern France in response to Austrian pressure, early in October 1792, infuriated Axel Fersen. All his months of diplomacy had been nullified. The French general Dumouriez promptly reoccupied Lille, Verdun, Stenay and other towns, then launched an assault on the Austrian Netherlands. On 7 November 1792, the Austrians removed their archives and gold from Brussels. Axel visited Mercy to ask 'if he had taken care of Josephine's diamonds' – an unmistakable reference to Marie-Antoinette's jewels, sent to Brussels for safe-keeping in 1791; but Mercy, slippery as ever, was deliberately vague about them. He left Brussels the following day with Archduchess Marie-Christine and Count Metternich.

Axel and his friends (Crawford, Eleonore and the Russian Baron Simolin) made frantic preparations to leave Brussels once it became clear that French troops would simply be allowed to walk in.

> *9 November.* It was decided to get into our carriages. They tried to persuade me to burn the portfolio containing the Queen's letters, but I did nothing of the sort. I placed it with mine in Simolin's carriage[1]

Axel had 'decided the day before to give it to Lord Elgin to be sent to England', but Eleonore Sullivan refused to part with Marie-Antoinette's portfolio when Elgin's footman came to collect it. It was an extremely precious deposit for Axel, marked on the outside in Marie-Antoinette's handwriting, '*papiers à mon ami*'. Her *ami* and his party set off at noon on 9 November for Germany. They passed hundreds of wounded soldiers and many French émigrés fleeing on foot before the French advance. With a lack of post-horses, extremely heavy traffic, and detours to skirt battle lines, it was 6 p.m. on 18 December 1792 before they finally reached the safety of Düsseldorf. Here Axel received news of Louis XVI's trial.

The King had been separated from his family since 11 December, and although he was granted defence lawyers, his fate was virtually sealed. The new Republic had to establish its legitimacy; killing Louis XVI was an effective way of depriving royalists of a cause. Popular demonstrations of support for the King once his answers to the Assembly's charges were published (there was a riot in Rouen, and unrest even in Paris) simply guaranteed his death at the hands of the Jacobins.

Axel was in torment. His intolerable suspense was exacerbated because news from Paris took a week to reach Düsseldorf, and letters were often intercepted. On 12 January 1793 a British diplomat, Mr Murray, informed him that Britain had threatened France with war unless the royal family were released and there was an immediate cessation of hostilities on the Continent. Murray also told Axel that Danton, Sainte-Foix, Robespierre and Marat were in Orléans's party. 'They want to exterminate the royal family and replace it with that of Orléans, and if they can't place the father [the Duc d'Orléans], at least they want his son [Louis-Philippe].'[2]

This rumour also reached the American ambassador in Paris, Gouverneur Morris, who passed it on to Thomas Jefferson on 21 December 1792, with the comment:

It is strange that the mildest monarch who ever filled the French throne, one who is precipitated from it precisely because he would not adopt the harsh measures of his predecessors, a man whom none can charge with a criminal or cruel act, should be prosecuted as one of the most nefarious tyrants who ever disgraced the annals of human nature.[3]

Needless to say, the Duc d'Orléans, now known as 'Philippe Egalité', sat in judgement on Louis XVI in the National Convention and voted for his execution. The King was condemned to death on 17 January 1793. 'Out of 720 voters,' Axel wrote to Taube, '35 gave disparate votes, 319 were for life imprisonment and 366 for death; that makes in all a majority of only 12.' He had to be diplomatic with Taube. To his sister Sophie, however, Axel poured out his grief and fears. He clung to the hope of a stay of execution or a successful appeal against the sentence, but was terrified about what might now happen to Marie-Antoinette.

We shan't know the latest result until tomorrow, but my fears are unimaginable. Poor, unfortunate family, poor Queen – why can't I save her with my blood! It would be the greatest happiness for me, the sweetest joy for my soul. Ah, I well feel at this moment all I should feel, all I have ever felt. Think then how wretched I am and how dreadful my position is. Yes, my dear Sophie, it's almost unbearable. . . . I don't know how I support the state I'm in. The restraint I'm obliged to maintain increases the horror still more, and yet I can't hide it, and the few people I meet perceive it but too clearly.[4]

Louis XVI had been executed three days before this letter was written. All attempts to overturn his death sentence failed. On the evening of 20 January 1793 he was reunited for an hour and a half with his family, and he himself broke the fatal news to them. Cléry described this last farewell in moving detail; with the Queen, Madame Elisabeth and the children all in floods of tears, while Louis XVI's eyes remained dry. He had already written a testament in which he begged Marie-Antoinette's forgiveness for the sorrows he had brought on her and 'for any vexations I may have caused her during the course of our union'. Louis was concerned to be seen doing his Christian duty. He sat the Dauphin on his lap and made him swear not to seek revenge for his death – but he could not bring himself to say good-bye for ever. He promised Marie-Antoinette he would see them all again at seven the following morning, knowing full well the Convention would never allow it. As he tore himself from their arms, his daughter fainted. She never saw the father she adored again.

On 21 January 1793, the thirty-eight-year-old Louis XVI was escorted from the Temple by 1600 soldiers, along the Paris boulevards to the guillotine on the Place de la Révolution (formerly Place Louis XV, now Place de la Concorde). The city and the crowds were silent. Louis XVI's last words to his subjects were drowned out by a roll of drums, but when his head was presented to them by the executioner, Sanson, at 10.20 a.m., cries of '*Vive la République!*' and '*Vive la Nation!*' rang out. The death of 'the Tyrant' did not, however, produce the carnival atmosphere some more fanciful revolutionary journalists described. 'The greatest care was taken to prevent an affluence of people,' Gouverneur Morris told Jefferson five days later. 'This proves a conviction that the majority was not favourable to that severe measure. In effect the great mass of the Parisian citizens mourned the fate of their unhappy prince. I have seen grief such as for the untimely death of a beloved parent.'[5]

Grief was certainly not confined to Paris. In Düsseldorf Axel's uncertainties over the fate of the royal family were finally, horribly, ended.

Saturday 26 [January] .... I spent the whole day in uncertainty and in a dreadful state. El[conore] cried; I was desperate at not being able to be alone with her to cry, but we were never alone. Ah, how much I felt I loved *Her* [Marie-Antoinette], and how much I suffered. At nine in the evening Baron von Lillien, Director of the Imperial Mail, came to see me . . . he had been told a courier had brought M. de Valence news that the King had been executed and the whole family massacred. . . .[6]

Axel was devastated. The false news of Marie-Antoinette's death obliterated the certainty of the King's execution from his mind. He scrawled a desperate letter to Sophie expressing all his passionate love for the Queen. Gone was his self-control, his icy reserve, that deceptive air of diplomatic reticence. Here was a man howling with grief for the loss of the woman he adored.

26 January

My tender, kind Sophie. Ah, pity me! Only you can know the state I'm in. I've now lost everything in the world. You alone and T[aube] are left for me – ah, don't abandon me! *She* who was my happiness, she for whom I lived – yes, my tender Sophie, because I have never stopped loving her, I couldn't, not for an instant, and I would have sacrificed absolutely everything for her, I well feel that at this moment – she whom I loved so much and for whom I would have given a thousand lives, is no more. Oh my God, why do you destroy me so, what have I done to deserve your anger? She no longer lives! My grief is overwhelming and I don't know how I stay alive. I don't know how I bear my sorrow, it is extreme and nothing will ever efface it; she will always be present in my memory and I shall weep for her for ever. Everything is over for me, my dear friend. Ah, why didn't I die at her side and for her – for them – on 20 June [1791]. I would have been happier than dragging out my miserable existence in eternal sorrows, in sorrows which will end only with my life, because never will her adored image be effaced from my memory, and you insulted me by even imagining for a moment it could be. You don't know me, you don't do justice to my heart. This heart is truly wretched and will be now for as long as it lives: your own feels too deeply not to pity me. Ah, I have real need now of my friends. They alone support me at the moment, and to crown my horrors at this cruel time I still have the wretched task of writing down these sad and dreadful details. I don't know how I have the strength. . . .

27th

It's midnight. We receive the sad certainty of the King's execution. My heart is so torn I haven't the strength to tell you more. There is no word of the rest of the family, but my fears are terrible. Ah, my God, save them and have mercy on me![7]

Axel's indignation at Sophie's belief that he no longer loved Marie-Antoinette indicates that the apparent cooling of their relationship in 1791 was definitely the work of Louis XVI, since the Queen's feelings for her lover never altered. Only Varennes and the interference of a husband had effectively ended Axel's liaison with the woman he called 'my happiness'.

Eleonore Sullivan wept openly and copiously when official confirmation of Louis XVI's execution was received, but Axel still had to play the diplomat. 'I was desperate at having to contain myself. The most heart-breaking memories came into my mind. I sent off a courier in the evening to inform the Regent [Duke of Södermanland], and this dispatch caused me great pain.'[8] Eleonore was his sole consolation, the only person who understood his grief, shared his tears and kept him sane. He clung to her like a drowning man, but though he was fond of her, he yearned for Marie-Antoinette. Eleonore Sullivan never could, and never did, take the Queen's place in Axel Fersen's heart – a heart which was slowly breaking as rumour and counter-rumour trickled through from Paris.

Axel correctly deduced that official silence on Marie-Antoinette and her children meant they were still alive, but he was almost crazed with fear that she would soon follow Louis XVI to the guillotine. On 31 January he, Crawford, Simolin and the Comte de La Marck discussed the possibility of asking Emperor Francis II to demand the Queen's freedom 'as a private individual' – but they were all afraid this would simply precipitate her trial. Axel, at Sophie's insistence, wrote his sister frequent letters in which his despair was all too evident. Sophie herself was indignant at the laconic way the Duke of Södermanland received news of Louis XVI's execution. Her distress at the position of the Queen she regarded almost as a sister-in-law was enormous. 'Alas, my dear Axel,' she wrote on 15 February, '*She* is not yet dead, but destined for fresh sufferings and a thousand deaths. What a position! And how it grieves me. . . . There are no words which can express the horror of her situation and my fears and my grief.'[9]

On 3 February Axel heard a horrible rumour 'that they want to declare the Dauphin a bastard, shave the Queen's head and shut her up in the Salpêtrière', a story which even reached Sweden.[10] Such tales only increased his anguish. 'My soul is so tormented and rent by memories of the loss I have just suffered and my fears for the future, that I can hardly think about anything else,' he told Sophie. 'In vain I try to console myself, in vain I want to hope, in vain the people I live with try to console me with rational arguments (which I even make myself), but they are themselves too distressed to dare to believe them.' By 9 February, however, he was calmer. 'I'm beginning to have a little hope about the fate of the Queen and her family; there is no talk either of her or her trial.'

Axel was nevertheless bitterly frustrated by his inability to do any-thing. 'I cannot be calm or reassured; sometimes I hope, then I de-spair, and the forced state of inactivity in which I find myself and the few means there are of serving her increase my pains still more.'[11] The absence of news from Paris was an added torment. 'It's been ten days now since we had any letters from Paris or Liège,' he com-plained to Sophie on 15 February, 'the French stop them all.' Obliged to remain in Düsseldorf on the orders of the Swedish government, yet unable to help Marie-Antoinette or even visit his ailing father, Axel sank into a black depression.

> I feel a constant melancholy and a disgust for everything which I cannot conquer. My ideas are always about only a single object, and the image of Louis XVI mounting the scaffold never leaves me. Often I curse the day I left Sweden, that I ever knew anything but our rocks and our firs. I would not have had, it is true, so many joys, but I'm paying very dearly for them at the moment, and I would have spared myself many pains. I cry often all alone, my dear Sophie, and with E.[Eleonore] when we can, but she herself is too upset by what has happened and by her fears for the future to be able to console me – but at least I have the consolation of crying with someone. This good woman is excessively devoted to them [the French royal family], she has made many sacrifices for them, even exposing herself to danger, and that's what made me love her.[12]

News of the royal family, good and bad, finally reached Düsseldorf on 16 February 1793. 'Letters from Paris to the Hague say the Queen has grown very thin and altered, but is well,' Axel wrote in his diary; 'that the Dauphin is charming; his guards only leave him with tears in their eyes.'[13] Less reassuring news followed, that the Duc d'Orléans was making a final attempt to seize the throne, and had paid one Paris section (a local council) to denounce the Queen to the National Convention and demand that 'Louis Capet' (the seven-year-old Louis XVII) be removed from his mother's 'corrupting influence'. The war also escalated. British revulsion at Louis XVI's execution led to the withdrawal of the British ambassador from Paris; France declared war on Britain and Holland on 1 February 1793.

Axel would have been greatly consoled had he known that Marie-Antoinette was not without friends in her hour of need. Though she was not so changed as rumour suggested, her health was failing, and it seems likely she too was slowly succumbing to the tuberculosis which had killed her mother, brother Joseph and her eldest son. In February 1793, however, in the dark, desperate days after her husband's execution, the Queen had a real prospect of escape from the nine-feet thick walls of the Temple. Her beguiling charm had had a magical effect yet again – on the commissioner from the Paris Commune who was responsible for the royal prisoners in the Temple, François-Adrien Toulan.

Thirty-two-year-old Toulan was an ardent Jacobin from Toulouse who became a devoted royalist when he met the Queen and her family in their cheerless tower. His first act of kindness was to steal back the personal objects Louis XVI bequeathed to his wife, which the Commune had seized – the King's wedding-ring, his personal silver seal, and locks of his, the Queen's and their children's hair. Toulan then became a smuggler of notes from Marie-Antoinette to her loyal servants, the Chevalier de Jarjayes and his wife, who had miraculously survived the assault on the Tuileries on 10 August and were still at liberty in Paris.

Marie Antoinette did not consider herself in any danger of a trial at this time, but Jarjayes and Toulan (who was, of course, well aware of sentiment in the Commune) were extremely concerned for her safety. Together they planned an escape for the whole family. Jarjayes made all the travel arrangements with the Queen's faithful secretary, Goguelat, while Toulan persuaded Jacques Lepître, President of the Paris Passport Committee, to provide the necessary documents in return for cash. The plan was simple. Toulan would escort the Queen and Madame Elisabeth out of the Temple disguised as *sans-culottes*, while the children would be smuggled out by Toulan's cousin, M. Ricard. Once outside the prison, and using false passports (no one could leave or enter Paris or travel anywhere in France without one), Jarjayes would immediately drive the royal *sans-culottes* to Normandy, where they would board a boat for England.

The escape was fixed for 8 March 1793; then disaster struck. Riots in Paris over bread shortages led the Commune to close all the city's gates and suspend the issue of passports. Jarjayes and Toulan were not discouraged. They postponed the escape several times. Finally it had to be abandoned, but they were still determined to save the Queen, whose position was the most dangerous. No one thought any harm could possibly befall her children or Madame Elisabeth. Marie-Antoinette hesitated. Jarjayes and Toulan begged her to leave while she had a chance, and when Madame Elisabeth seconded their arguments, the Queen agreed to make the attempt. But she found it impossible to say goodbye to her children, and wrote to tell Jarjayes she could not leave them.

> We have had a beautiful dream, that's all. But we have gained a great deal by it, in finding once more on this occasion fresh proof of your complete devotion to me. My confidence in you is limitless. You will always find in me, at all times, character and courage; but the interest of my son is all that guides me, and however much happiness I would have felt at being out of here, I cannot consent to a separation from him. . . . Be assured that I appreciate all the goodness of your reasons for my own interest, and that this opportunity may not arise again. But I could enjoy nothing if I left my children, and this idea leaves me without even a single regret.[14]

The opportunity never did repeat itself. Jarjayes had to leave France in March 1793, fearing he might be arrested. Shortly afterwards Toulan was removed from his post at the Temple. He still tried to help the royal prisoners through a man inside the prison, M. Turgy, and was guillotined for his devotion in 1794. Mme de Jarjayes was also arrested, escaping execution only by Robespierre's downfall on 9 Thermidor (27 July 1794).

When Jarjayes bade her farewell, Marie-Antoinette entrusted him with Louis XVI's 'precious relics', to be given to her brother-in-law, Monsieur. She also gave Jarjayes a cryptic message for Axel Fersen. Axel finally received it on 21 January 1794, and copied her note to Jarjayes in his diary: 'When you are in a place of safety, I would like you to give news of me to my great friend, who came to see me last winter. I don't know where he is. . . . I dare not write, but here is the impression of my seal. Tell him when you send it that the person to whom it belongs feels that it has never been more true.' 'This emblem was a seal depicting a flying pigeon', Axel noted, 'with the motto *Tutto a te mi guida*. Her idea at the time was to take my arms and she took the flying fish for a bird.'[15]

Marie-Antoinette could no more stop loving Axel than he could her – her belief in *Tutto a te mi guida* ('Everything guides me to thee') is ample proof she still hoped to be reunited with him. Why she did not get Jarjayes to involve Axel in the escape plan is puzzling. They could surely have discovered his whereabouts from the Swedish embassy in Paris. Marie-Antoinette probably thought he was in Sweden, and doubtless feared he would be needlessly risking his life, since Jarjayes and Toulan were quite competent. However, there is no doubt that Axel's persuasion would have had a far greater effect than theirs, and might have convinced her to leave while it was still possible.

Axel's only hope that bleak March of 1793 was that the Queen would be kept alive as a hostage. He was denied the consolation of knowing she still loved him and was thinking of him. Instead on 13 March he received a bombshell from Sweden: 'The Duke has given me the London embassy. It was a bolt from the blue for me. I saw myself obliged to leave F.[leonore] and to remove myself from *Her* and from affairs which put me in a position to serve *Her* and to contribute to her liberation.'[16] The following day he refused this prestigious diplomatic post, unwilling to be diverted from affairs which kept him, however tenuously, connected to France. Two weeks later he received a letter from the Duchesse de Polignac in Vienna. 'She tells me she has received news of the Queen from a doctor; it must be La Caze.'[17] The news was not altogether good, as Axel later discovered, but he was soon in a state of elation such as he had not felt for many months. On 5 April 1793 he heard that the French general Dumouriez had defected to the Prussians with his entire army, which was ready to march on Paris to place the young Louis XVII on the throne. Axel now felt his refusal of the London embassy entirely justified, and immediately wrote Baron Taube a letter bursting with hope and fresh plans.

> Here is an account of the arrangement made between the P[rince] of Coburg and Dumouriez. I'm in a state of enchantment and I view this great affair as finished. According to all possible sources there is nothing to fear for the Royal Family and I wouldn't be astonished at having to tell you soon that they have been carried in triumph through Paris. You know, my friend, the late King's [Gustav's] instructions which were confirmed by the Duke, that I should present myself as ambassador to the King [Louis XVII] as soon as he is free. Try to find out if I should still be governed by that, or if I must wait for fresh orders, in which case they must be sent to me as soon as possible because this could all happen very quickly....[18]

Optimistic and very happy, Axel wrote a detailed political report for Marie-Antoinette, whom he was determined to see appointed Regent during her son's minority in place of Monsieur. It seemed to be a dream come true. Axel and Marie-Antoinette would be reunited permanently in Paris, with Axel playing the grand role as the Queen's lover and political adviser snatched from him at Varennes – an even grander role now Louis XVI was dead. His feverish preparations for this blissful reunion came to a cruel and abrupt end on 8 April, when it was learnt that Dumouriez's army refused to follow him, and he had defected alone with a handful of senior officers.

Axel was plunged anew into despair. He still hoped Austrian and Prussian successes against the French would continue, but his fears for the royal family returned in full force. The Netherlands had been liberated, so the diplomatic exiles in Düsseldorf returned to their former base in Brussels. Before he left Germany, Axel visited Dumouriez with Baron Simolin. The general was very interested in Marie-Antoinette's lover, even complimenting him on his appearance. He denied involvement with the Duc d'Orléans, declaring that he wanted to restore the monarchy, and had taken four revolutionary commissioners (including the French War Minister) hostage, to be traded against the royal family. Axel described him as 'a true Frenchman; vain, confident and hare-brained, having wit and little judgement'.[19] It was tragic that the Prince of Coburg did not pursue Dumouriez's hostage plan, but freed the commissioners. Axel was later assured by another captive member of the Convention that the royal family would certainly have been exchanged for them.

These disastrous political blunders by the allies made Axel's nightmare worse. Back in Brussels with his friends from the end of April 1793, he was again reduced to watching, waiting and suggesting ways of releasing his beloved and her family from their long incarceration. Sophie reproached him for not doing enough, clearly expecting heroic deeds from her brother. Axel, however, seemed powerless to devise, let alone execute a Scarlet Pimpernel-style rescue of the prisoners in the Temple. He was only thirty-seven but he was not the man he used to be, frequently complaining about his health and needing Eleonore to look after him. Whether he suffered from weakness resulting from the fevers he had contracted in the American war, or was simply suffering from nervous exhaustion, is unclear.

Gustav III's death had also deprived him of all official support for a rescue attempt; the false passports and papers Gustav supplied for his secret visit to Paris in 1792 would not be granted by the new Swedish government, who had no interest in saving the French royal family. Even with such documents, it would have been far from certain Axel could have reached Paris. War was raging on France's land and sea borders; getting into or out of the country was virtually impossible. Even had Axel achieved this, how could he have avoided detection by the ubiquitous army of police spies with their draconian powers? He no longer had useful connections in the French capital. His friends were either exiled or murdered, and the new government was an unknown quantity. Without inside help, he could not possibly have reached Marie-Antoinette in the Temple.

Axel was also crippled financially. Varennes had proved to be an expensive disaster. Dependent now on his diplomatic salary, he was bound by Swedish government inaction. Planning an escape, paying for all the necessary assistance (which even then could prove treacherous or unreliable), would have far exceeded his means. Added to these practical difficulties, there doubtless lurked the terror that any such rescue could fail, as at Varennes, and actually precipitate Marie-Antoinette's death or endanger her children.

Axel, ever the diplomat, hoped the French could be persuaded to yield the royal family in exchange for concessions as the allies advanced once again into northern France. He cursed Gustav's assassins, who had ended all Swedish involvement in the war, thus depriving him of a chance to take part in the military campaign. But his thinking was too conservative. He saw no alternative but military might supplemented by pragmatic diplomatic solutions. The problem was that while Axel wanted his Queen, Austria had only one objective in mind – French territory. The Austrians demanded not only the release of the royal family but the whole of northern France, Alsace and Lorraine in exchange for a cease-fire. No French government could possibly meet these terms, and Marie-Antoinette was thereby doomed, her value as a hostage reduced to nil.

Mercy, in charge of Austrian affairs in Brussels, was extraordinarily unresponsive to all Axel's suggestions. His indifference to the fate of Marie-Antoinette, who had trusted him implicitly for so many years, was yet another wound to her lover's heart. Axel lived on a diet of hope, rumour and diplomatic gossip. On 22 May 1793 he received

further details of the visit by Dr La Caze (formerly physician to the
Comte d'Artois) to the royal family.

> La Caze went to the Temple. He found the Queen little changed;
> Elisabeth was so unrecognizable he didn't know her until the Queen
> called her 'my sister'. *She* was in the room in a nightcap, dressed in
> a very plain chintz gown. Little Madame had ulcers over her whole
> body and was threatened by a dissolution of the blood.... They write
> from Paris that the young King has been ill and that the Commune
> refused the Queen the doctor she asked for on the pretext he was too
> aristocratic, and sent one of its own persuasion.[20]

Marie-Antoinette herself was soon in dire need of a doctor. In
June 1793 Axel heard she had been very ill, 'but she is well at the
moment and was extremely well cared for during her illness'.[21] Like
so much information from Paris, it was only half true. The Queen's
health was finally cracking under the strain of imprisonment, and
deteriorated steadily during the next few weeks. Good news from
the war zone encouraged Axel to hope he might yet see her again.
On 9 June he told Sophie: 'News on the august prisoners is very
reassuring, and at the moment there are no proposals or movements
against them. That gives me a little hope of seeing them one day
freed from their long captivity. If I could ever enjoy such a spectacle
what a moment for my heart!'[22]

Marie-Antoinette's tender devotion to her children had even made
a favourable impression in Paris; no one expected 'the modern
Messalina', the voracious sexual monster of popular myth, to reveal
herself as a patient, good-tempered, loving mother. On 10 July Axel
recorded in his diary that 'a woman who has come from Paris says
people are beginning to think well of the royal family; the Queen
takes the air and she is applauded when she can be seen. They even
cry "Long live the Dauphin!"'[23]

Such displays of popular support for the monarchy were exceedingly dangerous, and the Commune, now presided over by the monstrous editor of the Jacobin paper *Le Père Duchesne*, Jacques Hébert,
exacted a swift and brutal revenge. Early in July, Marie-Antoinette's
eight-year-old son was torn from her arms and taken to a cell immediately below the rest of his family. The excuse was that the Queen
and Madame Elisabeth had been abusing the boy and indoctrinating

him as a royalist. It was the cruellest blow Marie-Antoinette could have suffered. For days she heard her darling *Chou d'Amour* sobbing for her; but much worse followed. An illiterate cobbler named Antoine Simon was appointed Louis XVII's guardian. He was instructed to transform him into a model republican, and to this end used to beat him and get him drunk to make him sing bloodthirsty revolutionary songs, taught him to swear and made him curse his mother, and even tried to force him to masturbate (to provide evidence against the Queen, who was herself accused of this crime).

Axel was only too well aware of Marie-Antoinette's agony, though he would have been doubly horrified had he known of the dastardly treatment being meted out to her son. On 16 July he wrote: '... the reason for the separation terrifies me and I'm afraid they will seize the chance to try the Queen'; and four days later he noted: '... this separation causes me great pain'.[24] Even greater pain lay in store. On 2 August 1793 Marie-Antoinette was wrenched from her daughter and Madame Elisabeth and transferred to a fetid cell in the Conciergerie, the grim fortress on the Île de la Cité which housed prisoners who would most certainly be condemned to death by the Revolutionary Tribunal. In 1795 young Madame told her former governess Mme de Tourzel that from that moment she never expected to see her mother again, and their farewell was heart-breaking.

Axel was desperate when he received this unexpected news on 10 August 1793:

My soul was torn. I pictured *her* condition, her griefs, her sufferings, and I also felt keenly all I have lost since the arrest at Varennes. Eleonore alone was able to console me a little, but she couldn't stop me feeling deeply, and the uncertainty over what I should do made my position even more dreadful, for I regard *her* death as inevitable and yet I try to hope. It cost me a great deal of pain to hide my terrible grief.[25]

Only much later did Axel learn how desperately ill Marie-Antoinette was. Week and emaciated, she haemorrhaged blood even in the fiacre which took her from the Temple to the Conciergerie. Axel was told: 'The coachman didn't know who he was driving, but he had his suspicions ... when they arrived at the Conciergerie, they waited a long time before they got out; the men got out first and the woman afterwards; she leant on his arm, and he found his fiacre full of blood.'[26] There was little Axel could do now except wait for dreaded news of the Queen's trial. Diplomatically his hands were tied, but he had an ally in the Austrian Comte de La Marck (now known as Prince Auguste d'Arenberg), who was very attached to Marie-Antoinette. They approached Mercy with a rescue plan.

> *Sunday 11 [August]...* As I had discussed means of saving the Queen with La Marck, and we decided that all that was needed was to thrust a large cavalry corps straight on Paris, which would be all the more easy because there is no army in the way and the barns are full of supplies, I went to see the Comte de Mercy, and found him glacial on this idea.... He believed the Royal Family lost, and that nothing could be done for them.

Undeterred, Axel and La Marck persuaded Mercy to send letters to the allied generals, the Prince of Coburg and the Duke of York, pressing them to march on Paris. They also thought the Republic might yet negotiate for the Queen and on 19 August got Mercy to agree to send a French financier, M. Ribbes, a friend of Danton, to Paris, 'to find out what's happening and see if it's possible to negotiate for the Queen's deportation for money'. Mercy, who alone had the authority to negotiate, delayed Ribbes's departure for a fortnight. Axel was outraged.

> *13 September.* What will M. de Mercy not have to reproach himself with, he who has made us waste eight days by his stay in the country, and four more since his return, with all the difficulties he has made! It's horrible to think about it. God preserve *Her* and give me the satisfaction of seeing her again one day![27]

In the event, nothing came of Ribbes's mission. He made contact with Danton only by letter, then returned to Brussels. No answer was ever received. Danton's reluctance to press ahead with the Queen's trial in the spring of 1793 had already marked him out as an enemy of the Revolution. He was no longer in a position to help her, even had he wanted to do so.

Axel, clutching at these pitiful diplomatic straws, poured out his anguish in letters to Sophie. On 14 August, after hearing of Marie-Antoinette's transfer to the Conciergerie, he wrote:

I no longer live, because it's not living to exist as I do or to suffer all the pain I feel. If I could still do something to free her I think I would suffer less, but to be able to do nothing except through solicitations is dreadful for me.... I would give my life to save her and I can't; my greatest happiness would be to die for her and to save her. I would have this happiness if cowards and villains had not deprived us of the best of masters [Gustav III]. He alone would have been capable of saving her. ... His great soul would have been exalted by the recital of her misery, he would have dared everything and conquered all.[28]

On 4 September Axel told Sophie: 'I often reproach myself even for the air I breathe when I think she is shut up in a dreadful prison. This idea is breaking my heart and poisoning my life, and I'm constantly torn between grief and rage.' And on 8 September he wailed: 'Why did I have to lose all means of serving her?'[29]

He later heard of an attempt to extract Marie-Antoinette from the Conciergerie, along with distressing details of her condition, from M. de Rougeville, an eccentric who 'had spent his life in the Queen's antechambers and followed her everywhere'. Rougeville and a wealthy American lady, Mme de Tilleul, hatched an escape plan and approached a lemonade-seller and Commune member, M. Michonis, one of the officials who escorted Marie-Antoinette to the Conciergerie. 'Michonis's heart was with the Queen', Rougeville told Axel, 'and he refused the money he was offered.' One day he allowed Rougeville to accompany him to the Queen's cell. When she saw this ghost from her apartments at Versailles she almost fainted, and dropped the note Rougeville slipped her in a bunch of carnations. He had to leave with Michonis, but the Queen regained her presence of mind and summoned them back. While Michonis diverted her guards, she spoke to her unexpected visitor.

She told Rougeville he was risking too much. He told her to take heart, that she would be saved.... She said: 'Though I am weak and downcast *this*' – placing her hand on her heart – 'is not.' She asked him if she would soon be tried; he reassured her. She told him: 'Look at me, look at my bed, and tell my family and my friends, if you can escape, the state in which you saw me.'[30]

The escape plan very nearly succeeded. Michonis bribed the prison porter and one of the Queen's two guards, and came one night at 10 p.m. pretending he had an order to take her back to the Temple. He was on the point of escorting her from her cell when the second guard became suspicious and threatened to raise the alarm. With no papers to back up his claim, Michonis was obliged to leave alone. Rougeville, now in imminent danger of denunciation to the Revolutionary Tribunal, had to flee Paris.

He informed Axel that Marie-Antoinette shared a small, damp cell with neither stove nor fire with a *poissarde* and two guards 'who never left the room, not even when the Queen had needs or bodily functions to see to'. Her bedclothes consisted of a single filthy holed blanket and dirty sheets. 'The Queen always slept dressed in black, expecting at any moment to be murdered or led off to her execution, and she wanted to go in mourning.' Physically she was in appalling shape.

> Her hair,cut at the front and back, was completely grey; she was so thin it was difficult to recognize her and she was so weak she could barely stand.... The guards told Michonis that Madame wasn't eating, and she couldn't go on living like that; they said her food was very bad.... Rougeville said it made Michonis cry with grief: he confirmed that the Queen kept losing blood, and said that when he had to go to the Temple to get the black *caraco* and linen the Queen needed, he wasn't permitted to go until after a debate by the council.[31]

This failed escape was the Queen's last chance. On 5 October 1793 the Austrians captured Drouet, the postmaster who had stopped the King at Varennes (since then a member of the National Convention who had voted for Louis XVI's execution). He denied that Marie-Antoinette was being ill-treated, but said nothing now would save her; a prompt march on Paris would simply hasten her death, and even the eight-year-old Louis XVII was in danger of being murdered. Axel, who could never forget his failure at Varennes, went to see Drouet in prison. 'The sight of this infamous scoundrel made me furious,' he wrote, 'and the effort I made to say nothing to him, because of the Abbé de Limon and Comte de Fitz-James, who were with us, made me ill.'[32]

Axel was now prepared for the worst, and the calm diplomatic exterior he was forced to maintain increased his agony. 'I shall have lost too much if I lose *Her*,' he wrote in his diary on 10 October, a day without any news from Paris. On the 13th, at her lawyers' insistence, Marie-Antoinette wrote to the Convention asking for three days for them to read the mass of papers presented to them by the prosecution. 'I owe it to my children to neglect nothing which is necessary for the entire justification of their mother,' she wrote.[33] This request was refused. There was no possibility that the Queen – or anyone else brought before the Revolutionary Tribunal – would receive a fair trial.

That same day, Eleonore Sullivan, still living with Quentin Crawford, tackled Axel about their difficult relationship. It was hardly a propitious moment.

Eleonore spoke to me of her position; she is excessively tired of it. She assured me she would come with me, but that she couldn't go to Sweden because the climate was too cold, and she could finish nothing until I had made up my mind. That embarrassed me a great deal. I loved her, I would have been happy to live with her; moreover I need someone to look after me. But if *She* lives, I neither want to nor can I abandon *Her*.[34]

Axel was also worried about his finances. His income was about 50,000 *livres* a year, but he noted: 'I'm spending much more in the position I'm in. I've always maintained it in the expectation of having need of it, but if this expectation proves to be vain, I will have been a fool. Never mind, it was for *Her*, I had to.'[35]

The following day, 14 October, Axel heard that 'a type of Jacobin', Aubré, just arrived in Brussels, declared 'that he could have saved the Queen for 200,000 *francs* which had been offered, but she had refused it'. As Aubré also vowed she was being well treated in the Conciergerie, his claim was very suspect. Nevertheless the Baron de Breteuil decided to offer him 2 million *francs* if he succeeded in releasing the Queen. Axel, highly suspicious of Aubré's motives, insisted he be made to reveal how his rescue would be carried out, since he was terrified Marie-Antoinette might be released only to be hacked to death by a mob.[36]

It was far too late. In Paris that same day, Marie-Antoinette was hurtled towards the scaffold. The Queen's trial began on Monday, 14 October 1793 and lasted just two days. The only real charge against her – her correspondence with Mercy during the spring of 1792 – was lost in a heap of atrocious accusations, among them that she had sent 200 million *livres* to her brother Joseph, planned to massacre 'patriots' in 1789 and 1792, and, with Madame Elisabeth, had sexually abused her own son. This last vile charge was wrung from a drunk Louis XVII by Hébert and his guardian Simon. Simon took the boy to see his bewildered aunt and sister and made him recite the accusation. 'At the end of this dreadful scene,' Mme de Tourzel was later informed by Madame, 'the unhappy little prince, beginning to sober up, approached his sister and took her hand to kiss it.'[37] He was immediately dragged away. It was the last time his sister saw him. Marie-Antoinette remained silent after this charge was read out in Court. When pressed to answer it, she made a direct appeal to the gallery: 'If I didn't reply,' she declared, 'it is because Nature refuses an answer to such a question made to a mother. I appeal to all those who may be here!'[38] Even hardened *poissardes* were moved, and their cries of indignation forced a suspension of the hearing. A death sentence was, however, inevitable; being Austrian and a queen was crime enough. Marie-Antoinette was condemned on 15 October with her execution fixed for the following day.

The beautiful, charming, lively Queen with whom Axel Fersen had laughed at opera balls and fallen in love, whom he had held in his arms and caressed, was only thirty-seven. But she was now prematurely aged, frail and dying. Her trial may even have been brought forward to avoid the embarrassment and disappointment of her death in prison. The French were not going to be cheated of the spectacle of watching 'the Austrian whore' they had tortured for so many years die a horrible death. It was to her young sister-in-law Madame Elisabeth that Marie-Antoinette wrote her last letter from her wretched cell in the Conciergerie – a letter which was never delivered and found among the public prosecutor's papers only in 1816.

16 October, at 4.30 in the morning

It is to you, my sister, that I write for the last time. I have just been condemned, not to a shameful death – it is only so for criminals – but to go and rejoin your brother. Innocent as he was, I hope to show the same firmness as he did in his last moments....

She went on to leave blessings and instructions for her children, thanked her 'kind, tender sister' for all the sacrifices she had made for them, and begged Elisabeth to forgive her nephew for the accusation he had been forced to make against her. The Queen followed this request with a defiant affirmation of her Roman Catholic faith, begged God's forgiveness 'for all the faults I may have committed since I was born', and declared that she forgave her enemies. She repeated Louis XVI's injunction to her son that he should never try to avenge his parents' deaths. There was also a sentence which most surely applied to Axel. 'I used to have friends,' Marie-Antoinette wrote. 'The idea of being separated from them for ever and their grief is one of the greatest sorrows I shall carry to my grave; may they know at least that I thought of them until my last moment.'[39] But it was leaving her son and daughter which broke her heart. On a page of her prayer-book she scrawled: 'My God, have pity on me! My eyes have no tears left to weep for you, my poor children. Adieu, adieu!'

Seven hours later Marie-Antoinette, dressed in a plain white dress, her hands tied behind her back, was taken from the tumbril which had driven her from the Conciergerie to the guillotine. She was pushed up the steep steps of the scaffold, but to Hébert's intense disappointment betrayed not a single sign of fear. Minutes later her severed head was displayed to the crowd, and some hours afterwards it was dumped with her body in an unmarked grave in the cemetery of the Madeleine, near the bodies of Louis XVI and the hundreds of Swiss Guards who had died trying to defend the King and Queen on 10 August 1792.

Four days later, on Sunday, 20 October 1793, news of the Queen's execution reached Brussels. Axel was stunned.

It was on the 16th at 11.30 a.m. that this execrable crime was committed and divine vengeance hasn't yet struck these monsters! I was astonished myself not to be more deeply affected; I seemed to feel nothing. I was constantly thinking of *Her*, of all the horrible circumstances, of her children; of her unhappy son and his education which will be ruined, of the ill-treatment they may subject him to, of the Queen's misery at not seeing him in her last moments, of the doubt she might perhaps have had about me, about my love and my interest. This idea devastated me. Then I felt all I had lost in different ways:

love, interest, existence, everything was united in her, and all was lost. At last I thought of everything and of nothing. I even had moments of disgust for Eleonore: it isn't the same love – that delicacy, that solicitude, that tenderness.... I felt truly wretched and all seemed to be over for me.[40]

Axel went to cry with Marie-Antoinette's friend and former lady-in-waiting the Duchesse de Fitz-James, and with the Baron de Breteuil. The following day he went out riding, to be alone: 'I could think only of my loss; it was dreadful having no positive details. That she was alone in her last moments without consolation, with no one to talk to, to give her last wishes to, is horrifying. The monsters from hell! No, without revenge, my heart will never be satisfied.'[41]

Once the initial shock had lessened, Axel's despair and anguish deepened. 'If my health would have permitted, I would have joined the army to avenge her or get myself killed,' he wrote on 22 October, and inserted a piece of paper in his diary. 'Here is the arraignment, with the names of the murderous judges, to whom I vow an eternal hatred which can never end.' As his grief deepened and he received fresh details of Marie-Antoinette's trial and execution, his desire for revenge grew even stronger. It was, he told Sophie, the only thing which sustained him. True to his vow, he later recorded with satisfaction the deaths of every one of Marie-Antoinette's enemies, even that of Barnave, who was executed barely a month after the Queen. 'Her image, her sufferings, her death and my love never leave my mind, I can think of nothing else,' he wrote on 24 October. 'Oh! My God, why did I have to lose her and what will become of me!' And on the 26th: 'Every day I think of it and every day my grief increases. Every day I feel even more all I have lost.'[42]

Axel also vented his fury on all the countries whose political machinations had contributed to Marie-Antoinette's death, and he lashed out at people who failed to mourn her properly – particularly Mercy, who 'spoke a great deal of his attachment to the unfortunate Queen and his grief at her end, but always based on his respect for the memory of Maria-Theresa, because he has always affected to be attached to the Queen only because of her mother'.[43]

There was nothing equivocal about Axel Fersen's love for Marie-Antoinette. He adored her unconditionally, even after her death. His intense sorrow at losing her was exacerbated by feelings of guilt over his relationship with Eleonore. In November 1793 he wrote in his diary:

I want to gather the most minute details on the great, unfortunate princess I shall love all my life; everything of hers is precious to me. Oh, how I reproach myself for my wrongs towards her, and how I know at present how much I loved her. Eleonore will not replace her in my heart. What gentleness, what tenderness, what kindness, what solicitude, what a delicate, loving and tender heart! The other [Eleonore] hasn't got all that and yet I love her; I look on her as my only consolation and without her I would be too wretched, but one has to find the goodness of her character and her feelings through a thousand brusqueries and a thousand ill-humours which it pains me to put up with. Oh, how my existence has changed, and how little happiness it promises me after having been the finest in the world.[44]

Axel wrote letter after letter to Sophie during the winter of 1793, bewailing his unhappy fate, and pouring out his love for Marie-Antoinette. On 11 December he declared: 'I would have been much happier if I'd died on 21 June. Now it would be cowardice not to know how to suffer.' His father begged him to return home, but Axel refused. His reluctance to leave Brussels could well have been due to his desire to help Marie-Antoinette's children, should they be (as he hoped) released from their tower. On Christmas Eve 1793 he wrote to Sophie:

Losing *Her* is the grief of my whole life, and my sorrows will leave me only when I die. Never have I felt so much the value of all I possessed, and never have I loved her so much.... This child [Louis XVII] still interest me, his fate increases my pain yet more. And that unfortunate girl [Madame], what will become of her? What horrors, what humiliations will they not put her through – it breaks my heart to think of it.[45]

There were small consolations. Sympathy from the Queen's old friends, who would remind Axel of happier days at Versailles; a visit from Goguelat, Marie-Antoinette's most loyal secretary; an affectionate note of commiseration from the young Swedish King, Gustav IV Adolf. But there was no word on the Queen's children, no hope of being able to comfort them, love them and derive some comfort in return. Axel was always especially concerned and affected by news of Louis XVII – Marie-Antoinette's *Chou d'Amour*, a child about whom he knew absolutely everything, as his diary shows. Was it simply because he knew how deeply the Queen had loved her son, or did Axel himself have a true paternal interest in the boy King?

The answer will never be known. One thing is certain. Marie-Antoinette, the woman who loved Axel Fersen and gave him so much joy, never lost her place in his heart. After her death he felt free at last to express all his enduring feelings for her. There was no danger now of exposure or scandal. On 8 January 1794 he wrote in his diary: 'Every day I feel how much I lost in *Her* and how perfect she was in everything. Never have there been nor will there be other women like *Her*.' 16 October was a day of mourning and remembrance for Axel for the rest of his life. In 1794 he recorded it thus: 'This day was a memorable and terrible day for me. It's the day I lost the person who loved me most in the world and who loved me truly. I shall weep for her loss all my life.' Four years later his grief was no less acute. 'This is a day of devotion for me,' he noted in 1798, 'and I can never forget all I've lost. My sorrows will last as long as I live.'[46]

EPILOGUE

The Memory of a Dream

Remembrance was an obsession for Axel Fersen from 16 October 1793 onwards. Memories were all he had left of Marie-Antoinette, his truly *grande passion*. '*Her* image follows me and will follow me constantly,' he wrote to Sophie, 'and everywhere I like to talk only of her and recall the happy moments of my life.'[1] Trying to relive the happiness he had known with the Queen was the one way Axel seemed able to cope with her death – she ruled forever in his heart. Fresh griefs, however, lay in store.

Senator Fersen died in Stockholm on 24 April 1794. His eldest son was in Brussels, and his feelings of guilt must have been intolerable. Axel had not seen his father since 1788, and, still hoping to assist Marie-Antoinette's children, had resisted his father's request to return to Sweden after the Queen's execution. Their relationship had never been easy, but Senator Fersen had supported and indulged Axel for years, and certainly deserved a better return for his affection. On his death Axel came into a large inheritance. He also received a taste of the Duke of Södermanland's spiteful temper.

The Swedish Regent, no longer fearing Senator Fersen's wrath, sacked Axel from his Brussels post on the trumped-up charge that he had conspired to declare the sixteen-year-old Gustav IV Adolf of age (thereby ending the regency). The Regent disliked Axel for both political and personal reasons. Politically he detested all Gustav III's old friends and advisers; a French royalist like Axel Fersen might well obstruct his negotiations for an alliance between Sweden and the French Republic. On a personal level he found the Fersens too much in favour at the Swedish Court; his wife in particular seemed very attracted to Axel. She had confessed to Sophie in 1791 that she loved him, but was eventually forced to settle for his more co-operative younger brother Fabian. Axel's disgrace in 1794 was not sufficient for the Duke of Södermanland, who remained a bitter and danger-ous enemy of the man now expected by much of the nobility to suc-ceed his father as Sweden's elder statesman.

Axel, however, showed no alacrity to return home. He wanted to remain within striking distance of Paris, to greet the young Louis XVII and Madame when they were released from the Temple. Events in May and June 1794 altered his plans. The French army once again advanced into the Netherlands, and in Paris, where the Terror was claiming dozens of lives every day, Madame Elisabeth followed her brother and sister-in-law to the guillotine. Louis XVI's thirty-year-old sister, who had led a completely blameless existence, selflessly devoting herself to her orphaned niece (Louis XVII remained sep-arated from his family), was executed at 6 p.m. on 10 May 1794. This totally unexpected and barbaric crime dramatically increased Axel's fears for Marie-Antoinette's children, even though it was gen-erally considered they were too young to be charged with any counter-revolutionary activities. But anything seemed possible from a murderous regime that now parcelled up teenagers and octogenarians of both sexes and from all classes for disposal by the horrifyingly efficient guillotine. No one in Brussels waited to find out if the same fate awaited them. Axel left the city at the end of June, just before the Republic's forces moved in.

Eleonore Sullivan and Quentin Crawford moved to Frankfurt. Axel left them there and travelled home to Sweden, finding great comfort in Sophie's welcome. His sister knew only too well all he had lost, and was able to give him the sympathy and consolation he craved. Sophie's husband had died and she at least was finally lucky in love, setting up home with her beloved Baron Taube. Their idyllic happi-ness was much envied by the grieving Axel, who, on 19 March, re-ceived a surprising memento from Marie-Antoinette. It came from his old friend Mme de Korff, who had advanced 300,000 *livres* for the flight to Varennes and provided the royal family's passports: 'Mme de Korff sent me the end of a note from *Her* to me – here it is – which gave me great pleasure. It seemed to me to be a final adieu, and I was deeply moved. I don't know how it was left in her hands and I've written to her to find out.'[2] The scrap of paper, carefully pasted into Axel's diary, bore the words 'Adieu, my heart is all yours' in Marie-Antoinette's unmistakable handwriting. Was it the end of a letter written in happier times by the Queen to her lover, or had she managed to smuggle it out from the Temple or Conciergerie? Axel does not appear to have recorded the explanation he demanded of Mme de Korff, but whatever its provenance, he took this precious fragment as a definite sign that Marie-Antoinette had loved him to her dying breath. This last adieu, arriving when it did, seemed to be a message from beyond the grave, and was soothing balm to his fractured heart.

There was no hope, however of an end to Axel's woes. He was still in Sweden when he received a final, crushing blow from France:

Sat 27 June [1795]. The post arrived and brought me the fatal news of the death of the young King Louis XVII. This event caused me real pain. He was the last and only interest left to me in France.[3]

The final sentence here is highly significant. Marie-Antoinette's daughter still remained alone in the Temple. Why was her brother, the *Chou d'Amour*, Axel's '*last* and *only* interest' in France? His words and reactions suggest a very close link indeed to the ten-year-old Louis XVII ('this poor beloved child'), though even had he known the boy was his son, he would never have dared say so openly.

Axel refused to believe Louis XVII had died of natural causes, as the French claimed, suspecting instead that he had been poisoned. On 7 July 1795 he wrote in his diary after reading newspapers from France: 'There is also the report on the autopsy of this unhappy child. What they say about the scrofulous tissue is plausible for the public but cannot be right for him. His burial was nothing. It's all too painful for me to think of, and gives me only too many sad memories and heart-breaking sorrows.'[4]

Axel's intimate knowledge of the health of 'this unhappy child', his 'heart-breaking sorrows' and the fact that it was too painful for him to contemplate are further indications of a much closer relationship to Louis XVII than history has ever recorded. The timing of Louis XVII's death was indeed suspicious. It was announced on 8 June 1795, when royalists were chasing Jacobins in the streets of Paris, just a month after most members of the Revolutionary Tribunal had been executed for mass murder. Ten thousand émigrés were preparing to invade Brittany to place Louis XVII on the throne. What better way to frustrate them than by killing the King?

Doubts remain to this day as to whether Louis XVII died in the Temple, and, if so, from what cause. He had been a robust child. After his mother's execution, he continued to be terrorized by Simon, who was in turn removed as Louis's guardian and executed in 1794. Why was the unfortunate boy not reunited with his sister? Was he in fact still in the prison? According to Mme de Tourzel, who interrogated prison warders, he spent some time utterly neglected in solitary confinement, but after Robespierre's downfall was supposed to have been well cared for. Mme de Tourzel was assured Louis remained 'very handsome', but that he refused to speak and slowly deteriorated, dying at a most convenient time. Surely he would have asked to see his family? And as his face looked so healthy, it seems improbable that he suddenly succumbed to an illness from which Axel Fersen believed he could not possibly have suffered. Madame never saw or heard of her brother after October 1793, and was not even informed he had died until some time afterwards. Since most of the people who had murdered her parents and aunt were themselves now dead, and she herself was in good health and properly looked after, the demise of Louis XVII seems even more mysterious.

Stories abound that the young King had been spirited away from the Temple and taken either to England or Germany, but all the pretenders who later claimed to be Louis XVII were disowned by the French royal family. Mme de Tourzel, his devoted governess, concluded from her exhaustive inquiries at the Temple that he had indeed died as the prison authorities claimed. It is interesting to note, however, that when Louis XVI and Marie-Antoinette were finally given a proper funeral in 1816, neither Louis XVIII nor the Comte d'Artois wanted to exhume the remains of their nephew Louis XVII – in case they could not find them?

Axel never doubted Louis's death, but was convinced he had been murdered. The only living relic of Marie-Antoinette was her daughter, Madame, who in the autumn of 1795 was permitted to receive three visits a week from Mme de Tourzel and her daughter Pauline. She broke down when she saw them, but they were surprised to find her 'tall, beautiful and strong'. It was the beginning of the end of her long agony. On 21 December 1795, two days after her sixteenth birthday, she was exchanged at Basle for French prisoners held by the Austrians, and journeyed to Vienna to meet her mother's family for the first time.

In late 1795 Axel left Sweden for Germany in anticipation of Madame's release. He visited Crawford and Eleonore in Frankfurt, where on 11 December he noted: '... that scoundrel Drouet [responsible for the arrest at Varennes] died at Freiburg, after falling from his horse.... He deserved another kind of death'. The following day was more to Axel's taste. 'Goguelat, who was here, dined with me. We talked of Paris and all we had lost there. That pleased me.'[5]

Further evidence of Axel's detailed knowledge of Louis XVII appears in his diary on 10 January 1796: 'The dog which Madame said she was permitted to bring with her and which belonged to her brother is doubtless an error. He couldn't bear dogs, and was afraid of them. It probably belonged to her mother.' This tallies exactly with Marie-Antoinette's information about her son's fear of dogs given to Mme de Tourzel when the latter became his governess in 1789. Axel soon had an opportunity to see this dog for himself. On 19 January 1796 he left Frankfurt for Vienna. 'The object of my journey did not satisfy me,' he noted. 'I wanted to succeed but I detest the role of beggar.'[6]

Axel's unpleasant duty was to try to get Emperor Francis II to repay the money he and his friends had advanced Louis XVI and Marie-Antoinette for the flight to Varennes. Mme de Korff was in particularly dire financial straits at this time, being dependent on Axel for money to survive forced moves as the tide of war ebbed and flowed across Europe, and banks ceased paying her interest. Repayment of the 300,000 *livres* she had lent the King and Queen of France would have been especially welcome. Though he resented having to ask for the money, Axel was hopeful of success. He possessed signed letters from Louis XVI and Marie-Antoinette ordering their heirs to reimburse him and Mme de Korff, and knew that Mercy had transported the Queen's diamonds and her money to Vienna before his death in 1794.

The second, no less important object of Axel's trip to Vienna was to see Madame. Not until 19 February did he succeed in getting a good look at her as she returned from Mass to her apartments in the Hofburg. He was accompanied by the Duc de Guiche, former Captain of Louis XVI's Bodyguard and son-in-law to the now deceased Duchesse de Polignac. It proved to be a highly charged emotional encounter.

She passed at 10.30 a.m. alone with Mme Chanclos. She is tall, well made, but she looks more like Madame Elisabeth than the Queen. Her face has developed but is not changed; she is blonde, has pretty feet but walks badly and is pigeon-toed. She has grace and nobility. She blushed as she passed, nodded to us, and as she entered her apartments turned round to look at us again; by her manners I recognized her mother, and I thought she looked as though she wanted to say something nice and tell us she recognized us. The impression was so keen that tears came into my eyes and my knees trembled beneath me as I went down the staircase. I had had a great deal of both pain and pleasure and I was very moved.[7]

Axel told Sophie he was pleased to report Madame's success in Vienna, 'but the sight of her, in bringing back painful memories, increased yet more all my sorrow and the feeling of all I've lost'.[8] He was determined to gain a private audience with her, to hear every last detail about her mother and brother, but the Austrians had other ideas. They would not even let Madame answer letters. Axel finally found himself in a group of seventeen people permitted to pay court to the French princess, which precluded any private discussion. Her conversation showed, however, that she had acquired the grace and polish he expected of Marie-Antoinette's daughter.

She talked to the Duc de Guiche about his children, to me about Sweden and the young King [Gustav Adolf], of his marriage, his majority, etc. etc., all with grace and spirit. Her face grows more animated as she speaks and then she looks prettier; her complexion is superb, but she has less of her mother and more of the Bourbon family, and I wanted the opposite. I noticed she was greatly embarrassed at having to see the Duc de Guiche and me in this manner. She looked at me often, but Mme Chanclos was attentive to all her movements.... The room where Madame held court was Joseph's bedroom, where he died. In the antechamber was Madame's dog, a type of red and white spaniel. It had belonged to her unhappy brother and was his companion in misfortune; when the prince died the dog was forgotten, but instinct led him to Madame's apartment, where he stayed by the door until he could get in. Madame, who did not know of her brother's death, recognized the dog and kept it, believing it had got lost.[9]

Madame's love of dogs was inherited from Marie-Antoinette, but she worsened steadily in Axel's opinion after this meeting. On 24 February he had an audience with Emperor Francis II, who declared he could not repay the money owing from Varennes. Axel informed Taube on 23 March:

> For what belongs to me personally I must wait until Madame comes of age and decides herself. I agree to that, and I'm working now only to obtain repayment for Mme de Korff or payment of interest. That, my friend, is how sovereigns value the attachment shown to their peers, and I'm not surprised they are not served, or served only out of self-interest, since people who do the opposite risk dying of hunger.[10]

Axel spent three more months in Vienna, finally leaving on 7 June 1796, disappointed and bitter. 'I have a very bad opinion of Madame's heart,' he told Taube. 'I'm afraid ... she is nothing like her parents; this idea grieves me, but a thousand circumstances confirm it.... I know she has discussed the repayment of these ladies like a lawyer in order not to pay.'[11] She would have been a successful lawyer. Axel himself had to repay both capital and interest; in all, the flight to Varennes cost him 1 million *livres* and brought him nothing but heartache.

Given the cruel blows fate had already rained down upon him, it was perhaps inevitable that Axel's life too should end tragically and brutally, despite a glittering career in Sweden. His personal life never recovered after Marie-Antoinette's death. Eleonore Sullivan, tired of his long absences and his uncommitted heart, severed all connections with him in 1796, and eventually married Quentin Crawford. Axel never married. In November 1796 Gustav III's son, King Gustav IV Adolf, attained his majority, and immediately recalled his father's old friend to office. Axel was sent as Swedish ambassador to the Congress of Rastatt, where Napoleon Bonaparte said 'he refused to deal with a man who had slept with the Queen of France'.

In 1799 Axel was appointed to the Council of regency which governed Sweden while the young King and his wife travelled abroad, and in 1801 he was made Grand Marshal of Sweden. Axel was now in a very powerful position indeed, but lost his influence in 1805 when he tried to restrain Gustav IV Adolf from a pointless war against France over Pomerania. Gustav IV Adolf was eventually forced to abdicate on 13 March 1809, after a disastrous war with Russia which led to the loss of Finland. Gustav III's brother, the Duke of Södermanland, now became King Karl XIII. He was childless, and selected a foreigner for Crown Prince – Christian of Denmark. Axel, the head of the old nobility, which lost considerable powers under Karl's new constitution, had supported the succession of Crown Prince Gustav (Gustav IV Adolf's son), but did not oppose Christian when he arrived in Sweden. All might have gone well had the new heir to the throne not died of a stroke at a military review on 28 May 1810. Axel suggested Prince Gustav be reinstated as Crown Prince. Karl XIII made the staggering choice of Napoleon's general, Jean-Baptiste Bernadotte.

The French Revolution finally destroyed Axel Fersen in a way he could never have foreseen. Bernadotte was not only a successful general of the French Empire, but had been an ardent Jacobin during the Revolution. Karl XIII, whose Jacobin sympathies had been so suspect, knew that Axel would never countenance Bernadotte as King of Sweden, yet Axel's backing was vital. The *Riksdag* always elected the Crown Prince; as head of the nobility, Axel could influence the parliament to reject Bernadotte. Karl XIII decided that Axel Fersen had to be eliminated.

The fifty-four-year-old Swedish Grand Marshal paid an appalling price for his loyalty to the legitimate heir, Gustav III's grandson, and his lifelong hatred of the French Jacobins who had murdered the woman he loved. Prince Christian's funeral was delayed so stories could be spread in the newspapers that Axel had poisoned him and intended to mount a *coup* in Prince Gustav's favour. Popular feeling against Axel in Stockholm had reached fever pitch by the time Christian's state funeral took place on 20 June 1810. It was the anniversary of the fatal day Axel lost all at Varennes and wished he had died. Perhaps he had wished to die too often. As Grand Marshal, he led Christian's funeral procession. Karl XIII was warned Axel was in danger, but merely replied: 'It would be no bad thing for that proud lord to receive a lesson.' He took the added precaution of ensuring that soldiers lining the funeral route had no bullets and gave orders that force was not to be employed against rioters.[12]

Axel's carriage was stoned as soon as it crossed the bridge into Stockholm's old town. Just before it turned towards the royal palace it was ambushed, and he was dragged by the mob into the street. He managed to escape into the Riddarhus (where the nobility held its parliamentary sessions), but was attacked and pulled away from the guards who came to escort him to safety. Generals Aldercreutz and Vegesach withdrew with their troops, allowing the mob to carry their victim off to the Town Hall. Here, already badly injured, Axel was given a glass of water before being bundled out into the courtyard and mercilessly bludgeoned to death in full view of rows of soldiers. General Aldercreutz was rewarded for permitting this brutal assassination by the gift of Läckö Castle, former home of Axel's ancestor, Jacob De La Gardie.

It could have happened in Paris during the Revolution. Instead the fate Axel had so dreaded for his adored Marie-Antoinette befell him in his native city, nineteen years to the very day that he had driven her out of the Tuileries on a doomed escape from the web of unhappiness destiny seemed to have imposed on them.

Notes

Abbreviations for works referred to in these notes are as follows. Further details are given in the Bibliography

Bombelles	*Journal du Marquis de Bombelles (1780–1789).* 2 vols.
Campan	*Mémoires sur la vie privée de Marie-Antoinette* by J.L.H. Campan. 2 vols.
Geffroy	*Gustave III et la Cour de France* by A. Geffroy. 2 vols.
Girard	*Correspondance entre Marie-Thérèse et Marie-Antoinette* ed. by G. Girard
Klinckowström	*Le Comte de Fersen et la Cour de France* ed. by R.M. Klinckowström. 2 vols.
MA Letters	*Lettres de Marie-Antoinette* ed. by de la Rocheterie & Beaucourt. 2 vols.
Mercy/Jo	*Correspondance secrète du Comte de Mercy-Argenteau avec l'Empereur Joseph II et le Prince de Kaunitz* ed. by Arneth & Flammermont. 2 vols.
Mercy/MT	*Correspondance secrète entre Marie-Thérèse et le Comte de Mercy-Argenteau* ed. by Arneth & Geffroy. 3 vols.
Söderhjelm	*Fersen et Marie-Antoinette: correspondance et journal intime inédits du Comte Axel de Fersen* by A. Söderhjelm.
Tourzel	*Mémoires de Madame la Duchesse de Tourzel.* 2 vols.

N.B. For multivolume works, the volume number is in roman numerals, followed by the page number(s).

Prologue: The Opera Ball

1 Söderhjelm, 34.
2 Ibid.
3 Ibid., 37.
4 Campan, I, 153–4.
5 Söderhjelm, 38.

1 *A Mésalliance*

1 Campan, I, xxxv.
2 Ibid., 37.
3 Ibid., 38.
4 Bachaumont, *Mémoires secrets*, 409; Levron & Van der Kemp, *Versailles and the Trianons*, 114.
5 Campan, I, xxiv–xxv.
6 *Mercy/Jo*, II, 365.
7 Ibid., 357–8.
8 Campan, I, 47–8.
9 *Mercy/Jo*, II, 366.
10 Campan, I, 48.
11 Tilly, *Memoirs*, 68.
12 *Mercy/Jo*, II, 373, 388.
13 Girard, 74.
14 Ibid., 71.
15 *Mercy/Jo*, Introduction, lii.
16 Campan, I, 32.
17 Ibid., 30.
18 Ibid., 90.
19 Ibid., 84.
20 Tilly, op.cit., 280.
21 Girard, 30.
22 *Mercy/Jo*, II, 381.
23 Girard, 27.
24 Geffroy, I, 293.
25 *Mercy/Jo*, II, 506.
26 Geffroy, I, 255.
27 Campan, I, 102.
28 Ibid., 112.
29 Ibid., 343.
30 Ligne, *Fragments de l'histoire de ma vie*, I, 113.

31 Campan, I, 134.
32 Ibid., 45.
33 Ibid., 49.
34 Ibid.
35 Girard, 136.
36 Campan, I, 105.
37 Ibid.
38 Ibid., 107.
39 Girard, 150.
40 Ibid., 155.
41 *Mercy/Jo*, II, 452.

2   *The Hero of a Novel*

1 Gustav III was the first king for a long time who actually spoke Swedish.
2 Geffroy, I, 138–9.
3 Söderhjelm, 191.
4 Geffroy, I, 113.
5 Klinckowström, I, xii.
6 Söderhjelm, 29.
7 Klinckowström, I, xv.
8 Ibid., xviii.
9 Ibid.
10 Söderhjelm, 37.
11 Klinckowström, I, xviii.
12 Geffroy, I, 359.
13 Söderhjelm, 65–6.
14 Tilly, op. cit., 283; Geffroy, I, 361.
15 Söderhjelm, 66.
16 Ibid., 21.
17 Ibid., 176.
18 Ibid., 48.
19 Ibid., 51.
20 Geffroy, I, 358.
21 Söderhjelm, 52.

3   *From Austria with Love*

1 *Mercy/Jo*, II, 450.
2 Girard, 127.

3 *Mercy/Jo*, II, 450.
4 Campan, I, 80–1.
5 Ibid., 98–9.
6 Ibid., 216.
7 Ibid., 214–15. *Tric-trac* was a type of backgammon.
8 Ibid., 127.
9 Ibid., 250.
10 *Mercy/MT*, III, 114.
11 See Chapter 8.
12 Campan, I, 151.
13 *Mercy/Mt*, III, 2.
14 Ibid., 31.
15 Ibid., 52.
16 Ibid., 50.
17 Ibid.
18 Ibid., 57.
19 Ibid., 74.
20 Ibid., 56.
21 Ibid., 62.
22 Ibid., 82.
23 Ibid.
24 Ibid., 54–5.
25 Ibid., 79.
26 Ibid., 138.
27 Ibid., 80.
28 Bernier, *Imperial Mother, Royal Daughter*, 217–18.
29 *Mercy/MT*, III, 84.
30 Ibid., 86.
31 *Mercy/Jo*, I, 70–1.
32 *MA Letters*, II, 49.
33 Girard, 212–13.
34 *Mercy/Jo*, II, 510, 512.
35 *Mercy/MT*, III, 137–8.
36 *Mercy/Jo*, II, 514.
37 *Mercy/MT*, III, 180.
38 Ibid., 188.
39 Ibid., 194.

4   *An Old Acquaintance*

1   Söderhjelm, 54.
2   Ibid., 55.
3   Ibid.
4   Klinckowström, I, xxii–xxiii.
5   Söderhjelm, 57.
6   Ibid., 58.
7   *Mercy/MT*, III, 189.
8   Klinckowström, I, xxviii.
9   Ibid., I, xxix–xxxii.
10 Söderhjelm, 60.
11 Ibid., 61.
12 Campan, I, 189.
13 *Mercy/MT*, III, 279.
14 Ibid., 278.
15 Tourzel, I, 45.
16 Geffroy, I, 296.
17 *Mercy/MT*, III, 290–1.
18 Ibid., 298.
19 Ibid., 302.
20 Geffroy, I, 360–1.
21 *Mercy/MT*, III, 322.
22 Campan, I, 197.
23 Söderhjelm, 70.
24 Ibid., 68.
25 Geffroy, I, 360.
26 Wrangel, *Lettres d'Axel Fersen à son père*, 52.
27 Ibid., 50–1.
28 Ibid., 51–2.
29 *Mercy/MT*, III, 399.
30 Wrangel, op. cit., 53.
31 Ibid., 59.
32 *Mercy/MT*, III, 417.

5   *Worlds Apart*

1   Söderhjelm, 70.
2   Klinckowström, I, 40.
3   Söderhjelm, 73.
4   Ibid., 71.

5 Klinckowström, I, 40, 42.
6 Ibid., 45.
7 *Mercy/MT*, III, 450.
8 Ibid., 478.
9 Bombelles, I, 42.
10 *Mercy/MT*, III, 496.
11 Ligne, op. cit., I, 91, 115.
12 *Mercy/Jo*, I, 16.
13 *MA Letters*, II, 2–4.
14 *Mercy/Jo*, I, 54.
15 Tilly, op. cit., 280.
16 Geffroy, I, 351–3.
17 Campan, I, 201–2.
18 *Mercy/Jo*, I, 71.
19 Klinckowström, I, 54–9.
20 Wrangel, op. cit., 114.
21 Ibid., 123.
22 Klinckowström, I, 58.
23 Wrangel, op. cit., 145.
24 Ibid., 157–8.
25 *Mercy/Jo*, I, 89, 121.
26 Ibid., 151.
27 Bombelles, I, 208.
28 Ibid., II, 76.
29 Ibid., I, 147–8.
30 Klinckowström, I, 72.
31 Söderhjelm, 74.
32 Ibid., 75.
33 Wrangel, op. cit., 176.
34 Ibid., 177.
35 Ibid., 178.
36 *MA Letters*, II, 21–3.

6 *'Josephine'*

1 Söderhjelm, 76–7.
2 Ibid., 90.
3 Ibid., 79; Geffroy, I, 362–3.
4 *MA Letters*, II, 25–7.
5 Söderhjelm, 91.

6 Bombelles, I, 244.
7 Ibid., 262–3.
8 Tilly, op. cit., 283.
9 Bombelles, I, 244; Söderhjelm, 386.
10 Söderhjelm, 81–2.
11 Ibid., 322.
12 Bombelles, I, 252.
13 Ibid.
14 Ibid., 255.
15 Wrangel, op. cit., 185.
16 Ibid., 184–5.
17 Söderhjelm, 99.
18 Geffroy, II, 13–14.
19 Söderhjelm, 91.
20 Geffroy, II, 22.
21 Bombelles, I, 271.
22 Ibid., 280.
23 *MA Letters*, II, 30.
24 Bombelles, II, 106–7.
25 Geffroy, II, 411.
26 *Mercy/Jo*, I, 264.
27 Bombelles, I, 326.
28 Söderhjelm, 385.
29 Klinckowström, II, 54.
30 Söderhjelm, 99.
31 Bombelles, I, 329.
32 Ibid.
33 Geffroy, II, 349.
34 Söderhjelm, 100.
35 Ibid.

7 *'Le Chou d'Amour'*

1 Söderhjelm, 101–2.
2 Bombelles, I, 340.
3 *MA Letters*, II, 39.
4 Ibid., 42.
5 Ibid., 42–3.
6 Ibid., 52.
7 *Mercy/Jo*, I, 421.
8 Geffroy, II, 444.

9 Bombelles, II, 41.
10 *MA Letters*, II, 64.
11 Nicolardot, *Journal de Louis XVI*, 43–4.
12 Söderhjelm, 103–4.
13 Ibid., 104–5.
14 See Chapter 5 of *Before the Deluge* by Evelyn Farr (Peter Owen, 1994), where the Necklace Affair is discussed in detail.
15 *MA Letters*, II, 76.
16 Ibid., 81.
17 Bombelles, II, 77.
18 Ibid., 90.
19 Ibid., 75.
20 *MA Letters*, II, 86; *Mercy/Jo*, II, 3.
21 *Mercy/Jo*, II, 12–13.
22 Ibid., 16.
23 Ibid., 31; Bombelles, II, 152; Nicolardot, op. cit., 44.
24 Bombelles, II, 161.
25 *Mercy/Jo*, II, 37.
26 Ibid., 80.
27 Bombelles, II, 194.
28 *Mercy/Jo*, II, 97.
29 Ibid., 140.
30 Söderhjelm, 110.
31 Campan, I, 175–6.
32 *MA Letters*, II, 105.
33 *Mercy/Jo*, II, 112.
34 Söderhjelm, 110.
35 Ibid., 113.
36 Ibid., 115.
37 Ibid., 116.

8   'Elle'

1 *MA Letters*, II, 112.
2 Ibid., Bombelles, II, 208.
3 Bombelles, II, 207.
4 Ibid., 214.
5 *Mercy/Jo*, II, 184.
6 *MA Letters*, II, 128.
7 *Mercy/Jo*, II, 196.
8 Söderhjelm, 119.

 9 Bombelles, II, 240–1.
10 Söderhjelm, 121.
11 Klinckowström, I, xliv–xlv.
12 Bombelles, II, 263, 273.
13 Söderhjelm, 132.
14 Bombelles, II, 284.
15 *Mercy/Jo*, II, 224.
16 Söderhjelm, 125
17 Morris, *A Diary of the French Revolution*, I, 67.
18 *Mercy/Jo*, II, 239.
19 Bombelles, II, 325.
20 Ibid., 331.
21 *MA Letters*, II, 130.
22 Young, *Travels in France and Italy*, 148–9.
23 Campan, II, 49.
24 Ibid.
25 *Mercy/Jo*, II, 256–7.
26 Ibid., 258.
27 Young, op. cit., 178.
28 Tourzel, I, l.
29 *MA Letters*, II, 140.
30 Ibid., 141.
31 Klinckowström, I, xlvii–xl.
32 Söderhjelm, 132.
33 Ibid., 134.
34 Tourzel, I, 8.
35 Söderhjelm, 135–6.
36 Tourzel, I, 10.
37 Ibid., 17–18.
38 Söderhjelm, 136.
39 *MA Letters*, II, 146.
40 Klinckowström, I, li.
41 *MA Letters*, II, 157–8.
42 Ibid.
43 Söderhjelm, 138.

9 *Her Majesty's Secret Agent*

1 Söderhjelm, 141.
2 Ibid., 140.
3 Ibid., 148.

4 Klinckowström, I, liv; Söderhjelm, 150.
5 *Mercy/Jo*, II, 273.
6 Tourzel, I, 80.
7 Söderhjelm, 145.
8 *MA Letters*, II, 173.
9 Campan, II, 217.
10 Söderhjelm, 151.
11 Ibid., 152.
12 Ibid., 149.
13 Ibid., 153.
14 Ibid.
15 Tourzel, I, 143.
16 Ibid., 203–4.
17 Geffroy, II, 228.
18 Söderhjelm, 159–60.
19 Ibid., 155.
20 Ibid., 158.
21 Ibid., 159.
22 *MA Letters*, II, 215–18.
23 Söderhjelm, 160.
24 Ibid., 161.
25 Klinckowström, I, 130.
26 Ibid., 122.
27 *MA Letters*, II, 241; Morris, op. cit., II, 157.
28 Söderhjelm, 166.
29 Ibid., 180–1.
30 Geffroy, II, 137.
31 Klinckowström, I, 132.
32 Ibid., 103–4.
33 Ibid., 105, 108.
34 Söderhjelm, 172–5.
35 Klinckowström, I, 137.
36 Söderhjelm, 187.
37 Tourzel, I, 304.
38 Ibid., 306.
39 Ibid., 311.
40 Klinckowström, I, 139.

10   *Adieu, My Love*

1   Klinckowström, I, 46.
2   Tourzel, I, 324.
3   Klinckowström, I, 2–3.
4   Söderhjelm, 183.
5   Ibid., 243–4.
6   Ibid.
7   Campan, II, 141.
8   Klinckowström, I, 5; Söderhjelm, 244.
9   *MA Letters*, II, 245–55.
10 Söderhjelm, 204.
11 Klinckowström, I, 141.
12 Söderhjelm, 184.
13 Ibid., 185.
14 Geffroy, II, 189.
15 Ibid., 186.
16 Klinckowström, I, 30.
17 Ibid., 15, 20.
18 *MA Letters*, II, 307.
19 Geffroy, II, 458; Klinckowström, I, 221.
20 Klinckowström, I, 19.
21 *MA Letters*, II, 308–311.
22 Heidenstam, *The Letters of Marie-Antoinette, Fersen and Barnave*, 40; *MA Letters*, II, 266.
23 *MA Letters*, II, 270–1.
24 Morris, op. cit., II, 71, 275.
25 Ibid., 275.
26 Klinckowström, I, 196, 213; *MA Letters*, II, 321.
27 *MA Letters*, II, 321.
28 Klinckowström, I, 196, 256–7.
29 Ibid., 231; *MA Letters*, II, 348.
30 Klinckowström, I, 233, 258–9.
31 *MA Letters*, II, 342–6.
32 Söderhjelm, 252.
33 Ibid., 236.
34 Ibid.
35 Klinckowström, I, 275, 296.
36 Söderhjelm, 240.
37 Ibid., 241; Klinckowström, II, 177.
38 Söderhjelm, 241–2.
39 Ibid.

40 Klinckowström, II, 179.
41 Söderhjelm, 245–7.

11 *The Death of Kings*

1 Klinckowström, II, 11.
2 Ibid., 230.
3 Tourzel, II, 74–5.
4 Klinckowström, II, 242–3.
5 Morris, op. cit., II, 403.
6 Klinckowström, II, 12.
7 Söderhjelm, 252.
8 Klinckowström, II, 230.
9 Campan, II, 195.
10 Morris, op. cit., II, 433.
11 Ibid., 436.
12 Klinckowström, II, 286, 298.
13 Campan, II, 205.
14 Klinckowström, II, 315.
15 *MA Letters*, II, 405–10.
16 Klinckowström, II, 43.
17 Ibid., 323.
18 Morris, op. cit., II, 473.
19 Geffroy, II, 356.
20 Klinckowström, II, 28.
21 Ibid., 43–5.
22 Ibid., 29; Söderhjelm, 269.
23 Campan, II, 242, 245.
24 Klinckowström, II, 374.
25 Ibid., 34.

12 *Love Lies Bleeding*

1 Söderhjelm, 273.
2 Klinckowström, II, 60.
3 Morris, op. cit., II, 591–2.
4 Söderhjelm 275–6.
5 Morris, op. cit., II, 602.
6 Söderhjelm, 277.
7 Ibid., 277–8.
8 Ibid.

 9 Ibid., 283.
10 Klinckowström, II, 62.
11 Söderhjelm, 281.
12 Ibid., 282.
13 Klinckowström, II, 63.
14 *MA Letters*, II, 433–4.
15 Söderhjelm, 323.
16 Ibid., 284.
17 Klinckowström, II, 67.
18 Söderhjelm, 289.
19 Klinckowström, II, 71.
20 Söderhjelm, 295.
21 Klinckowström, II, 74.
22 Söderhjelm, 296.
23 Klinckowström, II, 76.
24 Söderhjelm, 296–7.
25 Ibid.
26 Klinckowström, II, 100.
27 Söderhjelm, 297–8; Klinckowström, II, 92.
28 Söderhjelm, 299–300.
29 Ibid.
30 Klinckowström, II, 101–2.
31 Ibid.
32 Ibid., 93.
33 *MA Letters*, II, 440–1.
34 Söderhjelm, 309.
35 Ibid.
36 Klinckowström, II, 95.
37 Tourzel, II, 318.
38 *MA Letters*, II, 443.
39 Ibid., 441–4.
40 Söderhjelm, 310.
41 Ibid.
42 Ibid., 311.
43 Ibid.
44 Ibid., 315.
45 Ibid., 318.
46 Ibid., 322, 330, 366.

Epilogue: The Memory of a Dream

1 Söderhjelm, 317.
2 Ibid., 335.
3 Ibid., 337.
4 Ibid., 338.
5 Ibid., 342.
6 Ibid.
7 Ibid., 343.
8 Ibid., 348.
9 Ibid., 349.
10 Ibid., 348.
11 Ibid., 355.
12 Klinckowström, I, lxxii.

Biographical Notes

Artois, Charles-Philippe de Bourbon, Comte d', later Charles X (1757–1836), Youngest brother of Louis XVI, a fop and a womanizer. Strongly opposed to constitutional reform, he emigrated in 1789, and was the head of the reactionary nobility (the 'Ultras') at the Restoration in 1814. Crowned King after the death of Louis XVIII in 1824, his right-wing policies led to the July Revolution of 1830 and his renewed exile. Married to Maria-Theresa of Savoy (d. 1805), from whom he lived apart for many years. His abdication in favour of his grandson, the Duc de Bordeaux, was thwarted by Louis-Philippe's seizure of the throne.

Barnave, Antoine-Pierre-Joseph-Marie (1761–93). A Protestant lawyer from Grenoble, he represented the Third Estate at the States-General in 1789. A gifted orator and radical legislator, he became President of the National Assembly in 1790 and also reformed the Jacobin Club. Secretly negotiated with Marie-Antoinette over the 1791 constitution, but lost his seat when it came into effect. Retired to Grenoble in 1792, but was arrested and executed on 29 November 1793.

Bombelles, Marc-Marie, Marquis de (1744–1822). Soldier, diplomat, courtier, bishop, he was also an indefatigable diarist, although only a small portion of his immense journal has been published. After a successful military career, he entered the diplomatic service under the protection of the Baron de Breteuil (q.v.), serving at The Hague and Naples before becoming ambassador to Ratisbon (Regensburg) in 1774, Lisbon (1785–8), and finally Venice (1789–91). Refused to accept the constitution, resigned, and lived as an émigré. After the death of his wife in 1800 he became a priest in Germany, returning to France in 1814. Bishop of Amiens from 1817.

Bouillé, François-Claude-Amour, Marquis de (1739–1800). A French general who distinguished himself during the American war. Deeply involved in the royal family's 1791 escape attempt, he fled into exile when it failed at Varennes. Died in London.

Breteuil, Louis-Auguste Le Tonnelier, Baron de (1733–1807). He held a succession of important diplomatic posts from 1758, including Stockholm (1763–8), where he became friendly with the Fersen family, and Vienna (1775–83), where he met with Empress Maria-Theresa's (q.v.) complete approval. Consequently a friend to both Marie-Antoinette and Axel Fersen. Minister of the King's Household from 1783, he resigned in 1788, but was recalled to office in July 1789. After the fall of the Bastille he emigrated, and served as Louis XVI's secret Foreign Minister until the fall of the monarchy in 1792.

Brienne, Etienne-Charles Loménie de (1727–94). A great friend and protector of the Abbé de Vermond (q.v.), he was Archbishop of Toulouse (1763) and of Sens (1788) before his appointment as Prime Minister in 1788. Forced to resign when his budget failed to meet with approval. Died in prison while awaiting trial by the Revolutionary Tribunal.

Calonne, Charles-Alexandre de (1734–1802). Son of a magistrate, he held various legal posts before becoming Intendant of Metz (1768) and Lille (1774). Appointed Controller-General in 1783, he convened the Assembly of Notables to discuss fiscal reform, but was dismissed from office in 1787, believed to have enriched himself at public expense. A counter-revolutionary during his exile, he died soon after returning to Paris in 1802.

Campan, Jeanne-Louise-Henriette, née Genet (1752–1822). After an initial Court appointment as reader to the daughters of Louis XV, she joined the household of Marie-Antoinette, whom she served until the Court no longer existed. Married to the Queen's valet, Campan, she separated from him in 1790, and lost other members of her family in the Revolution. Later established a popular school for young ladies near Paris.

Coigny, François de Franquetot, Duc de (1737–1821). Equerry to Louis XVI and a member of Marie-Antoinette's set, he was often assumed to be her lover. Emigrated in 1789 and joined Condé's army. Returned to France in 1814.

Crawford or *Craufurd*, Quentin (1743–1819). A Scottish author and collector, he made a vast fortune in India before settling in Paris in 1780 with his mistress (later his wife), Eleonore Sullivan. Forced to emigrate in 1792 because of his strong royalist connections, but returned to live in Paris in 1802.

Esterhazy, Valentin, Comte (1740–1806). Soldier and courtier, he was descended from a French branch of the famous Hungarian family. A close friend on Marie-Antoinette for many years, he served with Axel Fersen in the Royal-Suédois regiment and emigrated in 1790.

Fitz-James, Marie-Claudine-Sophie, Duchesse de, née de Thiard de Bissy. Married the Duc de Fitz-James, a great-grandson of the Duke of Berwick (James II's son by Arabella Churchill) in 1768. A friend of and lady-in-waiting to Marie-Antoinette for many years. Emigrated in 1791.

Goguelat, Baron de. A technical artist and engineer from Château-Chinon, he came to Marie-Antoinette's attention when he drew plans for her of the Petit Trianon and St Cloud. The Queen promoted his military career by getting him a commission as ADC to Valentin Esterhazy (q.v.). Reported on debates in the National Assembly for the Queen, and by degrees became her secretary, secret courier, and trusted aide to Axel Fersen in the plan to extract the royal family from the Tuileries. Imprisoned after Varennes in 1791, 'Gog' was released in an amnesty and continued to serve Marie-Antoinette up to 10 August 1792. Managed to escape from France and was made a baron at the Restoration in recognition of his devotion to the royalist cause.

Jarjayes, François-Auguste-René Pelisson, Chevalier de (b. 1745). An army officer married to one of Marie-Antoinette's *femmes de chambre*, he undertook many missions for the Queen during the Revolution and tried to rescue her from the Temple, but was forced to emigrate in 1793. Carried her last message to Axel Fersen.

Joseph II von Habsburg, Holy Roman Emperor (1741–90). Co-ruler with his mother Maria-Theresa (q.v.) after his father's death in 1765, he was an 'enlightened despot' at home, reforming the Austrian legal, medical, fiscal and educational systems. Also suppressed hundreds of monasteries in an attempt to curb ecclesiastical power. His foreign policy, however, was largely unsuccessful, and his territorial ambitions led to costly wars. Married twice, but both his wives died of smallpox and he had no surviving children.

Lafayette, Marie-Joseph-Paul-Yves-Roch-Gilbert du Motier, Marquis de (1757–1834). Married young to Adrienne de Noailles, and consequently a member of one of the most prestigious families in France, he hankered after military glory. Arrived in America in 1777 and joined Washington's army as a volunteer, distinguishing himself in action. Promoted *maréchal de camp* in 1782. A Freemason and close friend of Washington, he was an early leader of the French Revolution. His Declaration of the Rights of Man was accepted by the National Assembly in August 1789, by which time he was also commander of the Parisian Garde Nationale. Instrumental in keeping the royal family confined in the Tuileries until his resignation in 1791. After the collapse of the monarchy in August 1792 he fled across the frontier, and was imprisoned by the Austrians until 1797. Sat in parliament during the reign of Louis XVIII, and his last political act was his open support for Louis-Philippe in 1830.

Lamballe, Marie-Thérèse, Princesse de, née de Savoie-Carignan (1749–92). Widowed at nineteen after barely two years' marriage to the son of the Duc de Penthièvre. A close friend of Marie-Antoinette, her appointment as Superintendent of the Queen's household in 1774 caused an outcry. Left Versailles when Madame de Polignac (q.v.) became the Queen's confidante, but the Queen often visited her in Paris and their friendship grew stronger during the 1780s as the Polignacs' influence waned. Loyal and steadfast to the end, she returned from a brief exile in 1791 to be with the Queen, was imprisoned after the assault on the Tuileries on 10 August 1792, and massacred on 3 September at the prison of La Force.

Lauzun, Armand-Louis de Gontaut, Duc de (1747–93). Duc de Biron from 1788. Courtier, soldier, roué, revolutionary, he was at one stage a member of Marie-Antoinette's circle. After his fall from favour, he took part in the American war and later joined the Orléanist faction. Elected to the States-General in 1789, he became an ardent revolutionary. Served as a general in the republican army, but was guillotined in 1793.

Maria-Theresa von Habsburg, Queen of Hungary and Bohemia, Holy Roman Empress (1717–80). The eldest daughter of Emperor Charles VI, she became heir to the Habsburg crown after the death of her brother. Her accession in 1740 sparked off the War of the Austrian Succession, and her reign was marked by several conflicts with her neighbours, particularly Frederick the Great of Prussia. Married Francis of Lorraine (Emperor Francis I), had sixteen children, including Marie-Antoinette, and was admired as a humane and practical ruler.

Marie-Thérèse-Charlotte of France (1778–1851). The only member of her family to survive imprisonment in the Temple, the daughter of Louis XVI and Marie-Antoinette was released to the Austrians in 1795. Married her first cousin, the Duc d'Anoulême (d. 1844), but they had no children. After exile in Germany and England she returned to Paris at the Restoration in 1814. Dauphine from 1824, but the 1830 Revolution forced her to spend the rest of her life abroad. Died in Italy.

Mercy-Argenteau, Florimond-Claude, Comte de (1727–94). Born in Liège, he entered the Austrian diplomatic service in 1752. After posts in Paris, Turin, St Petersburg and Warsaw, was appointed ambassador to France in 1766. Helped to negotiate Marie-Antoinette's marriage to the Dauphin, and reported all her activities to her mother for years after the wedding in 1770. Supported constitutional reform during the Revolution. Appointed Governor of the Netherlands in 1791, but continued to advise Marie-Antoinette by post from Brussels. Died in London shortly after arriving to take change of the embassy there.

Morris, Gouverneur (1752–1816). Born in New York and educated at King's College (now Columbia University). Became an attorney at the age of nineteen, was a member of the New York Convention in 1775, and strongly supported the cause of independence. Lost part of one leg after a carriage accident in Philadelphia, where he practised as a lawyer before being sent on private and state business to France in 1789. Succeeded Jefferson as American ambassador in 1792, a post he held throughout the Terror, and left France in October 1794.

Necker, Jacques (1732–1804). A Swiss banker and darling of the Parisians, he also represented the city of Geneva in France from 1768. Appointed Controller-General by Louis XVI in 1777. Forced out of office by Maurepas, he was recalled twice (1788, 1789), before his final resignation in 1790. Published several works on the administration of French finances, though his talents as a banker did more to enrich Swiss banks than reduce the French deficit.

Orléans, Louis-Philippe-Joseph de Bourbon, Duc d', Duc de Chartres until 1785 (1747–93). A perennial thorn in the King's side, his hatred of the Queen was one reason for his machinations against the Court. Plunged eagerly into politics when the States-General met in 1789, supported revolutionary policies from the outset, and joined the Jacobins in 1791. After the fall of the monarchy in 1792 he dropped his title to become 'Philippe Égalité'. As a member of the National Convention he voted for the execution of his cousin Louis XVI, a move which prompted his son, the future King Louis-Philippe, to defect to the Austrians. Arrested in April 1793, he was guillotined on 6 November that year.

Ossun, Geneviève, Comtesse d', née de Gramont (1751–94). A niece of the Duc de Choiseul, she was a loyal friend of and lady-in-waiting to Marie-Antoinette from 1781. Guillotined on 26 July 1794.

Piper, Countess Sophie, née Fersen (1757–1816). Axel Fersen's beloved sister married Count Adolf Piper (d. 1794), and divided her time between her children and her official duties as lady-in-waiting to the Queen of Sweden. *See also* Baron Taube.

Polignac, Gabrielle-Yolande-Claude-Martine-Jeanne, Duchesse de, née de Polastron (1749–93). Intimate friend of Marie-Antoinette from 1775. Her husband, Comte Jules de Polignac (duke from 1780), was made the Queen's equerry so that she could remain at Court. In 1782 she was appointed governess to the royal children. Resigned and emigrated in 1789, and did not long outlive the Queen, dying in Austria after a long illness in 1793.

Provence, Louis-Stanislas-Xavier de Bourbon, Comte de, better known (as the King's eldest brother) as Monsieur, later Louis XVIII (1755–1824). Not altogether trustworthy, he took a more liberal political line than the Comte d'Artois (q.v.), and did not emigrate until 1791. However, once across the frontier he threatened counter-revolutionary action which jeopardized the safety of the King and Queen, and he was quick to style himself Louis XVIII after the reported death of his nephew in prison in 1795. Ruled France from the Restoration in 1814. As King, he was a moderate constitutional monarch, though he had to combat 'Ultras' in parliament. Married Josephine of Savoy in 1771 and was childless.

Saint-Priest, François-Emmanuel Guignard, Comte de (1735–1821). Enjoyed a highly successful diplomatic career before his appointment to a cabinet post in 1788. Advocated counter-revolutionary measures which Louis XVI refused to implement, and resigned and emigrated in 1790.

Stedingk, Kurt, Count (1746–1837). A good friend of both Axel Fersen and Marie-Antoinette, he had an illustrious career both as a soldier and a diplomat. In the French army from 1766, he commanded an infantry brigade during the American war. Recalled home in 1787 by Gustav III to fight against Russia, and later attained the rank of Field-Marshal. In 1791 he was appointed ambassador to Russia. Swedish ambassador to France from 1814.

Taube, Evert, Baron (1737–99). A lieutenant-general in the Swedish army and First Gentleman of the Bedchamber to Gustav III, he also advised the King on French policy. Lived with Axel Fersen's sister Sophie (*see* Piper) from 1794.

Tourzel, Louise-Elisabeth-Félicité, Duchesse de (1749–1832). Daughter of the Duc d'Havré, she was married to the Grand Provost of France. Succeeded Mme de Polignac (q.v.) as royal governess in 1789, and remained with the royal family until she was imprisoned in the Abbaye in 1792. Escaped the September massacres, survived a second imprisonment in 1794, and was made a duchess by Louis XVIII in 1816.

Vermond, Jacques-Mathieu, Abbé de (1735–1806). Tutor and later reader to Marie-Antoinette, he proved a most useful spy on the Queen's activities for the Comte de Mercy (q.v.). Emigrated in July 1789 and died in Brno.

Select Bibliography

Place of publication is London, unless otherwise stated

Aubert, Raymond (ed.), *Journal d'un bourgeois de Paris sous la Révolution* (Paris: France-Empire, 1973)

Bachaumont, Louis Petit de, *Mémoires secrets de Bachaumont*, ed. P.L. Jacob (Paris: Garnier, 1874)

Bernier, Olivier (ed.), *Imperial Mother, Royal Daughter: The Correspondence of Marie-Antoinette and Maria-Theresa* (Sidgwick & Jackson, 1986)

Bombelles, Marc-Marie, Marquis de, *Journal (1780–1789)*, ed. J. Grassion & F. Durif, 2 vols. (Geneva: Librairie Droz, 1978–82)

Campan, Jeanne-Louise-Henriette Genet, *Mémoires sur la vie privée de Marie-Antoinette, Reine de France et de Navarre*, 2 vols (Henry Colburn & Co. & M. Bossange & Co., 1823)

Geffroy, A., *Gustave III et la Cour de France: suivi d'une étude critique sur Marie-Antoinette et Louis XVI apocryphes*, 2 vols (Paris: Didier, 1867)

Girard, Georges (ed.), *Correspondance entre Marie-Thérèse et Marie-Antoinette* (Paris: Grasset, 1933)

Heidenstam, O.G., *The Letters of Marie-Antoinette, Fersen and Barnave*, trans. W. Stephens & Mrs W. Jackson (Bodley Head, 1926)

Klinckowström, Baron R.M., *Le Comte de Fersen et la Cour de France: extraits des papiers de Grand Maréchal de Suède, Comte Jean-Axel de Fersen*, 2 vols (Paris: Firmin-Didot, 1877–8)

Lauzun, Armand-Louis Duc de, *Mémoires de Armand-Louis de Gontaut, Duc de Lauzun, Général Biron*, ed. E. Pilon (Paris: H. Jonguières, 1928)

DISCARD

Ligne, Charles-Joseph, Prince de, *Fragments de l'histoire de ma vie*, ed.
F. Leuridant, 2 vols (Paris: Plon, 1928)

Marie-Antoinette, *Lettres de Marie-Antoinette: recueil des letters authentiques
de la reine*, ed. Maxime de la Rocheterie & Marquis de Beaucourt, 2
vols (Paris: Alphonse Picard, 1896)

Mercy-Argenteau, Florimond, Comte de, *Correspondance secrète entre
Marie-Thérèse et le Comte de Mercy-Argenteau avec les lettres de Marie-
Thérèse et de Marie-Antoinette*, ed. Alfred Arneth & A. Geffroy, 3 vols
(Paris: Firmin-Didot, 1874)

——, *Correspondance secrète du Comte de Mercy-Argenteau avec l'Empereur
Joseph II et le Prince de Kaunitz*, ed. Alfred Arneth & Jules
Flammermont, 2 vols (Paris: Imprimerie Nationale 1889–91)

Morris, Gouverneur, *A Diary of the French Revolution*, ed. B.C. Daven-
port, 2 vols (Harrap, 1939)

Nicolardot, Louis (ed.), *Journal de Louis XVI* (Paris: E. Dentu, 1873)

Söderhjelm, Alma, *Fersen et Marie-Antoinette: correspondance et journal
intime inédits du Comte Axel de Fersen* (Paris: Editions Kra, 1930)

Tilly, Alexandre de, *Memoirs of the Comte Alexandre de Tilly*, trans. F.
Delisle (New York: Farrar & Rhinehart, 1932)

Tourzel, Louise-Elisabeth de Croy-Havré de, *Mémoires de Madame la
Duchesse de Tourzel, Gouvernante des Enfants de France*, ed. Duc des
Cars, 2 vols (Paris: Plon 1883)

Van der Kemp, G. & Levron, J. *Versailles and the Trianons*, trans. E.
Whitehorn (Nicholas Kaye, 1958)

Vigée-Lebrun, Elisabeth, *The Memoirs of Elisabeth Vigée-Lebrun*, trans.
Siân Evans (Camden Press, 1989)

Wrangel, Count F.U. (ed.), *Lettres d'Axel Fersen à son père pendant la
guerre de l'indépendance d'Amérique* (Paris: Firmin-Didot, 1929)

Young, Arthur, *Travels in France and Italy* (Dent, 1915)